From Jerusalem to the Edge *of* Heaven

ARI ELON

From Jerusalem

Contents

Foreword

Tikva Frymer-Kensky

I first met Ari Elon at a Berkeley-Stanford conference on "The Body in Judaism." We had each been invited to present papers about our work. As I listened to his paper, "The Torah as Esther" from *Alma Dee*, I became very excited. Somehow this Israeli man was reading texts with my eyes, understanding them with the same sensitivities that I had developed as an American Jewish feminist woman. When Ari had a similar reaction to my *Motherprayer* poems, I knew that we were onto something, and I began to read *Alma Dee*, the original, Hebrew edition of *From Jerusalem to the Edge of Heaven*. I read with a mounting sense of excitement, for I recognized the voices that were speaking. As I did so, I realized that aspects of my thinking that I had assumed were characteristically American and feminist were somehow part of a much broader contemporary international Jewish phenomenon.

In many ways, *Alma Dee* is characteristic of this new approach which, for want of a better term, we might call a postmodern approach to Judaism. *Alma Dee* is rooted in a great love of Jewish tradition and texts and a determination to remain part of the ongoing unfolding of Torah. At the same time, Elon has been profoundly influenced by Western philosophical ideas, by Zionism, and by modern sophistication. He is too restless and inquisitive to abide by the old orthodoxies, too philosophical and self-willed to grant others (rabbis–dead or alive) the authority to determine faith and truth. Nothing is accepted a priori; everything must be subject to examination, scrutiny, deliberation–an endless process of God-wrestling. This wrestling is accompanied by careful learning and scholarship, but the pursuit of knowledge is not purely academic, for he is unwilling to distance himself from the tradition in the manner of most modern Judaic studies scholarship *(Wissenschaft des Judentums)*. Moreover, the pursuit of learning is not purely intellectual, for it seeks more than knowledge or understanding. The tradition is not the authority to which Elon turns; it is not the object that he studies in a distanced, objective way. On the contrary, he internalizes the classic Jewish writings as the contrary part of his being and they serve as the inspiration for his thinking. The contemporary world is the prism through which Elon sees the talmudic texts; at the same time, the talmudic texts are the prism through which Elon sees the contemporary world. Life and Torah are a duality in a constantly interacting reality.

These were the aspects of *Alma Dee* that I found so familiar and so compelling, these the characteristics of my own explorations of the Bible and of Judaism. I had reached my own approach through my deveopment as a scholar, as a feminist, as an American Jew with deep loyalties to Israel. Ari Elon showed me that my approach was not unique and not limited to America or to women. At least some of our contemporaries in Israel had developed this same constellation of characteristics. I quickly offered to translate *Alma Dee* into English so that it could become part of the contemporary American discourse on Judaism.

Alma Dee presents a great challenge to a translator. The action in *Alma Dee* ranges over the Talmud, the *Haskalah* (the Jewish "Enlightenment"), Israeli intelligentsia, and the Israeli army. Ari Elon adapts his language to each change of scene: talmudic phrases give way to army slang. Moreover, part of Ari Elon's love of Jewish tradition is his love for Hebrew, the Jewish language, and he writes in a style that, while superficially simple, is full of double entendres, word plays, purposeful ambiguities, and multiple allusions. Ari Elon and I decided to work together: After I prepared a translation of each chapter, we would discuss the more intricate points and decide what to do. Sometimes I could duplicate the language games in translation, sometimes I could translate them by a matching wordplay in English, and sometimes they had to be sacrificed in the interest of clarity.

Many words in *From Jerusalem to the Edge of Heaven* have been left in their original Hebrew. For one pair of words, *datti* and *ḥiloni*, the reason is political: The term *datti* literally means "religious," and *ḥiloni* literally means "secular." In practice, however, these terms have acquired specific applications, particularly in Israel. *Datti* refers to the established government-supported Judaism of Israel, which is an Orthodox Judaism centered on *ḥalakhah* (Jewish law). In English, there is often confusion between the terms "orthodox," "observant," and "religious;" in Israeli Hebrew there is no confusion: *Datti* always means "orthodox." Similarly, a *ḥiloni* (secular person) can be quite spiritual, may even be an active synagogue goer but will never be classified as *datti*. Ari Elon is not a secular Jew, but in the Israeli context he would never call himself *datti*; on the contrary, he calls himself a *ḥiloni religiosi* (a religious secularist), an oxymoron in American English but not in Israeli Hebrew.

Another pair of untranslated terms are *rabbani* and *ribboni*, which Elon discusses in the body of the book. *Ribboni* is a recently invented term. Literally, it means "masterly," but in Elon's usage, it means "master of oneself and of no one else." It is the opposite of *rabbani*, literally "rabbinic." *Rabbani* means subscribing to a hierarchical view of truth and authority: One listens to one's rabbi, who explains the revealed Torah and determines what one should do. In turn, the rabbi relies on another rabbi for his authority. Nobody makes decisions without reference to others, and in this way authority and faith are always mediated by other people. This is the Orthodox system of rabbinic authority. Many of today's rabbis–Reform, Reconstructionist and many Conservative–do not believe in this paradigm and encourage community participation in all matters. For this reason, it would be unfair to say "rabbinic" when referring to the Orthodox paradigm, and we have chosen to say *rabbani*.

Many other terms have not been translated because they are part of traditional Jewish discourse and translating them removes the traditional flavor of the discussion. These include terms such as *s'mikhah*, (rabbinic ordination), halakhah, *mehitzah*, (a separation between men and women). These, and many others, are words that I use when speaking English, and it would seem strange and unlettered for me to use the English translations. Not everyone knows these terms, of course, so we have translated them twice: Once in the text when the term first appears and once again in a glossary at the end of the book.

A special set of untranslated terms should be mentioned separately. These are words that refer to the *beit midrash* (the academy of learning), where the sages of talmudic times assembled to study and argue about the tradition. This was a special world, a world out of time, a world that still exists today whenever we open a page of the Talmud. This world is populated by *talmidei ḥakhamim*, sometimes translate as "talmudic sages," who engage in the battle of the Torah, questioning and answering with their characteristic *pilpul*. The rest of the people, those who do not engage in this study, are the *amei ha'aretz*. All of these terms are translatable. The term *talmid ḥakham* literally means "student of the wise;" *pilpul*, literally "peppering," refers to the classic back-and-forth method of investigation through argumentation; *amei ha'aretz* (*am ha'aretz* in the singular) are literally "people of the land," the "folk." But translating these terms takes them out of their original context and makes them almost unfamiliar to people who are used to Jewish study. I have adopted a simple rule of thumb: Hebrew (or Aramaic) words that have been kept as cultural loan words in Yiddish are kept as cultural loan words here. Once again, they are explained when first used and are included in a glossary.

There is yet another problem in translation that needs to be addressed. In classic Jewish sources, God is always addressed as male. The pronoun used for God in Hebrew is always "He," "Him," or the form of "You" appropriate to addressing a male. When God is the subject, the verb appears in the masculine. To change some of these into the feminine would do violence to the tradition; to keep them all unchanged would be to continue to visit the sins of the fathers upon the children to the thousandth generation. God is not a man, and that should somehow be kept clear in translation. Sometimes the problem can be finessed: The epithet *Kadosh Barukh Hu*, literally "The Holy One Blessed Be He," can be rendered as "The Holy Blessed One" without disturbing the sense or the flavor of the original. But it is not easy to do away with the pronoun as the subject or object of verbs of action. Even if we keep the "He" in the direct quotation, we do not want to do so in the discussion of the text. But what can we substitute for "He"? To our anthropocentric eyes, "it" seems somehow less than human, and we are stuck with repeating the noun. This can result in the barbaric-sounding "God lifted God's hand Godself," or the distancing, "the Deity alone lifted Its hand," or the awkward and unpronounceable, "God lifted His/Her hand Him/Herself." Ultimately, English will develop a convention for referring to a third person animate being in a genderless way. Until then, I prefer to wind up with awkward passages sometimes rather than to continue the damage done by the consistent use of the masculine.

Preface to the English Edition

This book began as an issue of an innovative Israeli quarterly review called *Shdemot*, which is put out by the young intellectuals of the Kibbutz movement and its adherents. Shdemot is characterized by a combination of left wing liberal thought with an intense interest in Jewish classical texts. This combination, which has characterized *Shdemot* since its inception, is unique in Israel and matches my own interests and inclinations. Many of those who founded *Shdemot* were also active in the establishment of a Judaic texts program in Oranim, the college of the Kibbutz movement, which has become a fascinating secular quasi-yeshivah. Since joining the faculty of this program in the summer of 1977, I have been active in these circles. I became a contributor to *Shdemot*, and the editors suggested, at the end of 1989, that I write an entire issue of the journal. We wanted to keep the character of a typical journal issue, which normally includes scholarly, ideological, and literary articles, gathered together from various disciplines. This suited me perfectly, for it let me speak in many voices at once.

For over twenty years I had been filling notebooks with observa–tions, diaries, scholarly studies, and opinions. *Shdemot*'s proposal, which had a built-in deadline, functioned for me like a gallery's offer of an exhibition to an artist who has to be ready by a certain date. I started to review everything I had written, and little by little the fourfold structure of *Alma Dee* (the Hebrew original of *From Jerusalem to the Edge of Heaven)* began to coalesce. I began to realize that my output during these twenty years had concentrated on four areas: One, of course, was autobiographical; another, the political/ideological essays and lectures that I had produced during my fifteen years as an educator and activist in Israel; the third, the fruits of my scholarly endeavors in talmudic literature; and the fourth the military journals I had kept during twenty-odd years of army service. These were the areas that I would cull to create the "gates" into which *Shdemot* normally divided its issues.

I chose a few autobiographical pieces. This book would not be an autobiography, and I only wanted to provide a brief sketch of the events that had formed me. I was born into an Orthodox, God-centered world and had an intensely God-centered boyhood. During my teens, I lost my belief in God (as I the child had pictured God), and I mourned this loss as I continued to study in Orthodox schools, feeling increasingly isolated and alienated. In 1968 I joined the army. 1968, immediately after the six-day war, was a time of great national euphoria, and I threw myself wholeheartedly into the role of soldier; during my three years of army service, I neither prayed nor read. During these years I was able to ignore the metaphysical and philosophical turmoil that had preoccupied me since my teen years. After the army, however, I went to the Hebrew University to study philosophy and theology. I tried to resurrect my childhood God–but in vain. Then came the Yom Kippur war, which took me away from my studies to sit in the desert west of Suez for eight months. During these months, I began to long to leave Israel, to forget my tortured grappling with Judaism and to disappear once and for all into the wider world. I went to London to disappear, the first time this Israeli-born *Sabra* ever experienced *galut*. There I realized that I was a Jew, that I could never erase my Jewishness, and I became a Zionist. I went back to Israel in 1975, now aware of my absolute imperative to be a Jew, and tried actively to grapple with the anti-Jewish impulse that I had experienced and which was (and still is) very much alive in many secular Israelis. I felt compelled to study and learn the Jewish classical sources while emphasizing continually–at the same time–all the elements of Jewish existence that had nothing to do with "religion". Ever since then, throughout the late seventies and eighties I have followed two separate paths: The path of a secular Zionist at the center of political and intellectual activity, and the path of a talmudic scholar.

As I reviewed these writings for the *Shdemot* deadline, I began to realize to what extent I had been developing these two separate aspects of my identity: The politically active, committed educator and idealogue, and the modern version of a talmudic sage who found his rooftop in the Talmud far away from the hassles of ordinary life. Needless to say, during the fifteen years since my time in London as an Israeli Zionist man, I had also pursued a third course, that of an Israeli soldier. The autobiographical gate of *Alma Dee* provides the background material that enables the reader (and me) to understand these three worlds that I inhabited in my twenties and thirties: the Zionist political arena, the talmudic asylum, and the army.

The second gate is the Zionist gate. As soon as I returned from London, I accepted a job at the Institute of Zionist Education, a special educational project that had begun to give Zionist instruction to high school seniors. This project came out of the government's realization that the youth of Israel had very little Zionist consciousness. The initiative to start these institutes came from the right, and the first such institutes were set up by right-wing nationalist and religious-nationalist groups such as *Teḥiya* and *Gush Emunim*. They filled an ideological vacuum, and schools in Israel sent their students to learn Zionist ideology from them. The Department of Education (which was controlled at that time by the Labor party) eventually realized that it was supporting and encouraging Israeli students to learn a right-wing nationalist form of Zionism that included fundamentalist religious ideology and territorial aspirations to the West Bank. It realized that it would also have to set up Zionist institutes that taught a more peace-oriented Zionism. They had tried to interest me in the project before I went to London, but at that time, I was not the least bit interested. After my discoveries in London, I returned and immediately joined the project. I became first a teacher at the most liberal Zionist Institute in Jerusalem and then its director. In the years that followed, the staff at the Institute joined the core of the Peace Now movement. I accepted the challenge to create a liberal Zionist educational center for the Kibbutz movement. When several kibbutzim decided to send their teenagers to right-wing Zionist seminars, the ensuing uproar within the Kibbutz movement led to a decision to establish a Kibbutz Zionist seminar. This was to be located at Oranim, which is a major college of the kibbutzim. I directed this Institute, continuing the educational work that I had been doing but moving it outside Jerusalem into the heart of the kibbutz movement. Because of this, I became ever more involved with the intellectual activities of the kibbutz movement as I continued teaching, lecturing, mentoring, preaching, and counseling Israeli youth about the Zionism of Gordon, Katznelson, Brenner and Berdichevsky, Herzl, Bialik and Ahad Ha'am. The kibbutzim would invite me to give courses and seminars around the country, and I was ever more in demand as a public speaker who could present a form of Judaism alternative to the fundamentalism and militarism of the right wing in Israel. The Zion Gate in *Alma Dee* includes the speeches and articles that I wrote during those fifteen years.

These speeches remained fairly consistent during these years, but I continued to develop my thinking. The Zion gate also contains my reflections on the speeches written then and during the period in which I was preparing *Alma Dee* for *Shdemot*. It goes without saying that many of my ideas have continued to develop since then, and some of the ideas of 1980 or even 1990 seem a little unsophisticated to me today. I have included all these stages in my thinking because I believe that they are representative of an entire Israeli generation's struggles with these issues and because all of the opinions presented here are still held by many other people.

Ironically, the more I became a major voice of Israeli secular Judaism and the more occupied I was with public symposia and lectures, the more determined I became to learn more about the sources of Judaism and to read these texts through my perspective rather than the Orthodox perspective which I had been taught. I went back to the University in 1980. At the Hebrew University I was greatly attracted to the method developed by Jonah Frankel, a literary approach to talmudic literature, particularly to the narratives embedded in the Talmud. This literary approach opens the Talmud to nonlegal and nonhistorical study. The more I studied, the more I realized that the Talmud contains invaluable resources for modern Jewish thought. I further realized that many of the great Zionist thinkers had known this and had been attracted to Jewish scholarship for the same reasons that propelled me. I began to study talmudic stories intensively. Other people could deliver ideological lectures, and other people could create (what I believed at the time were superficial) transformations of holidays and rituals to incorporate and authenticate new Jewish ideas. I myself could go deeply into ancient Jewish texts and make these sources the roots of a profound new Judaism. The studies in the Ravine Gate were the curricula for courses that I delivered at locations throughout the Kibbutz world. At the same time, they re-involved me in the world of Israeli arts and letters, for Israeli artists came to understand that these talmudic stories were a Jewish mythology that could provide a Jewish source for the rich symbolism and psychological insights that artists have long sought in Greek mythology and Christian art.

During these years, I continued to be a reserve soldier, living the military life one month out of every year. I kept a journal of these months, and the final gate of *Alma Dee*, the "Dung Gate," comes from one of these journals. I decided to use the journal from the summer of 1988, because the intifada had impelled me to write about my political perspectives.

These, then, were the four gates of an issue of *Shdemot*, which corresponded so well to the different dimensions of my development. There was yet another element. *Shdemot* has a tradition of including artwork in its quarterly issue. Along with the commission to write an entire issue came the suggestion that I find an illustrator. I objected at first, feeling that an illustrated volume was more suitable for a children's book. However, as I collected and reviewed my material and as I became ever more conscious of the elements that connected them, I began to realize that all the gates had some connection to the world of children, specifically to children at play. "My Own Gate" clearly dealt with the play of the children of Sha'arei Ḥesed and the "Dung Gate" with the children of Gaza. Even the "Ravine Gate" presented stories which that portrayed the sages of the Talmud as children who never grow up, who continue to play games in their playground, the *beit midrash*. Behind the camouflage of serious *halakhah*, the sages of the Talmud play their intellectual games, and whenever I study Talmud, I look for these children. So too, behind the serious ideologue giving earnest Zionist speeches to counteract the Orthodox establishment lurks the perpetually childlike artist who feels a great empathy with the childlike sages of tradition who always hide.

Behind the two ideologues–the Orthodox and the secular–lie two children at play. They are like children on a seesaw. The seesaw was clearly an underlying motif and needed to be brought out in the artwork. We considered commissioning artists or photographers to capture the spirit of children at play, and then someone suggested that we use Breughel's "Children's Games." The moment the suggestion was made, it seemed the obvious choice. In this painting, 200 children are playing at their many games. It is a classic painting, traditional and contemporary at the same time. It forms a wonderful *midrashic* circle: The Breughel images are a *midrash* on the talmudic story-images, which are themselves sometimes a midrash on the contemporary scene.

The picture in its entirety is found on the frontispiece and was also used as the cover picture for the Hebrew edition. Parts of the picture are reproduced separately throughout the book, where they are surrounded by the text that they illustrate and that illuminate them. Reviewers pointed out that this layout had the appearance of a *Gemara*. It also looks like a children's picture book.

This book, culled from writings that span fifteen years, is a highly personal combination of the various dimensions of my life and interests. At first, I was sure that nobody would be interested in reading such a book. To my surprise, however, the book had considerable impact; it struck a responsive chord among many Israelis. I am not fully comfortable writing about this reaction of others, but it is clear that in many ways the book's idiosyncracies formed a great part of its appeal. Possibly because I didn't represent any single establishment and because the content is complex and obsessively interdisciplinary, it appealed to many people and portrayed some of the multifaceted dimensions of other people's experiences. I hope that *From Jerusalem to the Edge of Heaven*, the English version of the book, will evoke similar responses.

Prologue

THE STORY OF THE LAD ALMA DEE

This book is a children's book. It tells the tale of a lad called Alma Dee, who plays among hundreds of eternal children and cries out "Yitgadal veyitkadash shmei rabbah be'alma dee." The hundreds of playing children do not understand his cry because they have lost their ability to hear sounds and can only see them. They wander in their perpetual play from place to place and from language to language. Sometimes they are the children of Jerusalem's ghettos, playing hide-and-seek in Yiddish, throwing rocks at secular Jews who drive through their neighborhoods on Shabbat; Sometimes they are the children of the Gaza ghettos, playing hide-and-seek in Arabic, throwing rocks at Jewish soldiers who drive through their neighborhoods every day; Sometimes they are the children of Pumbedita Babylonia–talmidei ḥakhamim who refuse to grow up, playing in talmudic Aramaic, hiding from the world and throwing mental rocks at each other.

JUST LIKE EVERY CHILDREN'S BOOK *worthy of the name, this book has illustrations, and around each drawing, words of the book are arranged. The words surrounding the pictures are written in very large letters so that the children reading the book will not have to strain to read them—a little teaser so that in the end they will feel like devoting the effort to read the rest of the parts of the book, the many pages without illustration, the many words written in the small print of the books that grown-ups read.*

Visually, the illustrated pages look like pages of the Talmud. In the Talmud, each page is made up of a central section of the Talmud itself, surrounded by sections that contain commentary. The length of the central Talmud section varies, and so no one of the 5362 pages of Talmud looks exactly like another page. Just like no child looks exactly like another child. After all, each and every child is a unique combination of its center and its commentaries.

EVERY ILLUSTRATION IN THIS BOOK *is a* midrash *on a part of the main picture* "Children's Games" *painted in the sixteenth century by the Flemish artist* Peter Breughel *and found today in the* Vienna Museum *of the* History *of* Art. *This picture depicts hundreds of children who are playing dozens of games, most of which are still familiar and are still played by contemporary children. This book is a midrash that connects Breughel's children and games from the sixteenth century* Flemish *environment with three completely separate environments: with the* Jerusalem *of the late* 1950's–*the scene of infra-Jewish battles between* dattiim *(Israeli Orthodox) and* hilonim *(Israeli secularists); with Gaza in the late 1980's–the scene of Palestinian-Jewish combat, and with* Pumbedita–*the eternal scene of the battle of* Torah *which (despite the opinion of certain modern scholars) has no specific date.*

THE CENTRAL BUILDING *in the drawing also comes out of its* Flemish *context and wanders into these three other contexts. Sometimes it is the* Gra *synagogue, the central synagogue of the ultraorthodox* Sha'arei Ḥesed *quarter–a lively* House of God *in whose many rooms are held daily* 4-5 *simultaneous minyans for* shaḥarit, minhah, *and* ma'ariv *services. Sometimes it is the central mosque of* Gaza *on the way to* Palestine Square*–a lively* House of God *where entry is off-limits to conquerors like me; sometimes it is the great* Beit Midrash (*Academy*) *of* Pumbedita*–an* Olympus *full of eternal* talmidei ḥakhamim, *who uproot imaginary mountains, grind them into infinite slivers and build heaps of* halakhot *on each sliver.* The *broad expanse that surrounds the mosque-synagogue-academy is always full of hundreds of children playing without pause.* Countless *voices always rise toward me in a characteristic mix of* Yiddish-Aramaic-Hebrew-Arabic.

IN ALL THIS TUMULT, *the lad* Alma Dee *keeps on crying* "Yitgadal veyitkadash shmei rabbah be'alma dee." *Reciting and reciting the lad runs crying, or else he leaps, or hurls himself on the ground, or climbs the wall, or plays on a seesaw, or stands on his head, And the other children see* Alma Dee *crying out* "Yitgadal veyitkadash shmei rabbah be'alma dee," *and carry on playing in four languages.*

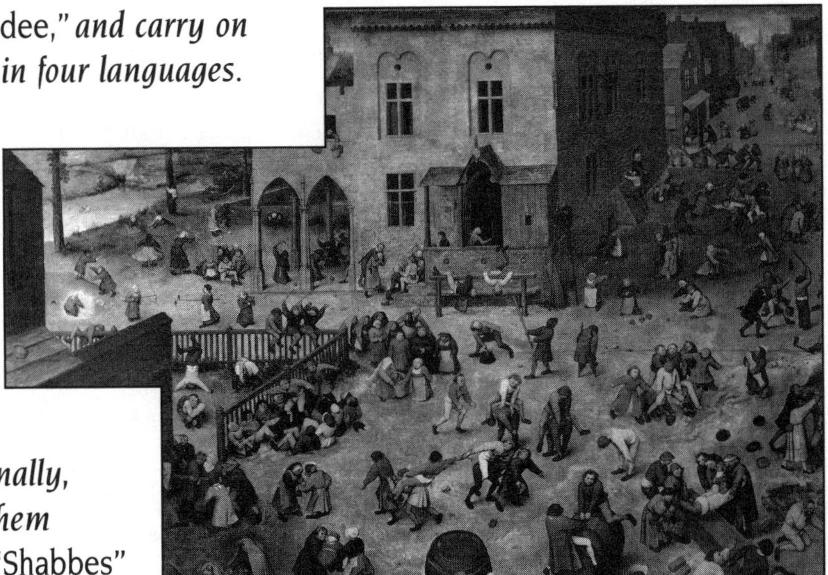

Occasionally, one of them shouts "Shabbes" *or* "Amen" *or* "Hineni" *or* "Al Yehud," *and keeps on running, and rolling on the ground, and shouting* "Oy," "Imma," "Shema Yisra'el," "Allah hu Akbar," *All the children see the voices of all the other children but none of them hears how* Alma Dee *keeps running and falling and crying* "Yitgadal veyitkadash shmei rabbah be'alma dee."

Sha'ar Atzmi:
My Own Gate

The Mourner's Kaddish: A Chapter from an Abandoned Novel Written in New York, 1978

On *Rosh Ḥodesh Elul* 5726 (1966), I murdered him out of mercy. I couldn't bear to see his suffering. During the whole of his last year, he would wander like a sleepwalker through the narrow streets of Jerusalem, a giant tallit wrapped around his Shabbat robe, his eyes dimmed, his lips murmuring with a mysterious stammer, "It is Shabbat today . . . it is forbidden to put on tefillin . . . it is forbidden to tear the strings that mark the Shabbat boundaries . . . it is Shabbat today."

Day after day, the children of Jerusalem threw stones at him and set their dogs on him. The dogs would tear his tallit from his shoulders, and he would continue to murmur, "It is Shabbat today, it is forbidden to put on tefillin . . . it is forbidden to throw stones at dogs . . . Why, children, do you throw stones at dogs? They will run off to the edge of town and tear the strings of the Shabbat boundaries, and then Jerusalem will not be marked off from the rest of the world . . . it is Shabbat today . . . it is forbidden to put on tefillin . . . ."

I could not watch his misery. I closed my eyes, and I bit my lips, and I tore the invisible strings that were his last connection to this world.

After that, I went out into the streets of Jerusalem and said *Kaddish Yatom,* the mourner's Kaddish. For three days and three nights I wandered through the streets and said Kaddish, murmuring with a mysterious stammer:

> *Yitgadal veyitkadash shmei rabbah be'alma dee.*
> *Be'alma dee yitgadal veyitkadash shmei rabbah.*
> *Shmei rabbah be'alma dee yitgadal veyitkadash.*[1]

For three days and three nights I wandered through the narrow streets of Jerusalem, and I recalled the wonderful days he had granted me as a child. Then I mourned him for seven straight years.

During my childhood, he used to carry me on the wings of his imagination, and he used to know all my thoughts even before I thought them. Every day he used to accompany me to school through the alleyways of Sha'arei Ḥesed, Naḥla'ot, and the Maḥane Yehuda market. Every day he would skip behind me over the roofs of the houses, and he would help me cross the streets in the days before there were traffic lights in Jerusalem. During prayers, he would hover between the synagogue chandelier and the ceiling and help me direct my devotions. And, when I went to the refrigerator on my tiptoes and opened it, he waited for me there, and I couldn't take a bite of ice cream until three full hours after my meat lunch. He never got angry. He only made me feel ashamed.

On Shabbat, he used to accompany me to the Betar soccer game. The YMCA field roared with thousands of fans who crowded outside the walls, on the rooftops of the houses and at the tops of the cypress trees. Above them rose the YMCA tower, which for many years was the highest building in Jerusalem—the stone closest to the sky. He hovered above the tower like an eagle, as far as possible from the horrible desecration of Shabbat, from the whistles and the vulgar language. Even there he didn't get angry at me. He only spread an additional flush on my cheeks so that they burned from shame throughout the whole game.

When we played hide-and-seek, he hovered above us and saw everyone hiding. And when I leaned my head against the counting stone and counted to a hundred (I counted very fervently, as if praying), then there on my right was Michael; on my left, Gabriel; at my front, Uriel; and at my back, Raphael:[2] "One, two three, I'm coming to get you."

The old women of Sha'arei Ḥesed had to climb the steep hill of Keren Kayemet. He used to push them from behind and help them overcome the earth's gravity. And when they would stop in their tracks, too tired to move, he would secretly support them until they gathered new strength for the rest of the ascent. At the top of the hill, he would shift their gears and merge them onto the level road.

At noon, he would stop the *ḥiloni* (secular) children coming out of school and hold them back at the curb until the speeding car that was coming around the corner had passed. And when the children of Sha'arei Ḥesed slid down the hill on wooden sleds they had made themselves, he would let their sidelocks fly in the wind and then brake their sleds at the bottom of the hill.

Once, secretly, I asked myself, "How come he gets to be God, and I don't? . . . What luck he has that he was chosen over everybody to be God . . . ." I was very jealous of him in those days, and I tried very hard to hide my envy from him. But at the top of Keren Kayemet Street, on the corner of Sha'arei Ḥesed, he told me that even my envy was known to him. And I blushed intensely.

He wasn't angry. But a dim and distant pain began to split me deep inside. The ache of heresy. The ache of an irresistible sadness. I envied him—I remember this with certainty—I envied him that he was God and I was not. This envy saddened my heart. But even sadder to me was the recognition that I could not hide my envy from him.

So I taught myself to envy in secret. Little by little, I taught myself to hide

HOW COME HE GETS TO BE GOD, AND I DON'T?

Once, secretly, I asked, myself, "How come he gets to be God, and I don't?... What luck he has that he was chosen over everybody to be God....

"I was very jealous of him in those days, and I tried very hard to hide my envy from him.

But at the top of Keren Kayemet Street, on the corner of Sha'arei Ḥesed, he told me that even my envy was known to him. And I blushed intensely.

He wasn't angry. But a dim and distant pain began to split me deep inside. The ache of heresy. The ache of an irresistible sadness. I envied him—I remember this with certainty—I envied him that he was God and I was not. This envy saddened my heart. But even sadder to me was the recogni-ion that I could not hide my envy from him.

my envy from him. "Why is he God and not I?" I asked myself, and he didn't know.

He didn't know.

And sometimes he couldn't even fathom the depths of my fervent devotion in prayer. Suddenly, I would find myself alone, in the depths of fervent meditation, and I was barely able to come back up without losing my breath. I was very frightened.

Every year, he became a little more tired. Sometimes he even fell asleep while I was saying my bedtime *Shema,* "Behold the Guardian of Israel neither slumbers nor sleeps—at My right is Michael, at My left is Gabriel. Nobody in front of Me or behind Me. One two three, I'm coming to get you."

I looked for him all night. I didn't sleep for a minute. I was afraid of the dark.

And I was afraid of my passion for devotion in prayer. The more fervently I prayed, the more I sensed fearfully that I was talking to myself. And the stronger the desire for fervent prayer grew within me, the more I feared the lies that I was telling myself . . . that I was telling myself.

I wanted him too much. Too much. I wanted him without intermediaries. Direct. I sang a song to him, direct. Day after day I sang a song to him. And I fastened crowns for his head; bands of unrequited love. With invisible strings I pulled him up from the ground and he was my kite. He was my rainbow in the clouds. I ran and pulled the strings of his kite. I ran and fell, cried, and rose again; I sang before him a new song and continued to run and fall, to cry and get up, and sing before him a new song.

I was drawn toward him with excessive force, and I pulled on his invisible strings with excessive force. I tore them, and he continued to fly in his empty skies, completely disconnected from everything.

And, disconnected from everything, he continued to wander the narrow streets of Jerusalem murmuring all the time, "It is Shabbat today . . . it is forbidden to put on tefillin . . . it is forbidden to tear the strings that mark the Shabbat boundary . . . it is Shabbat today."

The children of Jerusalem hurled rocks at him, and their dogs tore his tallit from his shoulders. He continued to mutter, "It is Shabbat today . . . it is forbidden to put on tefillin . . . it is forbidden to throw stones at dogs . . . . Why children, would you want to throw stones at dogs? They will run away to the outskirts of the town and tear the strings of the Shabbat boundary with their teeth, and Jerusalem will not be marked off from the rest of the world . . . it is Shabbat today . . . it is forbidden to put on tefillin."

For ten years I ran away from this murder that I had committed in my great mercy. For ten years I wandered between cities of refuge. I changed identities; I jumped borders; I trampled plantings and ruined vineyards. I left behind me destroyed gardens, orchards without owner. For ten years, I lived off the absence of authority.

When the *yetzer* (impulse) came upon me, I would dress in black and wrap myself in black and go out to whistle in the hide-and-go-seek field at the bottom of Keren Kayemet. One two three, I went to seek. Many hours I wandered through the hide-and-go-seek field whistling to myself the melodies of *Kol Nidrei,* the tunes of *Yedid Nefesh,* the whistles of *"Eli, Eli,* why have you forsaken me?"

I was very careful not to pass too close to a synagogue, lest the *yetzer* carry me inside. "They're only melodies," it would say to me seductively, "It's only the melodies that you are entering for, not the content, not the words that accompany the melodies. You will only make the sound, you won't even move your lips. They will think you are drunk, not praying. After all, it is not forbidden to sing the melodies without pronouncing the forbidden words." This was a very sophisticated heavenly trap.

I didn't come down to earth until the end of my period of mourning. I remained in the skies in order to erase all the real lines that I had drawn in my childhood that connected me to him, in order to tear all the invisible strings. Until this very day, when I lift my tired eyes heavenward, I see tens of thousands of lines of warp and woof. The warp, lines of my childhood, and the woof, erasures of my adolescence. I didn't fight him from the ground. With great ambition, I was eager to attack him in his heavenly base. It was a long war, one which I neither won nor lost.

And yet, when I returned to earth tired and bruised, I observed to my amazement that Earth had been flooded with new streams from the sky. We were drowning in sky and I, I didn't know where I was going.

Until one day I realized the tragic fact that the high wall that I had been so careful to build between me and him—he who is not—was in actuality a high wall between me and other people. An arrogant and intolerant wall.

A repressed rage started to gather in me, and I had nobody to direct it toward. A screen of erased lines divided me from the world. Black on sky. I was so angry at him that he never was and never will be, and I blamed him for leaving me without an address at which to direct my aims, toward which to devote my devotions.

And the more that the rage grew, the greater there grew in me a new desire, a passion for obligation, a passion to draw near to people. And my sleep (for which I had once urgently longed) began to lift from my eyes. My ever-increasing desire to be close to people forced me to speak in his name. Whatever will be, will be. But how could I come to them and cast a silence in the synagogue to announce that he is not?

And on the first day of *Elul,* 5736 (1976)—exactly ten years after his death, I cast a silence in a synagogue and began to speak in his name. Ever since then I have been a rabbi. Since then I have been beloved and revered.

Since then I have been the young rabbi of a congregation of elderly New

Yorkers in the old age home Sha'ar Hashamayim, which stands at the edge of the Lower East Side.

Since then until this very day, I have had only one mission—to make sure that until the day of their death, the old people will not taste the taste of his death. To make sure that they won't look back, I dedicate all my time to building a perfect system of illusions that will cause them to keep looking forward. Toward the East.

From this East—my East—I bring light to my world and its inhabitants. I hold on to the horns of the Holy Ark and spark fire with my sermons. "The *Kodesh Borukh Hu* hears," I bring the good news, "The *Kodesh Borukh Hu* sees . . . The *Kodesh Borukh Hu* knows." And their eyes sparkle. Oh, how their eyes sparkle!

Since then until this very day, I have trampled no plantings, I have denied neither the essential nor the incidental, and I have not changed anything in the *Shulḥan Arukh* (the law code) of my old people. At their age, changes bring doubt and anxiety to the heart. Everything that they keep, I keep. My one obligation is my obligation to them. Together we put on tefillin, together we keep our *Shabbatot.*

From Shabbat to Shabbat, the length of our weekdays grows shorter. From Shabbat to Shabbat, we retreat into ourselves.

From Shabbat to Shabbat, the pains of new longings form within me. The bittersweetness of *galut* (exile) cleaves my tongue to my palate, and nice old men spin delicate webs of dreams around me. Beyond them lies the violence of poor blacks. Beyond them, the violence of rich whites. I am their barricade in the face of the violence around us, and they—they are a wall of innocence that stands between me and Hell. They give content to my shortening days between Shabbat and Shabbat. They make me forget the sight of New York, a great octopus that extends her slow tentacles in every direction. From Shabbat to Shabbat, she destroys herself. From Shabbat to Shabbat, we sing the songs of the Shabbat's final meal deeper into the week.

By last fall we already remained around the white Shabbat tables until dawn. On that day we didn't put on tefillin. Since then we have not put on tefillin on Sunday mornings.

From Shabbat to Shabbat, dream webs are spun about Jerusalem, and mountains are folded into the web. And that wonderful pang of longing returns, "May our eyes see Your return to Zion, O come mercifully back to Your city Jerusalem, and dwell within her as You said . . . . "

I will never return to dwell in Jerusalem. She is no longer marked off from the rest of the world. Her western suburbs already reach those of the eastern plain, and the strings of her Shabbat barrier are completely torn. What do I have to do with a city without Shabbat barriers? I have chosen a congregation in a godforsaken city. The holy congregation Sha'ar Hashamayim on the edge of the Lower East Side. There I have set up my ladder and put wonder blocks at my head. There I labor to turn all the stones and trees of Jerusalem into words. Into prayers. Into dreams in Yiddish.

For the sake of my old people, I will not be silent. I climb an electric ladder for them. I carry their prayers up invisible rungs. The ladder is very high, and they are afraid to get near it. They have no grounding. I carry their prayers up to a higher heaven. To a level that doesn't exist. I am their porter; they shove tips into the many pockets of my overalls. The many coins make the climb more difficult for me. They pull me downward like weights. I climb with prayers and come down empty—climb up with another prayer and come down empty. And they walk back and forth on a platform and talk about this and talk about that and watch the automatic timetable whose letters race and whose hours change. All the while, trains are arriving. All the while, trains are departing.

Every once in a while, they put their right hands into an inside pocket of their coat, take out a gold watch, look at it, and compare the time on their watch to the time on the big clock on the wall. And when they return the watch to the inside pocket of their coats, they check to make sure that their return ticket is still there. They pat it one more time just to make sure.

They drink my words with tears of happiness. At the end of my sermon they pray with great fervor for their souls. I don't dare ask them to pray for my errant soul—my soul is their support, broken reed that it is. How could I dare proclaim in their ears that it is errant, lonely, lost, and accursed? Have I come to destroy their world? And who am I, and what is my accursed quest toward my accursed honesty compared with the eternal life of hundreds of innocent and sinless believers?

Every day I say to myself: Behold I place before you responsibility and truth. And you shall choose responsibility. Every day I choose responsibility.

Responsibility is my ability to sacrifice my private truth three times a day. To pray *Shaḥarit* to an empty sky. And *Minḥah* and *Ma'ariv.* And on Shabbat—the day of exaltation—to deceive myself four times a day. And on Yom Kippur—the Shabbat of *Shabbatot*—to pray *Ma'ariv* to empty dark skies, *Shaḥarit* to empty lightening skies, *Mussaf* to empty blazing skies, *Minḥah* to empty exhausted skies, and *Ne'ilah* to empty setting skies.

In the beginning, we had human sacrifices. Afterward, we had animal sacrifices—the substitute for human sacrifice. After that we had prayers—the substitute for animal sacrifice. And after that we have human sacrifices—the substitute for prayers. I, I am the human sacrifice—a daily sacrifice—burning live on my coals. Willingly offering my neck so that my believers will be able to pray.

I get up early every morning and wrap myself in a warm, white tallit. After that I close my eyes for a long moment in painful fervor. I listen inward to my inner conflict. To my daily conflict between truth and responsibility. And at the end of this long, fervent moment when responsibility wins out, I bind myself: I wind black straps around my arm, fasten them to my forehead, and say:

Yitgadal veyitkadash shmei rabbah be'alma dee
Be'alma dee yitgadal veyitkadash shmei rabbah
Shmei rabbah be'alma dee yitgadal veyitkadash

Then I experience a certain lightening of spirit that enables me to grasp the horns of the Holy Ark and spark fire in my sermons.

"Do not understand, my old ones, the Kaddish that you say evening, morning and noon. Jewish orphans have never understood their Mourners' Kaddish. Do not understand, my orphans; I will understand for you. I will understand for you, and you will say *Amen Yehei shmei rabbah be'alma dee.* Do not be afraid, my old ones; a day is drawing near that is neither day nor night, and on that day there will be a splendid platform—a terminal with velvet carpets. The cars will be covered in a red drape, and the bronze track will be a ramp. A ramp to heaven. You will walk peacefully on the splendid platform, and I will load the cars with your prayers. On every prayer I will write "heaven" in the giant letters used for *Kiddush Levanah* (The Blessing of the Moon). At the end of the journey, when you reach heaven, you will find your prayers moving before you on the luggage belts. You will locate them from a distance, and angels, bellboys in yellow caps, will push them in wagons for you. There, an elevator angel with a blue cap will wait for you. You won't move, but the elevator will go up and up and up. You will have a long Shabbat. A very long Shabbat. Without tefillin. Without torn threads. Elevators will mount to the sky and will mount beyond the sky, until you will break free of the sky's gravitational pull. You will go on. You, children, will go up and up and will not fall. You will not get dirty from the sandbox. There will be no sand. And there will be silence. The skies will have no sound. The skies will be calm. You will not know sorrow. You will not long for Jerusalem, for this will be your Jerusalem. And the sky, blue leaning toward purple fading into blue . . . .

Do not be afraid, my old ones, take a few possessions with you. The return ticket, the gold watch, and the prayer for a safe journey. Sing the prayer for a safe journey. Your song will have no sound—only your lips will move and you will be prayerful and drunk, drunk and prayerful. The whole sky will have no sound. Just blue leaning toward purple, blue fading to sky blue.

Alma Dee

Alma Dee was an orphan boy from the Reḥavia district. The children of Sha'arei Ḥesed gave him this nickname after the death of his father. Most reports say that Alma Dee left Israel in the mid-70's. But there is a stubborn rumor that he disappeared into the Sinai at the end of the War of Attrition; after that all traces of him were lost. In any event, nobody who knew him by the nickname Alma Dee knew his real name, so that there is no possibility of discovering what really became of him.

Before the death of his father, Alma Dee never appeared at prayer time and never visited the synagogue. After he was orphaned, his grandfather made him come with him every day to the Gra Synagogue in Sha'arei Ḥesed to say Kaddish.

During the entire service, he sat next to his grandfather and stared out the window at the large courtyard where the children of Sha'arei Ḥesed were playing catch, their forelocks waving in the wind as they ran. Every once in a while, he put his hand to his head to check that his *kippah* hadn't fallen off.

Toward the end of the service, when it was time to recite the Mourner's Kaddish, a tension arose in the room. In an instant, the children of Sha'arei Ḥesed stopped their game, crowded around the doorway, and waited for the Kaddish with mischievous tension.

Alma Dee would stand up and declaim the Kaddish with a mysterious stammer:

Yitgadal veyitkadash shmei rabbah be'alma dee
bara khiruteh veyamlikh
malkhuteh beḥayekhon uveyomekhon uveḥayei
dekol beit Yisrael be'agalah
uvizman kariv ve'imru
amen . . .

(Magnified and sanctified be His great name in that world which)
(He created by His will and is King.)
(His kingship in your life and days and in the life of)
(of all Israel speedily)
(and in the near future, and say you)
(amen)

All the children who crowded about kept themselves from laughing and answered, "amen" in chorus. Afterward, Alma Dee sat down in his seat and continued to stare out the window until the end of the prayer.

When he came out of the synagogue, he would run in front of his grandfather, kicking pinecones and little stones. The children would shout Alma

Dee to each other, and I never knew whether or not Alma Dee knew they were referring to him.

Five years afterward, in *Elul* 5726 (1966), the God of my childhood passed away. For three days and three nights, I wandered in the alleyways of Sha'arei Ḥesed, and I tried to say Mourner's Kaddish for him. That whole time I saw before my eyes that orphan of orphans: Alma Dee. Finally I closed my eyes and dared to say the Mourner's Kaddish with that mysterious stammer:

Yitgadal veyitkadash shmei rabbah be'alma dee
be'alma dee Yitgadal veyitkadash shmei rabbah
Shmei rabbah be'alma dee yitgadal veyitkadash

A few years later I would acknowledge the Mourner's Kaddish in that mysterious stammer as the key sentence of my life: *Yitgadal veyitkadash shmei rabbah be'alma dee,* which means in English, "Magnified and sanctified be His great name in the D world." The stammered Kaddish that I spoke revealed to me the secret of the existence of Alma Dee, "the World of D." "The world of D "—the imaginary world that lies beyond the boundaries of this world, that world where God dwells in splendid fullness.

Since then I have learned explicitly: God is dead in this world but lives eternally in the World of D; in it, magnified and sanctified is His great name. And I have learned further: The absolute prerequisite for the magnification and sanctification of God in the D world is the death of God in the real world. Only my decisive realization of God's death in this world and my feeling of being orphaned from God pushed me into my quest for the traces of God's fascinating presence in the infinity of all possible worlds.

I call this infinity of possible universes *Alma Dee,* "The World of D." And from here on I call the real world "World *Bet*" (the B world).

Why "world *bet*?" Because the world in which we live has the shape of the letter *bet.* That is what they explained to me when I began to learn to read the *ḥumash,* the five books of the Torah. When God created the world, God decided to create it in the square form of the letter *bet.* That is why God wrote, *"**B**ereshit **b**ara Elohim et hashamayim ve'et ha'aretz"* (In the Beginning God created the heavens and the earth). If God had wanted to make the world in the shape of the letter *gimmel,* God would have written *"**G**ereshit **g**ara Elohim et hashamayim ve'et ha'aretz."*

When I began to study *ḥumash,* the world was not yet round. The Copernican revolution was still far in the distant future, and the stars were gilded kites held in the sleep cords of children. When I began to study *ḥumash,* my world was shaped in the form of the letter *bet,* bounded with firm and secure borders on three sides. The heavens were its upper border, the deep its lower border, and the edge of Mamilla Street its eastern border.

We weren't allowed to approach the border. And when we did approach, we were cautioned not to point at the walls of the Old City because the Jordanian snipers hidden there could misunderstand our pointing fingers as the movement of guns. That, at least, was what the children of Mamilla Street told us very convincingly.

But it was even more dangerous to approach the border of the heavens. Even then we knew very well that there were questions that were simply forbidden to ask. For example, what is above the sky? And what existed before creation? And who created God? And can God create a rock that He can't lift? These questions we dared to speak to each other in our own rooms, but there were many even more terrifying questions that the heart didn't even dare reveal to the mouth. And the most terrifying: Why is He God and not I?

We already knew how to declaim in a trembling manner the rabbinic midrash that is found in many places in talmudic literature: "Why was the world created with a *bet*? To tell you, just as the *bet* is closed at its sides and open in front, so, too, you do not have the right to ask what is above, what is below, what is before, and what is after."

And yet, despite all the many years that have passed since then and even though it is now round, our world of reality is still bounded—even in these advanced days. It is still miserable and ridiculous compared with the infinity of possible worlds that the human imagination conceals. The heavens are still its firmest border, and the many midrashim that warn against questioning what is above and what is below are still extremely relevant.

Prolegomenon to Any Future Metaphysics

The night after Yom Kippur 5734—the 6th of October 1973—I was riding in a crowded pickup, shaking like a drunk with the DTs and trying to read (by flashlight) Kant's *Prolegomenon to Any Future Metaphysics.* All night the jeep drove amidst an unending convoy of vehicles that moved west on the rough roads of the Sinai.

I was scheduled to take an exam on Kant with Professor Rotenstreich on October 10, and I was convinced that I would get back to Jerusalem before the day of the exam. All night I concentrated on Kant and paid no attention to the march music that sounded constantly from transistor radios; no attention to the thousands of pickups, trucks, jeeps, tank cars, half-tracks, and tank carriers; no attention to the thousands of eager voices that obscured the *Prolegomenon to a Future Metaphysics.*

All night I shook and sang Kant to the tune of the *Hineni,* which had sounded from the mouth of Rabbi Abraham Shapira, who had been *Ba'al Mussaf* just a few hours before at the minyan of the Merkaz Harav Yeshivah. That Yom Kippur service was the first service I attended after I had stopped praying five years earlier. I was praying *Mussaf* with my brother Benny, a student at the yeshivah, when the sirens sounded. I never finished that *Mussaf.* Kant's

Prolegomenon, I finished before sunrise. I have never known Kant better than I did on that morning, October 7, 1973.

The sunrise itself I can't remember. I fell asleep while looking at clouds redden in the East before the Sinai sunrise. In my sleep I returned to the previous evening, walking the streets near the yeshivah. There was no sound as I walked in my white canvas sneakers. And there was no sound as an ancient man walked toward me, for he also wore white sneakers.

The silence of Yom Kippur spread to the horizon. No car disturbed it. I thought to myself that when the old man reached me, I would nod hello wordlessly so as not to disturb the silence. But he kept approaching me without ever reaching me. He had a white beard and white curls, wore a white robe, and his sneakers were as white as his curls.

I returned to the yeshivah in absolute darkness. I didn't want to turn on the light in the dormitory corridors, and I didn't remember whether my room was the third on the right or the third on the left.

I went into the study room, took out a copy of Rav Kook's *Orot Hateshuvah (The Lights of Repentance),* I went up to the roof, and tried to read by the light of the moon. I couldn't concentrate. I swayed back and forth with great devotion, but I couldn't understand a single sentence. The more powerfully I *shuckled* (swayed), the greater grew my hope that Someone could see me during this moment of inconspicuous rightful action. Then, after an hour of continuous *shuckling,* I clapped my head in my hands, deeply ashamed of my own hypocritical desire to be noticed as I performed an "unnoticed righteous act." I comforted myself with the thought that indeed there was no God in this place so that no one could see my disgrace. When I convinced myself that, indeed, there was no God here, I laughed in confusion. When my laughter died I was horrified. In my horror, I resumed swaying over *Orot Hateshuvah,* and I couldn't free myself of the hidden, despised hope that Someone, after all, was watching me.

As the darkness began to lift, the pines and cypresses of Jerusalem came alive with the wild chirping of thousands of birds hidden within them. I fell asleep, *Orot Hateshuvah* on my lap.

I awoke tramping through sand dunes. Thousands of confused men were treading ankle-deep in sand without making any forward progress. A painful metallic whine came humming out of the burning sun. We abandoned thousands of vehicles from our endless convoy on the rough asphalt surface of the Akavish route to the Sinai, and we followed with fearful trembling the columns of smoke that arose from the band of Sohoy bombers as they flew away. Suddenly, someone shouted, "They're coming back!" but the people around me continued to stamp in place without being able to move forward. I stamped with them, stumbling while fleeing, unable to get up, digging a pit with my fingers, scattering sand like a urinating dog. My mouth drooled, my knees trembled, my stomach cramped. "They're coming back!" someone cried again, and I whispered to myself, "This is it, I'm dead . . . I'm dead."

Two weeks later, I crossed the Suez canal. For the first time in my life, I left the continent of my birth—Asia—and I landed in the land of Goshen, which lies at the northeast boundary of Africa. In the long cool nights of the land of Goshen, during endless tank expeditions, I finally realized that the God of my childhood would never return. Finished were the seven years of religious searching that had begun on the first of *Elul* 5726 (1965), seven terrible years of pathetic attempts to conjure up my childhood God with a crystal ball. This realization that my childhood God was gone was accompanied by an overwhelming sense, *tremendans* and *fascinans,* that along with my God I would lose also my people and my homeland.

Many voices started to call to me through the endless tank sorties, "Go from your land, your homeland, your father's house to the land that I will show you." And a sweet taste of lusty adventure mixed with the fear that arose from the calling voices—the taste of *galut.* In the long cool nights of the land of Goshen, during the endless tank sorties, I planned my first exile. I spent my few leaves from the Army selling off my belongings, planning the trip, and holding a garage sale.

I was discharged in the spring of 1974. On the way from Africa to Europe, I passed through my home base—Israel—in order to get discharged and hand in all my provisions. In return, I got a one-way ticket from Tel Aviv to London and a wallet of travelers' checks in dollars.

From the moment that the plane took off, I gave myself over to the ancient sweet pleasure of Abraham—the pleasure of smashing idols. I trailed shattered pieces of gods behind me, shattered fragments of homeland, and broken bits of people. "Your people are not my people," I said *sotto voce* in the direction of the self-satisfied Israelis in the plane, "and your God is not my God. You have round-trip tickets, and I am only going one way. Period. I am going forth from my land, from my homeland, from my father's house, and I am flying to a new people and homeland. There, at the edge of the landing strip under the deep clouds, there a new god already awaits me. I am that god. Master of Myself. I and no other am the master who spoke from within me and said, 'go forth,' and I went."

So began the pseudo-self-mastery period of my life. Four hours later, the Boeing passed through the clouds over the English Channel on its way to the landing strip. I stayed in the clouds. It was a whole year later, at the end of the spring of 1975, before I managed to land. Not in London. In Israel. Among the ruins. Among the shattered gods. The hangover that came after the intoxication of smashing was very cruel. A broken voice called to me out of the depths, "Abraham, Abraham, why did you raise your hand against the boy? Cursed be you. All the days of your life, you will try in vain to rebuild your ruins. Until the day you die, you will piece together a puzzle of your shattered bits of your idols. Cursed are you and cursed is the ground that you walk on. You will be a wanderer in your land, in your homeland, in your father's house."

And since then I have been a wandering preacher in my land, in my homeland. Sometimes I strike fire with my sermons. Accursed am I.

The Vocabulary of Refugee Kids (Al Yehud)

A week after I returned to my homeland, I was called up by the army. A month later, I found myself in a refugee camp for the first time in my life. Each day, every day, I made thousands of horrified Palestinian kids run away. Every day, my job was to comb a portion of the alleys in the Jebalia refugee camp in the Gaza strip. The alleys were very narrow. Sometimes they were narrower than the weaponry hanging at the ready across my chest. In their midst was an open sewage trench. The air echoed with the happy cries of kids.

It was in the hot, early afternoon. At that hour, the men of the camp were on the scaffolding of construction sites in greater Tel Aviv. The women tried not to be seen. The old men sat in coffee houses and fingered colorful strings of worry beads. The big children were studying in U.N. schools in the camps. Only little kids cried joyously in the alleyways. Goats and chickens wandered among them over the open sewage.

We passed from alley to alley, more or less, just as we had practiced during the dozens of maneuvers that trained us for combat in built-up areas. Two men stood against the wall, guns cocked, eyes scanning the walls facing them. And I, with a tense and exacting movement, entered the new alley. In this way, I secured myself successfully from any potential ambush by any conceivable terrorist who might await me around the bend. But, whenever I suddenly entered a new alley, this is the scene that repeated itself: Dozens of kids romping in the alley ran away from me as from a monster. Less than two seconds passed before they all disappeared into the courtyards of houses or into other alleys. In an instant, the joyous cries of playing children changed into panicked screams. And when the screams died down, the alley became tensely still. In the air echoed the one word which accompanied the kids' flight: *Al Yehud* (the Jew).

"Al Yehud," they cried and ran away, *"Al Yehud, al Yehud, al Yehud."* One sole word from the small vocabulary of refugee children. They didn't yell, "soldiers," and they didn't yell, "monsters." Not "thugs," and not "bandits." Not "imperialists," and not "conquerors." Not "paratroopers," and not "border control." Not "Zionists," and not "Israelis." *"Al Yehud."* Thus, in one word, they defined me. That one word was enough to contain all the negative terms just mentioned, and many, many more. Never have so many characterized me so

AL YEHUD... AL YEHUD... AL YEHUD...

Whenever I suddenly entered a new alley, this is the scene that repeated itself: Dozens of kids romping in the alley ran from me as from a monster. Less than two seconds passed before they all disappeared into the courtyards of houses or into other alleys. In an instant, the joyous cries of playing children changed into panicked screams. And when the screams died down, the alley became tensely still. In the air echoed the one word which accompanied the kids' flight: Al Yehud (the Jew).

"Al Yehud," they cried and ran away, "Al Yehud, al Yehud, al Yehud." One sole word from the small vocabulary of refugee children. They didn't yell, "soldiers," and they didn't yell, "monsters." Not "thugs," and not "bandits." Not "imperialists," and not "conquerors." Not "paratroopers," and not "border control." Not "Zionists," and not "Israelis." "Al Yehud." Thus, in one word, they defined me. That one word was enough to contain all the negative terms just mentioned, and many, many, more. Never have so many characterized me so intensely–and with only one word, a word repeated thousands of times every day.

intensely—and with only one word, a word repeated thousands of times every day.

This nightmare lasted forty days. On the fortieth day, I was released, and an old Egged bus took me, along with the others coming off duty, to the Central Bus Station in Tel Aviv. For the first time in forty days, I found myself walking on a Jewish street, among the cassette stalls of the Central Bus Station. I had not even had time to pass the first platform before a smiling Lubavitcher Hasid approached me, a tefillin bag in his hand, "Soldier, do you want to be a Jew for a bit and put on tefillin?" I didn't want to. "What do you care? It only takes two minutes . . . Be a Jew for a moment." I didn't want to. "You won't miss the bus; you'll have a mitzvah . . . for free. Be a Jew for a moment, it won't hurt you."

On the bus to Jerusalem, I sat on the last bench and cried. Behind my sunglasses, of course.

Pumbedita: Every Day I Am Careful Not to Take an Overdose

The next day, I entered a senior class at a famous Jerusalem high school as a new teacher. My first classes in rabbinic literature had been postponed because of my reserve duty. Some of the boys in the class were wearing *kippot,* and the rest had their *kippot* at the ready on the tables before them. When I entered, some of the students told me, bemused, that I must be in the wrong classroom. They were waiting for a Judaism instructor—me they took for the army training instructor of the class across the hall. I told them I didn't know the meaning of the term "Judaism," and anyway, I couldn't be their Judaism teacher; however I was the one who was to teach them rabbinic literature, what they call, with a mocking tone, *Toshba.* After they recovered from the shock, they asked me where my *kippah* was and why was my appearance so different from that of a Judaism teacher? When I asked them what they meant by the appearance of a Judaism teacher, they explained that they meant someone with a *kippah* and beard and *tsitsit* (fringes) flying, someone like a yeshivah rabbi or at least a rabbinic assistant. Afterward I asked the boys if they wore *kippot* in their math class. They answered, as I expected, "Only in Jewish studies." And when I asked them what they meant by Jewish studies, someone answered, "The subjects of the *datti'im*" (Israeli Orthodox), and somebody added, "Subjects that the *datti'im* teach."

"And you—what do you have to do with Judaism? Are you Jews?"

"Us? Not so much. We're Jews a little—they are much more Jews than we."

The circle closes. In those days I lived with the sense that the Zionist movement was dissipating. That it had been a finite episode—a national liberation movement for the Jewish people—and that it was no more. This movement toward national liberation had been compelling and dynamic, but the Jewish people had remained static. In this way, Judaism had gone back to being a religion; its religion had gone back to being a rabbinic sect, and the rabbis had returned to being the exclusive spokesmen and teachers of Judaism. Full circle.

Seniors in high school were Jews for a bit—for two hours a week—the time that they wore their paper *kippot* in their *Toshba* classes. The next year they will get to be Jews for a bit at the places where soldiers assemble—at the terminals of the central bus stations. As the soldiers come back from refugee camps for weekend leaves, yeshiva students will wrap their bodies in black straps and will cover their heads with black paper *kippot.* At these gathering places for soldiers the yeshivah Jews will extend the Jewish passports of these boy-soldiers, lengthening for a few months their identity as Jews (Jews for a bit).

In those days, I lived with the sense that the Jewish people had voluntarily given up the certificate of liberation it had acquired in the Zionist revolution and had voluntarily gone back to the pre-emancipation ghetto, the period in which a Jew's identity was contingent on membership in a rabbinic sect. A time in which "Who is a Jew?" was not an issue at all, because a Jew was only someone defined as such by the rabbis.

Full circle. The rabbis who had been appointed the exclusive interpreters of the rabbinic beliefs of the rabbinic sect in exile have continued to be appointed the sole definers of Jewish peoplehood in its land. This people continues to appoint them. This people will not or cannot stop being a sect. What have I to do with it?

And the expatriate in me returned to pack his bags.

Ever since then my bags have been packed. Ever since then, to this very day, I leave my homeland every day and take off for an exile far more exciting and profound than London. I fly to Pumbedita, to the great city Pumbedita on the great river, the Euphrates. My take-off field to Pumbedita is the Babylonian Talmud. Ever since then I have been in the midst of the second emigration of my life. Every day I take off from Israel to Pumbedita. There I enter into discussions with Rashi and Rabbi Akiva about the debates of Abaye and Rava. There I pose twenty-four questions for Rabbi Yoḥanan, and he gives me twenty-four responses. And one page of Talmud stretches as long as *galut* itself, and Rav Reḥumi joins us together with Bar Yoḥai, Yehuda ben Ḥiyya, the Gaon of Vilna, Ḥoni, Resh Lakish, Elisha ben Avuya, and the rest of the children of Sha'arei Ḥesed.

The *Bavli,* the Babylonian Talmud, is the take-off field for my daily journeys to Alma Dee, the world of infinite possibilities. Israel is, after all, only the *bet* World, my secondary place of residence. Ever since *Elul* of 1975, Israel has served primarily as my landing field. The exile of Pumbedita is the land of unbounded possibilities, and Israel only a land of very limited possibilities. Israel is a very restricted land with harsh obligatory regulations which sometimes seem intolerable to me: traffic rules, and income tax regulations, and marriage laws. And worse of all: the rules about army reserve service and the need to make a living.

For my livelihood, I have to teach and preach. I have to come down from my rooftop and wander through my homeland, teaching about this and preaching about that. One can't make a living from the study of Torah in a nonrabbinic society. Such a society doesn't know how to value study for its own sake, doesn't subsidize the scholars or release them from reserve duty, and doesn't free them from bureaucratic entanglements. It doesn't admire them, and it doesn't give them the chance to be free of the equal democratic obligations that impinge on their poor enlightened souls. In short, because of my sins I am exiled from the place of Torah and have to come down from my rooftop and teach and preach for a livelihood. "I was young and now I am old," and I was never privileged to have my work done by others.

I obliterate the pain of making a living and of existence by studying the Torah of Pumbedita. As it is said, "Whoever feels pain in the head should study the Torah; whoever feels pain in the throat should study the Torah; whoever feels pain in the guts should study the Torah; whoever feels pain anywhere in the body should study the Torah."[3] The Torah of Pumbedita is my medicinal drug. As it is written: "'This is the Torah which Moshe placed *(śam)*'—don't read 'placed' but *sam* (drug)."[4] I am careful not to take an overdose and not to get too high. The Torah of Pumbedita is the taste of life, but it could very easily turn into the taste of death. As it is written, "If one is worthy it will be a medicine; if one is not worthy, a poisonous drug."[5]

Ever since *Elul* of 1975, I have been addicted to the *galut* of Pumbedita, which is more fascinating and more dangerous than any other conceivable *galut.* And because Pumbedita carries such great danger in its midst, I force myself to come down daily to the land of Israel. Every day I make myself come down from my rooftop, which is Pumbedita, to the land of Israel. This is the sum total of my present Zionism, told on one foot.

My frustrating first exile made me dream of going up to the land of Israel *(aliyah);* the exciting power of my second exile makes me come down to the land of Israel *(yeridah).*[6] No one can stand such enormous power as Pumbedita's for any length of time. We need our national home as a place to come down to—and to come down in—so that we can once again take off skyward with renewed strength.

My first exile was the direct result of the death of my childhood God who had created me in His likeness and image. My second exile is a living testimony to the birth of the God that I am creating in *my* likeness and image. Every day I create God for myself in my image and take off with Him for my rooftop in Pumbedita.

EVERY DAY I CREATE GOD IN MY IMAGE
AND TAKE OFF WITH HER FOR MY ROOF TOP
IN PUMBEDITA.

Everyday I make myself come down from my rooftop, which is Pumbedita, to the land of Israel. This is the sum total of my present Zionism, told on one foot.

My frustrating first exile made me dream of going up to the land of Israel (aliyah); the exciting power of my second exile makes me come down to the land of Israel (yeridah). No one can stand such enormous power as Pumbedita's for any length of time. We need our national home as a place to come down to—and to come down in—so that we can once again take off skyward with renewed strength.

My first exile was the direct result of the death of my childhood God who had created me in His likeness and image. My second exile is a living testimony to the birth of the God that I am creating in my likeness and Image. Every day I create God for myself in my image and take off with Her for my rooftop in Pumbedita.

Sha'ar Tzion:

Zion Gate

"How can we become not us?"

—Y.H. Brenner

Drowning in Sky

Until the Zionist revolution, the children of Israel had to float in the sky as in a Chagall painting. It's not important now who pulled their strings and caused them to hover—whether it was God who tugged them from above, as if they were marionettes, or whether the rabbis pulled them from below, as if they were kites. When they started drowning in the sky, the *ḥalutzim* (pioneers) appeared and brought them down to an emergency landing. That is how the children of Israel came to the Land of Israel.

The *ḥalutzim* gave this people the only down-to-earth revelation in its history. They gave a motherland to this people whose umbilical cord to the sky had not yet been cut. They brought the people down from exile. They bore the people the whole way on their hands while it slept.

In its dreams, new waves of sky break on the shore. They threaten to wipe the land and its dreamers from the face of the earth. The *ḥalutzim* do battle with the sky. They build little dikes with their fingers. They dry out the edges of the sky. They divert them into side channels.

The long night of winter continues. Like stagehands, the pioneers walk on the soles of their bare feet. They transfer the central stage of the Jewish people to the Land of Israel. During this whole long night they wrestle with God and continue to build. They build and continue to wrestle. When the dawn rises, they set Him free, and disappear after Him behind the scenery.

(Curtain Going Up)

The Red Flag

> **Once there was a wonderful violinist who made terrible faces while he played. From year to year his playing got better, and his faces got worse. Once somebody asked him directly, "You play well, but why do you make such terrible faces?" The violinist answered furiously, "I hate music."**
>
> —*variation on an old joke which I sometimes told at the beginning of lectures about Judaism*

Ever since the summer of 1975, I have been wandering through my land, my homeland, filling small neglected halls, as I give speeches about the Jewish identity of the *ribboni* (free-thinking) person and the *ribboni* character of the Jew, the separation of nationality from religion and the separation of religion from the state, on the liberation of our sources from the *rabbani* (rabbinic) stranglehold and on the need for a *ribboni* renaissance of classical Judaism; and other such slogans—correct slogans, indeed—but slogans, nonetheless. Sometimes I strike fire with my speeches. I am accursed.

Fifteen years have passed since then, and I still continue to wander with my lectern and set it up before temporary eastern walls and give my Sisyphus speeches. In all these years, my doubts have increased, but I continue to believe in what I am saying, and I clutch the horns of the altar of my *ribboni* belief. From year to year, I improve my speeches and learn to hide my doubts with impressive artistry. From year to year, I increasingly grow to hate the obnoxious and provocative tone with which I cover my doubts.

Sometimes I feel like a miniaturized version of Balaam. An angry prophet-for-hire of sinking secularism. A happening. A constant quester (a *"ḥozer be-she'elah"*) who sets his weight against the worrisome and dangerous tide of "dark Jewish fundamentalism." A kind of retro Jew—one of ours—who knows how to argue with the *datti'im* in their language. A kind of red flag that one can wave in front of the stormy rabbinic bull and shouting, "Hola!" Sometimes I feel like an intelligence prize—as if I were a Syrian pilot who had deserted with his plane—a fig leaf of a fading intellectual movement that cannot fight the cultural battle it is engaged in and is reduced to having its champions hurl projectiles and Molotov cocktails. We are these champions, frustrated questers and other unstable guerilla fighters who know how to cite a verse properly and draw a profit (when all is said and done) from the painfully honest spiritual metamorphosis that we have undergone in our lives.

Twelve years ago I wrote these words:

"During the four years that I have worked in the Jewish-Zionist educational institutes run by the Ministry of Education, I have been struck repeatedly by the phenomenon of *ḥiloni* (secular) high school students who claim that 'the true Zionists are really the *datti'im'* (Israeli Orthodox). The *datti* claim of our rights to the land has become more and more the claim that comes easily to the tongue of our young people, both *datti* and *ḥiloni*. In the universities, two or three professors continue to lecture to six or seven students about the secular socialist foundations of the Zionist movement.

"Right before our eyes a total confusion has taken root and sprouted about the basic concept of our identity. The expressions *"datti,"* "religious," and "Orthodox" have come to mean the same in Israeli Hebrew. Those who are not Orthodox are not considered religious and are pushed farther and farther to the wall, while being forced to define their very Jewishness. Jewish-national claims that Jewishness is a matter of destiny, historical identity, culture, ethnicity, or language are less and less accepted. The equation has even pushed further: Religious = Orthodox = Jewish. It now threatens to go even further and become a fourfold equation: The *datti* (Orthodox) is the religious, is the Jew, is the Zionist. And it still keeps on: is the believer, is the moral one, is the one with values, etc., etc. And, of course, *ḥiloni* (secular) is coming to mean just the opposite.

"During this same period, I met many teachers and principals in the national government school systems, particularly the kibbutz subdivision. Like a frustrated trader announcing his wares, I had to spell out to them the curriculum of the Jewish-Zionist seminar: A vital encounter with actual selections from the writings of the Zionist visionaries; a confronting of the world of the *ḥalutzim* and the early immigrants; the study of selections from Mishnah, Talmud, and Midrash; workshops on questions of Jewish identity and related topics. Several directors of kibbutz educational establishments responded to me in this fashion, 'You can hear about Herzl and Berl Katznelson in school. What interests our students is Mishnah, Talmud, and a little *yiddishkeit*. Since they are interested in Mishnah and Talmud, why should they learn them secondhand in Oranim when elsewhere they can meet authentic Jews whose study of Mishnah and Talmud is combined with hasidic song, a little prayer, a little bit of warmth, and religious experience?'

"In one of our conversations, a teacher in Emek Hayarden said, 'Gordon . . . Second Aliyah . . . That's Judaism?' Or I would encounter this very widespread argument, 'Why are you so dogmatic? Why are you afraid to have our children get acquainted with a world view that is different from yours? And if that world view is so attractive, maybe it really has something to it?'

"Afterward, I would meet with students and ask them if they were Jews.

"'Us? Sometimes we are Jews. They are much better Jews than we are. They are Jews every day.'

"'And Judaism—what do you think of Judaism?'

"'Judaism is nice. It's distant. It's ancient. It's found in the hills of Hebron, in the hills of Safed. Judaism is an experience . . .'

"Judaism is an experience. A child from the valleys makes a pilgrimage to it, to Jerusalem. The child listens intently to the guardians of his people's embers who prove to him from the Talmud and Mishnah that he is also a Jew. A good Jew. But . . . .

"His eyes open wide. Maybe hypnotized, maybe amused. Every ten minutes, the boy puts a trembling hand to his head to make sure that his paper *kippah* hasn't fallen to the ground. Don't move your arm, boy: the paper *kippah* has been made exactly for the measurements of your head. You are also a Jew. Even a good Jew. But . . . there are Jews with black *kippot,* Jews with crocheted *kippot,* Jews with paper *kippot.*

"Our boy is very satisfied to be a paper-*kippah* Jew. Perhaps that is the main reason that he wants to hear about his own identity in the Merkaz Harav Yeshivah rather than at home. There he participates, consciously or not, in a full spectrum of spiritual enterprises that grant him the following privileges:

"1. He acquires a ready-made spiritual identity.

"2. He avoids feeling any alienation from his national identity.

"3. He is exempted from being obligated.

"The representatives of the rabbinate do not place before him any real challenge. They do not compel him to actually confront the questions of his identity and world view. They do not disturb the process of his life. On the contrary, they give an a priori 'amen' to all his deeds and clap him on the shoulder in brotherly love.

"So why shouldn't he go up to them in annual pilgrimage? They will sing hasidic *niggunim* (tunes) mixed with patriotic songs, tell him stories of heroism crowned with glory, read to him legends cloaked in mystery. And before he leaves, they will stamp his identity card and extend the period of his Judaism for another year."

I wrote and published these words twelve years ago. At the same time, I wrote the following words which I didn't dare publish:

All Zionist seminars are a lip service paid by an ambitious Zionist revolution that climbed onto a high branch during the first generation, sat on it in the second generation, and then, by the third generation, reached the conclusion that it couldn't get down, and began to cut off the branch for the benefit of the fourth generation.

All these Zionist seminars are the tip of the iceberg, the heavy price that the young paper generations have to pay to this very day to their revolutionary grandfathers and grandmothers—the *ḥalutzim* who brought this movement's dream of liberation into reality. They pay with their bodies, as Hazaz wrote, "Why do you have to study Jewish history—go play soccer." With their spirits:

Nefesh yehudi homiah (the Jewish soul dwells within). And with their money: five hundred dollars, the cost of five days at a Zionist seminar for each young person. The more I am involved with the subject of these seminars, the more it seems to me that there is only one Zionist phenomenon more tragic and bearing a much steeper price: the service of the children of the third and fourth generation to the Zionist revolution in the occupied territories.

Only superficially is there no connection between these two Zionist tragedies. All this obsessive concern with the question of Jewish identity is an enormous waste of energy and a loss of wonderful potential for creativity. It would be much better for our ethical and spiritual might if we organized art seminars and sports seminars instead of all these Zionist seminars and Jewish identity seminars.

We will not be a normal nation as long as this obsessive preoccupation continues. As long as there remains in Israel even one circle of young people occupying themselves with the question, "How am I a Jew?," the Zionist revolution will not have been fulfilled, and it will not have accomplished its mission as a movement of national liberation—a movement for final and absolute liberation from the apologetic preoccupation with the rights of a person to assert his or her own identity.

The tragedy is that this self-preoccupation is unavoidable. And there is no more painful evidence of this tragedy than a young Jewish child, fourth generation in Israel, asking, "How am I a Jew?" in the ancient language of the Jewish people, which is not only her mother tongue, but her grandmother's mother tongue . . . .

And maybe these things will never come to pass? I argue with myself, "Maybe you are just an obsessively spoiled believer. Maybe it is only fear and laziness that makes you continue to grab the horns of the Zionist altar and hang yourself on the great cruel oak trees of the freethinking revolutionaries from the early twentieth centuries?"

After all, all those revolutionaries were Abrahams with an established freethinking agenda, who left their lands, their homelands, and their homes to hunt for a home environment they could fill with their fantastic program, one that has turned out to be decrees the public cannot endure. Maybe (I say to myself) the day has come that you should recognize that it is precisely your land, your homeland, your home, that prevents that freethinking *ribboni* agenda from being put into effect. Why do you not follow their example and leave? After all, the Moslem is telling you, "This is home only for me," and the *rabbani* tells you, "This is home only for me." The Moslem tells you, "Go away from here, you Jew!" and the *rabbani* tells you, "Go away from here, you non-Jew!"

So why are you still here? (I ask myself). "Don't you realize yet that the land has been lost? Are you so naive that you want your children to be taken in a cruel *jihad* in the wake of a future announcement by the Israeli Government that the third Temple is being built on the ruins of the Al Aksah Mosque? Maybe your primary ethical duty is to go to as many young people as possible and tell them, "Go! Neither the Moslem nor the *rabbani* will ever let you take root here."

Maybe it is not true faith that forces you to go from place to place to give your lectures about freethinking *ribboni* Zionism. Maybe it is just the terrifyingly awful obsession of a *galut* Jew who cannot settle down, who goes from place to place explaining his utopian dreams about Judaism in a national context and about Israel as a national home to settle into permanently and to furnish with democratic, humanistic, freethinking furniture, blah, blah, blah."

These words I also wrote twelve years ago, and since then—to say the least—things have not gotten better. I hope I am wrong, but I have this terrible feeling that in the next twelve years I will continue to be a *ribboni darshan* wandering the socialist ghettos and the *ḥiloni* settlements. A most furious fiddler on the insecure roofs of our almost bankrupt ideological centers. One who hews broken cisterns. A red flag.

Ribboni and Rabbani

The *ribboni* person is the master of himself or herself.

She has no other master in her world, and is not the master of the world or of other people. A *rabbani* person is not the master of herself or himself. He creates a rabbi for himself. The rabbi creates God for him.

The Jewish people is a typical *rabbani* people: *Am rav.*

From the Destruction until the National Renaissance movement, the *ribboni* minority was suppressed by the rabbinic leadership and wasn't able to expand. At the renaissance, *ribboni* tremors and lava flows began to appear. These tremors prepared the ground for the volcanic eruption of all the *ribboni* streams which had been suppressed for 2000 years. This lava provided the fertile soil that made the state of the Jews possible.

Internecine Warfare

The intra-Jewish cultural conflicts between the *rabbani* and *ribboni* Jews has three main fronts:

1. The people of Israel
2. The land of Israel
3. The Torah of Israel

On the people of Israel front there have been and will be many important battles around the question, "Who is a Jew?" Should the declaration of a

Jewish person's national identity depend on the rabbis or on the individual person?

On the Land of Israel front there are many battles around two essential questions:

1. What will be the final frontiers of this land—will these be secure *(ribboni)* borders, or will they be the "promised" (and *rabbani)* borders?

2. What will be the social and moral character of the State of the Jews for those who will live securely within these borders? Will it be a democratic *(ribboni)* state or a *halakhic (rabbani)*? state?

The Torah of Israel front is the most worrisome. Practically no battles are being fought on it. The silent majority of the Israeli people assume that the Rabbis have an exclusive monopoly over the cultural sources of the people of Israel and its tradition. One could even say that the *ribboni* leadership shows no enthusiasm to fight for its rights and obligations to liberate the Torah of Israel from the *rabbani* stranglehold. The *ribboni* leadership's continuing abandonment of the Torah front will cause them to lose the whole war on the other two fronts.

For the *rabbanim,* The Torah of Israel is first and foremost their source of authority. For the *ribbonim,* the Torah of Israel is only a source of inspiration. As long as the Torah of Israel continues to be the exclusive property of the *rabbanim,* they will continue to treat the Jewish people as their private property while they shake their threatening Torah at them. On the day that the *ribboni* leadership succeeds in wresting the Torah of Israel from the *rabbanim,* then each and every Jew will know the Torah has seventy faces. Seventy thousand myriads. From that day on, every single Jew will begin to treat the sources of his and her culture as private property. Then, for the first time, the Jews will begin to be a free people on their own land.

There are, of course, substantial differences between this internal-Jewish culture conflict that derives from the Zionist revolution and the external conflict with our Arab neighbors:

1. The external conflict with the non-Jewish enemy has outlived its function, while the internal culture conflict is still at its height.

2. The non-Jewish enemy is prepared to recognize my rights to self-determination in exchange for my relinquishing parts of the land that we have in common, while the *rabbani*-Jewish enemy is not prepared to recognize my rights to self-determination and definition.

3. The war with the non-Jewish enemy, which is by its very nature external, must be resolved outside the battlefield. The essentially internal war with the Jewish enemy will only be resolved on the battlefields.

4. The war with the non-Jewish enemy has to stop because by its very nature it is bloody and destructive. The war with the Jewish enemy has to continue because by its nature it enriches and fertilizes us. If the sides are smart enough to stick to conventional weapons, it will not even cause minor injuries.

5. If, God forbid, no solution will be reached in the conflict with the non-Jews, many tens of thousands of battle casualties of the next war will die a final, clinical death. On the other hand, the tens of thousands of casualties of the internal Jewish war, the *rabbani-ribboni* war, which will come upon us for our good fortune, will be felled with a kiss in the tent of Torah.

A Jew Is Anyone Who Looks at Himself or Herself in the Mirror of History and Sees a Jew

Who is a Jew? A Jew is anyone who looks at himself or herself in the mirror of history and sees a Jew. If for some reason, she doesn't look at herself in the mirror of history, then she is a Jew who doesn't look at herself in the mirror of history.

I, for example, am a Jew. Sometimes I like to look at myself in the mirror of history, and sometimes I don't. But I always see a Jew. The fact of my being a Jew cannot be erased. It can, of course, be shoved aside. I have occasionally made futile attempts to shove aside the fact that I am a Jew. Twenty years ago, in the pubs of London, for example, I used to declaim in halting English, "I've no country, I've no nation—I'm a Cosmopolitan from Somewhere." That may have sounded impressive, especially after the fourth beer, but it couldn't erase the fact that I am a Jew.

The fact of my Jewishness says nothing about my world view, my beliefs, my way of life. I can believe anything I want; I can look at the world from any perspective I choose; and I can participate in any lifestyle I wish, without any of it having any effect on the absoluteness of the fact that I am a Jew. If someone should someday convince me that Jesus was resurrected and brought salvation to the world, then I would be baptized and become a Christian Jew. If, on the other hand, someone should convince me that the mountain came to Mohammed, I would become a Moslem Jew. If I were to join Rabbi Kahanah's version of the Ku Klux Klan, I would be a Nazi Jew. And if I should dedicate my life to studying Torah in the Or Sameaḥ Yeshivah, then I would be a happy *rabbani* Jew. In the meantime, I continue to believe that a human being should be master-of-self-and-only-of-self, and that makes me a *ribboni* Jew.

My Jewishness indicates only that my existence has certain biographical-national components. These components are: language, homeland, culture, and tradition. My mother tongue is the language of the Jewish people; my homeland is the homeland of the Jewish people; the culture and tradition in which I was raised are Jewish culture and tradition. These four components are absolutely neutral and completely flexible. In other words, they do not imply any particular ideational complex. They are open to any possible interpretation. The language has seventy faces. The homeland has seventy faces. The sources have seventy faces. In other words, the fact that I am a Jew says nothing about my being part of any closed complex of ideas,[1] but rather of my being part of a totally open and flexible system. For this reason, I prefer to call the fact that I am a Jew my "Jewishness" *(yehudiut)* rather than my "Judaism" *(yahadut),* a contrast I invented long before I learned that it was well known in the English-speaking world. To me, the term "Judaism" has the connotation of an "ism"—a finite complex of ideas. The term "Jewishness," on the other hand, connotes an organic flow.

The finite complex of ideas we call "Judaism" comprised and comprises a concrete religion whose principles are: belief in a Commander (who created the world), acceptance of the authority of His commandments and obedience to them; acceptance of the authority of the Mosaic Torah as the exclusive filter through which this God's commandments pass; acceptance of the authority of the Oral Law and rabbinic literature as the legitimate and essential filter through which the divine command passes after it has come through from the Mosaic Torah; and absolute obedience to the commands that emerge through these filters. The rabbinic filter is the ultimate filter. This is what gives the entire system its unique final shape. According to this way of thinking, any system of life that does not pass through the rabbinic filter is not a Jewish way of life. In fact, the closed system of ideas called "Judaism" simply means the rabbinic religion. Theoretically, there have been and will be many attempts to create other Judaisms—in other words, other finite systems of thought alternative to the rabbinic one. I refer particularly to the Reform and Conservative systems of Judaism, but not enough time has elapsed to determine whether these experiments have passed the test of reality.

The constitution of Judaism as a rabbinic religion began around the time of the destruction of the Second Temple and received its final form in the late amoraic period.[2] From its beginning until around the time of the destruction, the people of Israel had what the scholars call *de facto* pluralism. Ever since the dawn of its inception, this people practiced different religions and various rituals to diverse gods. The Bible itself is the best proof that this pluralism actually existed. When King Ahab met Elijah, he didn't say, "You are not a Jew"; he just said, "Is that you, you troubler of Israel?" And Elijah didn't answer, "You are the one who is not a Jew," but rather, "I am not the troubler of Israel: It is you and your house." Even around the time of the destruction of the Second Temple, the Jewish people contained various differing sects. So too, there were many people who didn't belong to any sect—heretics, hellenizers, and just plain Tel-Avivis. They were all Jews: Those who looked at themselves in the mirror of history and saw Jews, and those who never looked at themselves at all. During this period, the Pharisees were only one sect among all the other sects active in Israel.

At some point, the leaders of the Pharisees gained control over the Jewish people, shoved aside all the other sects, as well as all the nonsectarian Jews, and turned the whole people of Israel into one sect. From that point on the Jewish people stopped being pluralist and became antipluralist. The Jews went from being a people to becoming a people-sect.

The Pharisees—by this later period they were called Rabbis—took the Jewish people out of history. They caused this people to stop looking at themselves in the mirror of history and to begin to see themselves in the mirror of halakhah. From this time on, being a Jew meant being a rabbinic Jew. From this time on, belonging to the Jewish people depended entirely on accepting the authority of the rabbis. From this time on, the rabbis became the only notaries authorized to extend the national passport of the Jewish people. Whoever wanted to have a Jewish identity card in his wallet had to have stapled to it a membership card from the rabbinic sect. From this time on, we have no example of any social or spiritual group that was able to maintain itself for long as a recognized and legitimate group within the Jewish people while it openly behaved in a manner opposed to the edicts of the rabbinic leadership.

During this entire period, there was a strange unwritten agreement between the leaders of the Jewish people-sect and the millions of Jews who assimilated about the indissoluble connection between Jewish national identity and the principles of the rabbinic religion. Both groups agreed that whoever did not accept the principles of the rabbinic religion had no further place among the Jewish people. During this entire period, the question, "Who is a Jew?" never arose because there was an absolute equation between belonging to the Jewish people and belonging to the rabbinic sect. A Jew was anyone who accepted the principles of rabbinic religion. Or whoever accepted the principles of rabbinic religion was a Jew.

This period witnessed the development of the now well-known myth that the acceptance of Torah and obedience to its commandments was the essential element keeping the Jewish people together during the Exile. This myth constitutes the visible, public explanation of Jewish survival. However, the hidden and repressed flipside of the coin is the fact that obedience to rabbinic authority "was in actuality compelled by the force of the *ḥerem* (excommunication), a mighty weapon that required people to choose between conforming to specific norms or leaving the congregation."[3]

The rabbinic system managed to keep the Jewish people a people-sect until the end of the eighteenth century. "Once the rabbinic power of *ḥerem* was taken away at the end of the eighteenth century, diversity and difference began to spread again."[4]

Once the rabbinic power of *ḥerem* was taken away, the Jewish people-sect began to go back to its original ways, toward a renewed *de facto* pluralism. So began the first stage of the Jewish people's journey toward national liberation, the Jewish people's striving to be like all other peoples. Ever since the end of the eighteenth century, the essence of being Jewish has been transformed and has returned to comprising many multicolored varieties. This renewed receptiveness to a more open Jewishness reveals that, in truth, varieties of nonrabbinic Judaism had never completely died or been extinguished but rather had continued to flicker with a low flame.

Since the end of the eighteenth century, the Jewish people has been trying to stop being a people-sect and has yearned to join the family of normal peoples—i.e., peoples who contain in themselves an infinite variety of practical and intellectual allegiances and do not reject any particular variety a priori. A great hope began to develop as the possibility arose that one could cancel the equation Jewish = rabbinic.

Since the end of the eighteenth century, the leaders of the rabbinic sect have refused to become once more a sect within the people and have continued to hope to turn the wheel backward, to restore the crown to its former glory, and to make the Jewish people again a sect/religion. The rabbinic leadership's rejection of this restored openness to Jewish existence, which has now been continuing for almost two hundred years, keeps the question, "Who is a Jew?" in the headlines. As long as this question continues to occupy us, then the Zionist revolution will not have been completed, and the Jewish people will not be a normal liberated people.

A normal liberated people is one that allows its members to continue to feel at home as they go from belief to belief. A normal liberated people is one whose sources contain the potential for various opposing beliefs. A normal liberated people is one that encourages its members to develop their various beliefs with the help of their common sources. An abnormal, constricted people is one that forces upon its members an *a priori* identification with specified beliefs and ways of life. A constricted abnormal people is a people that turns its sources into sources of authority and forces its members to let these sources lead to only one result.

The Zionist movement is a movement for the liberation of the Jewish people. It must not be content with the liberation of this people from the gentile world, but must also strive for the internal liberation of the Jewish people. This movement must seriously strive to enable the members of the Jewish people to be free in their own land. It must be the divider between the rabbis and the assimilationists; it must destroy the dangerous accord between them, and it must prevent them from continuing to govern the consciousness of the Jewish people. It must liberate the members of this people once and for all from the rabbinic concept (which is the same as the assimilationist concept) that whoever does not accept the authority of the Mosaic Torah has removed himself or herself from the Jewish people.

In fact, the question, "Who is a Jew" that arises in our days should not be presented in this way. The question being asked is essentially, "Who is a rabbinic Jew?"—or, to be more precise, "What are the conditions for being accepted into the closed system of rabbinic religion?" The argument between the Orthodox rabbinate and the Reform rabbinate is an internal dispute—interesting in and of itself—between two historical streams of the Jewish religion. With all due respect, I do not believe that either group can determine **my** national identity. I am not a member of any rabbinic sect or party—not Orthodox, not Conservative, not Reform, not Reconstructionist. No rabbi determines my way of life, my world view, or my ideological identity. So too, no rabbi can determine my national identity.

The real question is, "Can a *ribboni* Jew integrate into the Jewish people and gain absolute recognition as a Jew, or will the Jewish people sooner or later take away from him everything that cannot be reconciled with rabbinic authority?" It is very possible that the concept of the Jews as a nationality will turn out to have been an illusion of Zionist activists and visionaries. It is very possible that in another generation, the only thing remaining of these activists and visionaries will be the names of streets and that in another two generations these will also disappear. On the streets themselves, Jewishness and religion will have reverted to being absolutely identical, and the Jew will go back to being only the person who accepts the authority of the rabbis of that generation. If I should ever be totally convinced that this nightmare is unavoidable and that the equation Jewish = rabbinic is a necessary one, then I will not think twice. I will get up and leave Israel. The fact that my Jewishness cannot be erased doesn't mean I have to remain in Israel at any price. I stay because I believe in the rights and prerogatives of every person in the world to distinguish between his beliefs and his national identity. This belief is one of the foundation stones of my world view as a *ribboni* (as a human) and a Zionist (as a Jew). I believe—despite the worrisome signs around—in the possibility that the movement will free the Jewish people to finally distinguish between religion and nationality. I believe with perfect faith that my chances of being *ribboni* in my national home are much greater than my chances of being *ribboni* in *galut.*

This is what Proudhon—one of the Utopian socialists—answered to the person who suggested that he should emigrate from France to America and create there "a new people in a new land." "Here I tell you, under the sword of Bonaparte, under the rod of the Jesuits, under the eye of the Sécurité here is the place in which we must work for the liberation of the human species. We have no skies more amenable and no land more fertile . . . ."[5] And that is exactly what the Zionist in me says to the expatriate in me: Here, in the land

AS LONG AS THE
PALESTINIAN PEOPLE
DOES NOT
ACHIEVE
LIBERATION,
THE JEWISH PEOPLE
WILL NOT
BE LIBERATED.

As long as the Palestinian people does not achieve liberation, the Jewish people will not be liberated and the Zionist dream will not be realized. Since this is so, we have an obligation as Zionists to remove our yoke from the Palestinian people and release them from our shackles. And to stop keeping such a tight grip on them in making them sign all kinds of assurances and statements of obligation so that we can finally securely return to them what we have to return, so that they can settle down finally and finally concentrate on their internal culture war and leave us free to concentrate on our own culture wars, and thus the redeemer will come to Zion.
Amen.

for which our ancestors yearned, we will be able to work better for the liberation of the human species than in any other land. There are no skies more amenable nor land more fertile.

Everything that I have said about the internal *ribboni* liberation from rabbinic rule is also relevant *vis-a-vis* the Palestinian nation. They have a no less encompassing problem with their Moslem brothers (the position of women, the freedom of the individual, the sanctity of the land, etc). We can support them and identify with them in their internal struggle with their "rabbis," but that is not really our business. Their external liberation, on the other hand, is most definitely our business.

For as long as we continue to rule over another people, we will not be a *ribboni* people. Not even if we should arise tomorrow and find nationality separated from religion or our national life freed from rabbinic control. A *ribboni* people is master of itself and only of itself. For this reason, as long as the Palestinian people does not achieve liberation, the Jewish people will not be liberated and the Zionist dream will not be realized. Since this is so, we have an obligation **as Zionists** to remove our yoke from the Palestinian people and release them from our shackles. And to stop keeping such a tight grip on them in making them sign all kinds of assurances and statements of obligation so that we can finally securely return to them what we have to return, so that they can settle down finally and finally concentrate on their internal culture war and leave us free to concentrate on our own culture wars, and thus the redeemer will come to Zion. Amen.

Those Who Cannot Abide Dreams, and Those Whose Dreams Abide

> Until we can live with the feeling that the spiritual revolution of Zionism is more substantial than the spiritual revolution of the ancient Rabbis, we will not know how to fulfill either the obligation or the privilege that those Zionists placed on us to explicate our sources with at least the same degree of autonomy that the Rabbis permitted to themselves.
>
> The Rabbis, for example, decided utterly to transform the biblical image of David and to turn him into a talmudic *talmid ḥakham,* and the David that the Rabbis constructed is the one who entered the people's consciousness. If they were allowed to see David in the guise of Rabbi Yehoshua ben Ḥananiah, what prevents us from seeing the words of Rabbi Yehoshua—"It is not in heaven"—coming out of the

> mouths of these pioneers as the basis for their Zionist-*ribboni* but well-grounded world view? Yehoshua ben Ḥananiah is an important figure for me. Yosef Ḥayyim Brenner is even more significant. He and his colleagues sketched for us a framework for a Jewish spiritual revolution. I hope that our generation will not diminish this revolution into nothingness. These revolutionaries had such great power that the generations that came after them were left stunned. We, who come a bit after the shockwave, can allow ourselves to approach the mountain, to gather from its base and its summit the vessels—intact and broken—and to fill the framework with a new/old content.
>
> —Drowning in Sky *by Ari Elon (1980)*

The *ribboni* revolutionaries placed an exalted challenge before the Jewish people: To turn the Torah of Israel from a source of authority to a source of inspiration. Their heirs were not able to rise to this challenge and left Israel's Torah in the hands of the *rabbani* leaders.

The abandonment of Israel's sources to the rabbis was, in effect, a hidden mutual agreement between the rabbis and the heirs of the *ribboni* revolutionaries. This hidden agreement turned into a lament for the generations and almost defeated both sides of the dogmatic coin. One side compelled its children to believe in the presence of the God who floats menacingly through the holy writings. And the other side compelled its children to believe in the absence of that very same God who floats in those very same holy writings.

That is the spiritual package deal into which many of the Sabras were born. Neither of these two dogmas permitted the generations that followed to confront Scripture in a direct manner and internalize it. One dogma was afraid that a rupture might occur between the sources of Israel and the authoritative God of Israel; the other dogma was afraid that a connection might be created between these two. In this way two opposing and arbitrary approaches were created in Israel: The tendency of those whose dreams abide toward *dattiyut* (orthodoxy) and of those who cannot abide dreams to *ḥiloniut.* At some stage it appeared that these two arbitrary approaches would become two parallel streams that could bring national destruction.

However, in the 1970s, two groups tried to connect the *ḥilonim* with Israel's sources. The first group hoped a return to the sources would be a first step toward accepting the authority of these sources. The other group wanted to create a connection with these sources out of the belief that one can transform them from a source of authority to a source of inspiration.

On the surface, it seems that the first group has been more successful. They knew how to market their ideas, and with the help of the media they have created the impression that the Jewish people are setting out on the way to "return." The other group has done nothing at all to market its conception or to create a public. Even today they are not known widely, and from the little that is known about them, the impression has been created that this is a group of spineless naifs whose souls yearn for a little *yiddishkeit.* Many of this group—which includes this writer—unconsciously played into the sophisticated hands of the *rabbani* establishment, and a few of them eventually even became a kind of neo-*rabbani* stream.

It may be that this group will disappear in the end, and the rabbis will finally have control over the sources of Israel and ultimately over the people of Israel and the land of Israel. I believe that this will never happen. This belief of mine is an absolute prerequisite to my being a *ribboni* Jew in my land and homeland. It is absolutely necessary to my deepening sense of self-identity and to the erasing of the national frustration and alienation in which I grew up.

I arrived at my *ribboni* belief through the Talmud and the other sources. And when I want to strengthen my *ribboni* sensibility, I go to the Talmud and learn it in my way and find in it much support. For me, the interaction between the *ribboni* experience and the sources of Israel is extremely palpable. I believe that someday it will be as palpable and unremarkable to many others.

The *rabbani* person sees Israel's Torah as a source of authority. The *ribboni* person cannot relate to this Torah as a source of authority, for that person is the source of authority for himself or herself. So the *ribboni* person can approach the classical sources with great freedom and can claim them as her own. She can learn from them much about herself, her people, her collective memories; he can learn much about his passions, his repressed urges, etc. The *ribboni* finds in these sources an endless field of organic symbols.

Of course, in order to be able to harvest these symbols at will, the *ribboni* must be familiar with the actual field in which they grow. In order that *ribboni* refinements should not be artificial, they must be anchored in the classical heritage. Innovation without tradition creates alienation and sows a short-lived field of rootless symbols doomed from their inception. Tradition without innovation strangles a person's chances of being *ribboni.*

A people does not give birth to new symbols in one day. One cannot import symbols. One cannot invent them. They must arise organically from the roots of the tradition and sources. The question is: Who governs the growth of these organic symbols? Who guides their direction? Who will liberate self and people by releasing these symbols?

A normal people supplies the same sources to individuals of diverse and opposing viewpoints. The same common sources carry the collective symbols that different people combine differently to express their differing beliefs. If we unite only around common ideas, then we will always have to invent new symbols. But symbols cannot be invented, for invented symbols are always disjunctive symbols.

> An organic symbol has the ability to supply a fixed form to the unfolding of life. The disjunctive symbol has no actual reference to the life of the people in their generations. Its momentary existence is confined to the imaginary world of airborne spirits, phantoms. The organic symbol is slowly and increasingly woven into the fabric of the people, of the citizens, strangers, widows, and fishermen. It flows silently until exceptional individuals come and release it to a new meaning.
>
> —*Meir Ya'ari,* Disjunctive Symbols *(1923)*

An organic symbol is raw material that contains an inspirational payload for varied and opposing meanings. An organic symbol is a ladder whose foot is on the earth and whose top reaches the skies. It is anchored in an innocent (and graceless) mundanity that addresses the lowest common denominator, and it kisses the resplendent celestiality of exceptional, creative individuals.

Only leaders who can manage to set up their Jacob's ladder in the place where children and simple people dream will be able to change the society in which they live. Their ladder may be humanistic or it might be chauvinistic. It may be democratic or it might be totalitarian. It may be *ribboni,* or it might be *rabbani.* It may be open, or it might be closed-minded.

The only way to cultivate organic symbols is midrash. As a discourse, midrash is completely different from scientific discourse. Science grinds raw symbols in the mill of analytic conceptualization; midrash turns concepts into raw symbols. Scientific discourse abstracts; midrashic discourse makes things concrete. Scientific analysis delimits; midrash breaks all limitations. Scientific analysis strives to reveal the conceptual world of the creators of symbols; midrash tends to ignore the conceptual world of these symbol-creators. Scientific analysis sees the symbol as a means to reach the past; midrash sees it as a way to reach the future. Scientific discourse aspires to be objective; midrashic discourse is intentionally subjective. Midrashic discourse takes symbols out of context; scientific discourse strives to place symbols in their contexts.

Analytic, scientific knowledge is necessary for being *ribboni,* but it is not sufficient. The one who does not know how to ask, "Who was the person who created *ex nihilo* the sentence, 'In the beginning God created heaven and earth'?" cannot be *ribboni.* Only one who strives to understand both the manifest and latent motives of each generation's god-creators can be *ribboni.*

But a scholar who doesn't know how to speak to his or her child in science-fiction language about the chaos that preceded God's creation of the world also cannot be *ribboni.* That scientist's academic rank may reach the highest heavens, but his ladder does not extend down to earth.

In short, only a *ribboni beit midrash* for science-and-midrash enthusiasts will bring *ribboni* leadership. Only creative workshops in the discourse of midrash—its vocabulary, its grammar and syntax, its many sources—will emancipate the Torah of the Jewish people in the wake of the liberation of its homeland and its language.

Such a *ribboni beit midrash* could be a crucible for taking the organic symbols that are part of the fabric of many generations and processing them into treasures of liberated expression.

Children do not like to be spoken to in the analytic mode of discourse. They are eager for midrash of organic symbols. At a very young age, they discover that the world is round, but their inner world stays pre-Copernican, and angels climb up the ladders of their world and slide down slides into their sandboxes. If we really want them to grow up autonomous *(ribboni),* knowing how to be their own divinity, we have to teach ourselves how to give them many midrashim about gods, angels, demons, and spirits. After all, we created God, and only in *aggadah* can our creature rise against its creator. A *ribboni* isn't afraid of legends. A *ribboni* loves them.

High and Low, Low and High—Nobody Here But You and I

Once there was a *ribboni* master of midrash—Ḥayyim Naḥman Bialik. He recorded the essence of his *ribboni* power in this poem:

> ***nad ned nad ned***
> ***red 'aleh 'aleh vared***
> ***mah lema'alah***
> ***mah lema'atah***
> ***raq 'ani, 'ani ve'atah***
>
> Back and Forth and High and Low
> What is above and what is below?
> High and Low, Low and High
> Nobody here but you and I.

The question: "What is above and what is below" is the *rabbani* person's most forbidden question:

> Whoever looks at these four things would have been better never to have come into the world: What is above and what is below, what is before, and what is after.[6]

> Our sages taught: Can a person ask, "What is above and what is below, what came before and what comes after?" . . . . You may ask from the edge of the heaven to the edge of the heaven, and you do not ask what is above and what is below, what came before and what comes after.[7]
>
> Why was the world created with a *bet*? Just as the *bet* is closed at its sides and open in front, so you can not ask what is above and what is below, what came before and what comes after.[8]

The rabbinic world was created in the form of the letter *bet,* a world bounded and sealed. Its ceiling is the heaven, and its floor is the deep waters. The rabbinic masters of *halakhah* defined the boundaries of the world of the rabbinic person and marked the forbidden boundaries with the giant letters of *Kiddush Levanah* (Blessing the Moon): "You must not ask what is above and what is below."

Bialik, the *ribboni* master of *aggadah,* on the other hand, allows himself to ask, inquire, and look. He even includes little children in his attempt to reckon what is above and what is below. Bialik and the children go up together and come down, they swing, and they seesaw. Together they go into the *aggadic pardes* (the garden of thought), and come out safely with their answer in their hands:

> High and Low, Low and High
> Nobody there but you and I.

The child on its swing sees what Moshe Rabbenu never saw. Even he was afraid to look at what is above and what is below. God tried to show him, even at their first meeting in front of the burning bush. God looked him directly in the eye, but he lowered his eyes because he was afraid to look at God. Only after many years did Moshe dare try to see what is above and what is below through the eyes of God, but by then it was already too late. God said to him, **"You cannot see my face, for none can see my face and live . . ."**[9]

Moshe's tragedy was stunningly expressed in a midrash attributed to Rabbi Yehoshua ben Karḥa:

> **And Moshe hid his eyes—Rabbi Yehoshua ben Karḥa says, "Moshe did not do well when he hid his face. For if he had not hidden his face, the Holy Blessed One would have revealed to Moshe what is above and what is below, what has been, and what will yet be. And in**

the end, he wanted to see this, for it is written, 'Show me your glory.' The Holy Blessed One said to Moshe, 'I came to show you my face and you hid your face; now I say to you that none will look upon my face and live. When I wanted, you didn't want. Now that you want, I don't want.'"[10]

According to rabbinic tradition, Moshe reached the highest level possible for human beings. The rabbinic Moshe reached this level despite God's refusal to show him God's face. The reason? God permitted him to see God's back, something that God permitted no other mortal. God placed Moshe in the cleft of the rocks and walked opposite him, while covering him with the divine hand. Only after God turned about-face did God take away the hand.

Yosef Ḥayyim Brenner was one of the greatest *ribboni* Jews ever. The strength of his *ribboni* belief did not allow him to be content with striving for the level of Moshe, which is the highest rabbinic level. He yearned for more:

Hear, O child of Israel; listen, O child of sorrow. Lift your head, lift your head, and the eternal gates will rise up. No rest and no self-deception whatever. No fear of results, whatever they may be. No grain of deceit or tenderheartedness. Shoo away the clouds. Come out of the cleft of the rock. Take God's hand away, approach the mist, go up to the *pardes*. Look upon the face of Being. Grasp its essence, its glory. Be sanctified. Become holy.[11]

Yosef Ḥayyim Brenner demands that the child of Israel achieve what Moshe Rabbenu, the greatest of the rabbinic Jews, could not: Leave the cleft of the rock, take away the hand of God, look upon the face of Being. Yosef Ḥayyim Brenner was a *ribboni* Jew. He had the spiritual strength to enter the dark rabbinic *pardes* in order to prune its plants and let light in. He had the spiritual strength to look directly upon the face of Being and see that only the human being is a master-commander in his world.

Ḥayyim Naḥman Bialik was a *ribboni* Jew. He had the spiritual strength to ask the most forbidden question–what is above and what is below?–and had the bravery to look directly at the face of Being and say, "Nobody there but you and I."

Bialik's "Song of the Seesaw" begins where "Scroll of Fire" leaves off. At the height of passion, Bialik wrote "Scroll of Fire" and added a second title, "From the Legends of Destruction." "Scroll of Fire" became a *ribboni aggadah* prophecy of the redemption-not-to-come.

"Scroll of Fire" relates that two hundred naked boys and two hundred naked girls were taken after the destruction of the Temple to a remote desert island. A giant cliff divided the island into two, and the deep that stretched out from it separated the young men from the women. The eyes of the two hundred young women were shut and facing heaven; the eyes of the two hundred young men were shut and facing the deep. And the deep was reflected in the heaven, and together they formed a vertical axis before them.

All the young men drowned in the deep that was reflected in the sky. All the young women drowned in the sky that was reflected in the deep. There remained only one curly-haired young man lifting clear eyes to the empty sky and one young woman pure of body, direct of gaze. Their glance met for an instant, but the young man was afraid to look at the young woman and lowered his glance to the deep:

> *. . . and he looked, and there in the high crags facing him, innocent and pure as the angel of modesty and humility, there stood before him one pure of body with sorrowful eyes, looking straight at him under her lashes, and at her head rose the doe of dawn.*
>
> *And the heart of the boy beat, and he lowered his glance for the first time in his life and turned his modest eyes to the ground. And his glance sank to the river and rested on the image of the girl as it was reflected with the morning star.*

The fate of the young man with clear eyes will be like the fate of Moshe. Moshe lost his once and forever chance when he hid his face at the moment of grace when God tried to reveal Godself and show him what is above and what is below. And Moshe would carry the mournful taste of that missed encounter to every place he went. So too the boy with the clear eyes: He is destined to cling for his whole life to the painful memory of the once-in-forever chance that he lost forever. All his life he is destined to be a young man climbing toward a young woman, reaching and yet not reaching, touching and yet not touching. He is destined to fall into the deep before the longed-for touch. He will always fall into the deep. And there in the deep, a spark of redemption will be lit, the spark of illusion, which will be for him like the end of a rope or the ring of a life-saving ring, like a guy wire he is destined to climb and fall. He will always fall again.

For his entire life, the young maiden will change forms and faces before the clear, suffering eyes of the young man. She has dozens of veils, like the dozens of elusive signs of the doe of dawn. Sometimes she is the *Shekhinah* and sometimes a whore. Sometimes a holy one, and sometimes a harlot. Sometimes the doe of love, and sometimes the doe of dawn. Sometimes she is Venus reflecting toward him from the deep, and sometimes she is Venus who rises before him with the morning star. She is always redemption. She is always redemption-not-to-come, and redemption-not-to-come says, "I came to show my face to you and you hid your face. Now I tell you that none can see me and live. When I wanted, you didn't want; now that you want, I do not want . . . ."

Until that critical meeting, the young man had lifted his eyes only to the sky. The young woman's direct gaze made him look down in the deep for the first time in his life.

And the young man's heart beat, and for the first time in his life he lowered his modest eyes to the ground, and his glance sank into the river and rested on the image of the young woman reflected to him with the morning star.

The image has the sense of the imitation, the statue, the idol, the toy.

The young man cannot look directly at the original—at the direct eyes of the young woman. He flees to the image, to the idolatrous copy that is reflected to him by both sky and sea. The young man is not able to look directly on the horizontal axis—the original—and he flees to the vertical—the distorted—axis of sky and sea. The axis of illusion. The axis of the redemption-not-to-come.

And he kneels before the image and exposes himself with an awesome and terrible confession. The essence of this confession is the repeated description of this Sisyphus nightmare: He is always a young man climbing toward the young woman, reaching and not reaching, touching and not touching, falling before the final touch, always falling to the depths of the sea, the depths of despair. There a spark of illusion is lit—of redemption. The end of a rope. The end of a guy-wire. He climbs the guy-wire, climbs it, and falls. Always falls again.

Much has been written about the content and substance of this young man's confession. Very little, if anything, has been written about the manner in which it was said—about the fact that such bravely revealing words were said in a foxhole, in the aversion of his glance downward. Or about the fact that the bravely revealing words were said on bended knee before an image. Without being able to look directly at the original, at the face of Being, at the face of one desired young woman, pure of form and sorrowful of eyes. Only at the end of the confession does the young man stop bowing before the image with shut eyes and dare return to look at the place where the girl had been.

And when he looked, he became like a stone. The young girl disappeared from the craggy heights and was no more. But her image was still captured in the river like the impression of a seal. She and the morning star reflected back at him from the black depths.

The girl disappeared, and was no more. Only her image remained. The once-and-forever confession had been made in vain because it was the confession of a lad before a shadow, of a boy before a toy.

And the waters disgorged the lad in a very distant land. In a strange land, the land of galut. *And he wandered through all the lands and joined the exiles. He passed among them like a legend from long ago and a vision of the future. And he was strange and a riddle to all. And he looked at the heavens, and they were alien to him. And he looked at the earth, and it was foreign. And he taught his eyes to look straight ahead—to the edges of the universe. Just as the image of that girl had looked at him on that dawn. When did he see that dawn?*

And the lad wandered in the land like a derelict star in cosmic space.
And he went naked and barefoot with direct gaze . . . .

With this description, the last section of "Scroll of Fire" begins—with the description of the tragic metamorphosis in the spirit of the lad with the clear eyes. He changes into a riddle strange to everyone. The heavens are alien to him, the deep is foreign to him, and he trains his eyes to look straight ahead, straight on the horizontal axis. Until now he has always journeyed on the perpendicular. He looked for redemption in heaven—the redemption-not-to-come, fell into the deep, and sang the song of despair. He always went up and down, down and up. He seesawed over the face of the deep, until he finally fell into it for good. Until the deep disgorged him onto the land of *galut,* and since then he has wandered naked and barefoot with straight gaze—just like that girl with the direct gaze on that dawn. However,

> *Nobody could withstand his direct gaze. There were some who would have their eyes escape upwards from the gaze of that boy, and there were those who had them dodge his gaze by looking down.*

The only line that passes through the level horizontal plain in which he now lives is the line that comes out of his eyes and goes nowhere. To use more precise scientific terms, this is not so much a line as a vector. A vector that comes out of his eyes and continues till infinity. Never reaches a destination. It never meets even one pair of eyes that could save it and make it finite, a bounded line of sight. The eyes of the other people in his world aim along a vertical axis. They look to the endless skies or the endless deep. He is the only one in the world who looks straight ahead. To the ends of the universe. And the only one in his world whose glance disappears into the final horizon.

After "Scroll of Fire," Bialik devoted himself, among other things, to editing *Sefer Ha'Aggadah.*[12] He opens the first chapter of *Sefer Ha'Aggadah,* the chapter on the creation of the world, with two of the quotations on what-is-above-and-what-is-below that are quoted above. And he also includes in the book the other two midrashim. As is well known, *Sefer Ha'Aggadah* contains only a small fraction of the midrashim that the Rabbis wrote. The fact that he included most of the what-is-above-what-is-below midrashim indicates Bialik's attitude toward this motif, an attitude that is also manifest in Bialik's creative works. In fact, we can often learn about the importance of motifs in Bialik's own creative endeavor by their appearance or absence in *Sefer Ha'Aggadah.*

The study of Bialik's work as editor of *Sefer Ha'Aggadah* provides unending insights into the creations of Bialik the poet. We should ask ourselves why it is specifically Bialik—the greatest of Jewish poets ever—who found it appropriate to dedicate a great part of his strength to editing the rabbinic *aggadah.* He could have let Ravnitzky do it together with some Judaic studies professor or other.[13] We could be satisfied, perhaps, with the explanations that Bialik himself brings in his foreword to *Sefer Ha'Aggadah,* ". . . Whoever wants to understand the people of Israel . . . must go to *aggadah* despite himself" or ". . . . Through the *aggadah* one enters the absolute living center of the soul of the people of Israel and looks at his innermost parts."

But this type of explanation is completely typical for Bialik, the national poet who tried to give back to his people their cultural, literary, and national sources. Without a doubt, *Sefer Ha'Aggadah* was intended to be a bridge between the generation that didn't know *aggadah* and the ancient Rabbis, the masters of *aggadah.* In this aim, Bialik and Ravnitzky achieved considerable success. Many thousands will continue to pass over this bridge. I myself testify that I have met many good people who would never have dared open the Talmud and midrashim to look at them if not for *Sefer Ha'Aggadah.*

Despite this, I am inclined not to be satisfied with Bialik's open declarations about his commitment to *Sefer Ha'Aggadah.* These declarations belong to Bialik, the ideologue of the Hebrew Renaissance movement, and not to Bialik, the young man with clear eyes and the man of riddles who is strange to all. I came to Bialik in a most unusual fashion: I came to Bialik through the rabbinic *aggadah.* I climbed onto the bridge from the other side. And I take the risk, I dare to express this heretical view: *Sefer Ha'Aggadah was intended to be a bridge between the generation that knew no aggadah* and one of the greatest masters of *aggadah* that the Jewish people has ever had: Ḥayyim Naḥman Bialik. Bialik, of course, didn't dare proclaim this in his introduction to *Sefer Ha'Aggadah,* and it may be that Bialik never dared acknowledge this even in his innermost chambers.

And more: Bialik prepared *Sefer Ha'Aggadah* as a code book for emergencies. As a lifesaving bridge for himself. Maybe through this code book someone could be found who would not avert his eyes; maybe through this code book, people would stop seeing him only as another ideologue traversing the perpendicular to discuss the fruitless eternal issue, heaven or earth.

Bialik prepared another code book—children's songs. He stopped investing his astonishing vocabulary in adults. After all, adults see such a treasury of words only as decorations to place on the walls of the ideological heaven and earth that lie on the limitless perpendicular. To use such vocabulary for grown-ups wastes fields of fertile symbols. It is a waste of energy. A futile confession. He has enough with the simple words in the innocent first 100-word vocabulary of a child. Above. Below. You. I. What. Nobody. Up. Down. High.

THE CHILDREN ON THE SWING SEE WHAT MOSHE RABBENU NEVER SAW.

The rabbinic masters of halakhah *defined tbe boundaries of the world of the rabbani person and marked the forbidden boundaries with the giant letters of* Kiddush Levanah (*Blessing the Moon*): *"You must not ask what is above and what is below."* Bi*alik, the* ribboni, *master of* aggadah, *on the other hand, allows himself to ask, inquire, and look.* He *even includes little children in his attempt to reckon what is above and what is below.* Bi*alik and the children go up together and come down, they swing, and they seesaw.* T*ogether they go into the* aggadic pardes (*the garden of thought*), *and come out safely with their answer in the hands*:

H*igh and* L*ow,* L*ow and* H*igh*–N*obody there but you and* I.

T*he children on their swing see*
what M*oshe* R*abbenu never saw.*
E*ven he was afraid to look at what*
is above and what is below.
G*od tried to show him, but...*

Low. "The Song of the Seesaw" conceals the entire vocabulary of "Scroll of Fire." With simple words Bialik, the children's poet, says more than he was able to tell adults with the exciting vocabulary that he thereafter hid. The Bialik who speaks to children is the strange man of riddles—the same one who taught himself to go naked and barefoot with direct eye. He has no need to beautify himself with words. He has no more need to intoxicate. He seeks the most simple, the first things. Maybe the children will help him find it. Maybe the children will be the final bridge that will enable him to look into the *pardes* full of eyes, into the lost garden of paradise.

It is of these children that he asks the question what-is-above-what-is-below. It is not Rabbi Akiva to whom he poses this most forbidden question, but to little ones, kids. And he not only dares pose this most forbidden question to them, he even dares answer it in front of them:

High and Low, Low and High
Nobody Here but You and I
weighed-in on a balance scale
under heaven, over hell.[14]

It is as if Bialik is saying to a little child:

"Enough singing songs to grown-ups. They kill them. They change them into ideological decorations. With you, child, it is not ideology. With you it is everything. With you, child, I can swing on the paradise swing in which you and I are weighed in a balance under heaven and over hell. The Law of the Seesaw is the human race's law of balance. This seesaw is the human balance. We don't weigh merchandise in this balance, we don't weigh ideology. But when you and I are weighed in this balance, then our fervent wish for horizontality can be realized.

Only two who know how to teeter-totter are able to live balanced between heaven and earth. If the two do not know how, one will always be underneath and the other above. Only after we learn teeter-totter technique can we achieve the condition of being balanced over hell and under heaven. The condition in which we can hover, our eyes looking toward "nobody but you and I."

How does one learn teeter-totter technique? The first step is investigation and inquiry. Back and forth, above, below, down and up, up and down. Go to the ends of the universe. Do not be afraid. Ask whatever you want. Investigate what you want. Ask, "What is above, what is below, what came before, what comes after, one, two, three, go and seek! Have you found it? Is it true that there is nothing below and nothing on high excepting only you and I?"

The second stage is the stage of "you and I." How can you and I be balanced between heaven and hell? How can we create three parallel lines that will never meet: the line of the sky, the line of you and I, and the line of the abyss? How can we avoid the Scylla of the deep and the Charybdis of heaven? What is the right dosage of dreams and legends that will give us the ability to stay balanced between heaven and earth without getting drunk on the rapture of the deep? When do our eyes meet most of all?

Just so that we shouldn't drown in sky. If we drown in sky, then we lose the chance to have our eyes meet. Two hundred young men drowned in the deep, and two hundred young women drowned in the sky. Those who cannot abide dreams will drown in the deep; those whose dreams abide will drown in the sky. To Bialik it is the same. The skies are just the reflection of the deep, which is only the reflection of the sky. God is just the reflection of Satan, who is only the reflection of God. Everything is an image.

Only the human being was not created in an image. Only you. You and I.

(*p.s.* It is one of the ironies of history that despite Bialik's clear intentions and despite the clarity of his poem, none of the children who now go about singing the teeter-totter song actually says, "What is above and what is below" but instead sings something like, "Who is above, who is below?" or, "from above to below." Can there be some Providence that prevents children from asking the most forbidden of all questions?)

The Voice Is the Voice of Esau and the Hands Are the Hands of Jacob

Scholars are perpetually divided on the question of whether there ever was a historical Abraham. Was he invented or did he actually live? In the meantime, masters of *aggadah* create many Abrahams in their own images and forms. In their own image, likeness, and form they even create gods who say to their Abrahams, "Get out of your land, your homeland, your father's house, to the land that we will show you."

The one Abraham—the biblical—goes west. From Babylon, his homeland, he goes to the Land of Israel, which his god YHWH shows him. Coming toward him—without his being aware of it—is the rabbinic Abraham on his way east. From the land of Israel—his homeland—to Babylonia, the land that the *Kadosh Barukh Hu,* (the Holy Blessed One), the rabbinic god, is showing him. "You will be brought to Babylon," says the Holy Blessed One, "and there you will remain until I take note of you."[15]

The rabbinic Abraham promises the Holy Blessed One that he will not try to return to Israel by his own powers; he will not go up as a wall and will not rebel against the nations and will not force the end of Exile.[16] The rabbinic Abraham will remain in Babylon until the Holy Blessed One will turn to him again and say, "Go out of your land, your homeland, your father's house to the land which I will show you." He is still in Babylon. The *Kadosh Barukh Hu* has not yet appeared to him.

The biblical Abraham builds an altar to YHWH who appears to him in the Land of Israel. Later he will cut into two a three-year-old heifer, a three-year-old goat, a three-year-old deer, a dove, and a pigeon. YHWH will appear to him between these cut pieces to make a covenant and cause his seed to inherit this land from the river of Egypt to the river Euphrates, which is in his Babylonian homeland. Afterward this biblical Abraham will bind his son—the biblical Isaac—to an altar. There, too, YHWH will appear to him from above the altar.

The rabbinic Abraham doesn't build altars in Babylon. He builds *batei midrash,* study-houses. The Holy Blessed One prefers a single day that he sits and studies Torah to the thousands of sacrifices that the biblical Abraham sacrifices to YHWH on the altar.[17] For many generations, the rabbinic Abraham has been sitting in the study-houses of heaven and earth studying Kiddushin and Bava Metzia and other talmudic tractates. During all of these generations, the biblical Abraham has known nothing about the existence of these talmudic tractates.

The biblical Abraham also knows nothing of a fixed liturgy for the morning prayers. This despite the fact that—or even because of the fact that—the rabbinic Abraham is the creator of this liturgy. When the biblical Abraham arises on the morning of the binding of Isaac and loads his donkey, it never occurs to him that on that very same morning the rabbinic Abraham also arises, puts on tefillin, and establishes the morning prayers.[18] Scholars and historians are perpetually divided on the question of whether or not there ever was a historical Abraham, whether he was born or invented. Meanwhile, the artist-masters of *aggadah* create many Abrahams in their likeness and image. In the likeness of their form and image, they even create gods that say to their Abrahams, "Go out of your land, your homeland, to the Land that we will show you."

One of the most fascinating Abrahams that creators have made is the *ribboni* Abraham. The *ribboni* Abraham, like his predecessors, rebelled against the tradition of his fathers. He broke the gods of the rabbinic Abraham. He went out of his homeland, his father's house, to the land shown to him by the god who spoke from within him. Abraham himself is the god who spoke from within him. The lord of himself. The master of himself. That self-direction that he seeks is his divinity. He broke the rabbinic God, the one external to him, into smithereens. The *ribboni* Abraham rebelled against the three great negative promises of his rabbinic fathers. He went up against the walls of the ghetto, rebelled against the nations of the world, and forced the end of exile. This end he called liberation—liberation of self and liberation of nation.

The *ribboni* Abraham instilled in Isaac all his fear of and hatred for the rabbinic Abraham. Hatred for the yeshivah student. For the world of the *beit midrash.* For the astonishing innocence. For the bowed head. For pallor. Abraham transferred to Isaac everything he wanted to be and didn't totally succeed in being. He bequeathed to him his working hands, his ability to do things. To make things happen. A good-enough capacity for having wells dug by servants. For exemplary agriculture. For extraordinary industry. For the national water pipeline. For an army to be proud of.

Isaac is a rough-edged Sabra. He has never left the Land. The son of immigrants. A son of *ḥalutzim* in whose recessive genes lurks the yeshivah-*bocher* part of his father. Like a golem. Like the raw material for a silk shirt. Isaac learned to go out into the field and achieved results that are not at all bad, whether in the cornfields (fields in the valley of . . . .) or on the battle fields. Isaac went to fields.[19] He went.

But something was always bothering him. Something prevented him from being totally devoted to the field. A memory of a childhood full of fire and the slaughter knife made him sing melancholy hassidic songs around the campfire . . . . Even though he was a complete man of fields and a complete man of production, a certain spiritual nightmare kept pursuing him. The world of devils and demons was his spiritual world. The spirit of rebellion threatened him through the flashing eyes of his father who forced him onto the makeshift altar.

Isaac never heard anything from his father about his grandfather Terach. Abraham and Sarah were careful not to speak about Terach in Isaac's presence. Occasionally, Abraham would hum a song without words out of the depths of his heart, and this melody had a pagan-hassidic flavor. Sometimes Isaac would secretly listen to the strange things that his father would say to his mother, ". . . Our fathers, Sarah were, of course, innocent and *galut* idol worshippers, but they knew how to sing. Oh, how they knew how to sing . . . ." And Sarah laughed in the tent door. Enjoying the powerful *ḥalutz*-sarcasm of her Abraham. Abraham also laughed. Ricochets of round laughter and of destroyed idols flew in the air. But afterward Sarah went inside the tents, looked at the yellowing picture of her father and mother, looked right and left, and cried in secret as she covered her face with the palms of her hands.

Isaac will never forget this melody and the aroma of grandfather Terach that wafted from it. The aroma of hassidic songs without words that are swallowed up in the darkness. In the fields. Only in the darkness of the fields would Isaac allow himself to sing from the bottom of his heart. He walked in the light of the fields. He stormed. He carried pipes. He carried the wounded. But Isaac knew nothing about the heritage of his grandfather Terach against whom Abraham had rebelled. And he also knew nothing about the revolutionary heritage of his father. The only heritage Isaac knew very well was the *Heritage of battle.*[20] Both the first of Tishrei and the first of May were left on the abandoned altar with the wood and the slaughtering knife.

Now Isaac is old. His eyes have gotten dim. Jacob and Esau are also not so young. Now Isaac is getting a little confused. He doesn't know which of his sons to bless. He loves Esau with a love as strong as death. He hasn't related too well to Jacob, leaving him to the care of Rivkah. Rivkah wasn't born in Israel. She passed her childhood in Ur of the Chaldees and did not internalize ideological hatred of grandfather Terach to the same great extent as Isaac. Jacob is his mother's child; Esau his father's. Esau went to work in the field—his father Isaac committed him to do so—and called him Esau as in "to essay."[21]

So Jacob found out somehow about his great-grandfather Terach's melodies. Esau didn't even know they existed. He worked in the field and engaged in industry and couldn't abide dreams. A hunk. Half a head taller than his father, and a full head taller than his grandfather. Wears size thirteen shoes. Knows how to take apart any engine you give him. Drives a tractor at nine years old. Has been reaping harvests for fifteen years.

During all this time, Jacob tries to dream but is ashamed of his dreams. He wants to be a tent sitter and live in the world of Torah, but he is ashamed before Isaac. The whole time, Jacob has been secretly learning the despised and tragic learning. Rivkah loves and spoils him. But this nurturing embarrasses Jacob. It is hard to be mother's boy in a society which is so supportive of father's productivity. He forces himself to be a practical man. He too knows how to tear down engines. In the wee hours of the night, he studies poetry.

Now Isaac is old. His eyes are dim. He still loves Esau with an open and fierce love, but something deeply buried in him starts to love Jacob. In his old age, he is less ashamed of his rejected sources of inspiration. So, in a moment of weakness, which means in a moment of truth, he confuses Jacob and Esau and blesses both of them. "The voice is the voice of Jacob and the hands are the hands of Esau." Isaac is still blessing his son in confusion. He still hears the voice of Jacob in his son and sees the hands of Esau. He still dreams that his vision will be realized. We dream with him.

Isaac has to dream. At his age, he can't do anything else. We, on the other hand, cannot allow ourselves to rest content with dreamimg of this longed-for mixture of the voice of Jacob and the hands of Esau. If we don't do something to help this sweet dream along, it will change into a nightmare right before our eyes. Right before our eyes a mysteriously frail monster will grow whose syndrome will be known far and wide—the voice is the voice of Esau and the hands are the hands of Jacob. A vocabulary of three digits and two left hands.

When You Go Out To War: A Sermon for the Portion Ki Tetzei

For our ancestors, the Shabbat was a modest and revered revery-space and the six weekdays were an exhausting reality. The rabbis guarded the fruitful tension between the earthly world of reality and the ladder of their dreams. Every Shabbat had its portion of the week, which was the launchpad for these earthly dream ladders. The rabbis attached our ancestors to their prayer-benches with safety belts and then counted backwards carefully. The people who walked in darkness saw a great light.

> **When you go out to war against your enemy, and the Lord your God gives him into your hand, and you take captives, and you see among the captives a beautiful woman and want her and take her for your wife . . . .**

Every one of our forefathers would shut his eyes, take off his tallit, and go out to war against his enemy. And when HaShem gave his enemy into his hand, our forefathers, with closed eyes, would each choose a beautiful captive.

At the end of the sermon, the rabbis would reattach our forbears to their prayer benches and let them land gently onto Saturday night. The sharp smell of herring floated in the air, and our forefathers would sadly cling to the songs of the final Shabbat meal.

We have lost that wild and wonderful tension. A part of us has erased the dreamy Shabbat from our hearts, placing us in an unending and exhausting cycle of seven weekdays with no place for revery. The other part of us has erased the six days of the week from its calendar, and has placed itself into a wild vicious cycle of seven holy days that have no places for sane reality: the days of the Messiah. One part of us has abiding dreams, the other part cannot abide dreams.

Those of us whose dreams abide drag ourselves around moonstruck in the foundering traces of the Messiah, lift Helmish eyes[22] to heaven, and bury our heads in holiness. Those of us who cannot abide dreams bury our hearts in the mundane earth and purge all romantic notions from our heads.

Those of us whose dreams abide have lost the dreamy uniqueness of the Shabbat. The whole week is one long Shabbat that rides on the birth pangs of the Messiah and the hunger pangs of many, many children. The rabbis who knew how to give our ancestors an exact dose of dreams have lost control over them. Other rabbis have gained control over those of us whose dreams abide and have taken off their safety belts. They have turned the portion of the week into a rocket launchpad. They constantly shoot rockets from our ancestors' dreamland and explode them outside our windows. They always go out to demonstrate in the name of the portion of the week.

Our ancestors' rabbis knew how to keep our ancestors' dreams burning on a low flame. The new rabbis aren't interested in this at all. They are always setting fire to those whose dreams abide and burning them with the fires of Hell. They always see a great light. A happy light. The light of the seven heavens. The lights of redemption. The lights of repentance. All seven days of the week. Twenty-four hours of the day. Those whose dreams abide now have bombs abiding.

We who cannot abide dreams face off with those whose dreams abide in a Malkhei Israel Square of the mind. We Yuppies. Contemporary, city-paper writers, super-sophisticates, falsely-autonomous assimilators. Negative words for rhetorical beauty. Nonsyntactical sentences. Nonobligatory meaning. Devoid of subject, object, verb. A story from the movies. Really something. The heirs of Bialik, Brenner, Berdichevsky—those pillars of fire who burned alive in order to commit us to give a *ribboni* answer to the *rabbani* threat. We are pissing out these pillars of fire. We take the bridge over God that was built by Bialik, Brenner, Berdichevsky, Feirberg, Shenk-in, Shenk-out,[23] and we hold pissing contests off it. As far as we are concerned, those with dreams abiding can continue to bury their heads in holiness, to await their Messiah-who-will-not-telephone.[24] We will continue to bury our hearts in the mundane earth and will continue to try to achieve self-actualization as part of our movement for strumpet liberation.

They will continue not to know who they are. We will continue not to know who we are.

Those whose dreams abide and those who cannot abide dreams have lost their self-knowledge because they burned all the portion-of-the-week bridges that connected them to their collective dream "I."

This portion of the week can be a faithful reflection of this "I." In the same breath, it commands us not to oppress the hired hand and to stone our rebellious children to death; not to hate the Egyptian and to wipe out the memory of Amalek; not to execute children for the sins of their parents and to execute the adulterous man and woman; to have mercy on a mother bird and to cut off the hand of a woman who dares touch the genitals of a strange man during a dispute.

What is all this absurd mishmash if not an ugly and beautiful reflection of our rejected collective "I?"

They whose dreams abide promote the concretization of all these connections here and now in a monstrous state governed by halakhah; they who cannot abide dreams are trying to cut themselves off from the whole primitive matter. These and these relate to this Torah as a normative authoritative system we should promote or reject. These and these completely ignore all the layers of their own psychology that are wrapped up in this glorious myth. These and these relate only to the visible tip of the iceberg of their myth. Just as they relate only to the visible part of themselves. These and these will eradicate each other in the Malkhei Israel Square of the mind.* Until their very last day they will not know who they are.

*Alas, five years after this was written, Yigal Amir, whose dreams abide, killed Yitzhak Rabin in the real Malkhei Israel Square, which is now called Rabin Square.

Sha'ar Hagai:

Ravine Gate (Bab el Wad)

Why is the Torah compared to the doe of love? To tell you: Just as the doe has a "narrow womb"* and stays as desirable to her mate each time as she was the first time, so the Torah always stays as desirable to those who study her as she was the first time. (BT Eruvin 54)

WARNING!

We have not yet discovered the Torah written by women. The Torah that we know was written by men. Thousands of men participated in the making of the Written Torah and the Oral Torah. As far as we know, not a single woman participated, at least in the writing of the Oral Torah (the rabbinic writings). Even the women who are written about in these texts were written about exclusively by these thousands of men.

The reader can only bear witness to the world of the writer of the material being read. So, in the coming pages, I cannot write about the world of the woman being written about, but only a little of the world of the men who write about her. In fact, reading about the women in Torah is a good way to enter the complex world of the men who were writing her. We can see them in what they wrote about the written woman and the oral woman, the revealed woman and the hidden woman.

This woman (the Torah) has seventy faces. The men who discourse about her knew how to reveal her many faces in their studies. They know how to keep looking at her in order to find everything in her.

The Torah as Esther

The Torah has a "narrow womb" and seventy faces. Each time she is as desirable to the men who learn her as the first time. About her it has been written: **May your source be blessed and rejoice in the wife of your youth—a**

*A narrow womb, of course, is a catastrophe that makes it impossible for a woman to carry a pregnancy. What the Rabbis meant was a tight vagina (colloquially we use a coarser term). However, they either didn't have or didn't record for us a separate word for the vagina. Of course, a tight vagina isn't very good for women, either, but it is a well-known male fantasy. (Translator's note)

doe of love, a graceful gazelle. Let her breasts satisfy you at all times, and always be infatuated with love of her.[1]

She is the wife of his youth; at the same time her presence satisfies completely the man who is with her ("let her breasts satisfy you at all times"), and she is the only object of his love ("always infatuated with love of her"). She is the target of all his fantasies. She is past, present, and future. She is reality and vision, order and madness. The most necessary object in the world of her lover and yet the freshest.

One can only love somebody or something that is known. The familiar taste of the beloved is a necessary condition for the lover. Nevertheless, it is not sufficient. An additional necessary condition is freshness. Only the familiar that is also fresh can be beloved. But even these two necessary conditions are not sufficient. For the freshly familiar can also be hated or feared. The third necessary condition is delight. Only the familiar whose freshness is delightful can be beloved.

The doe of love is the most beloved woman a man can imagine. She is the most familiar, the freshest, and the most delightful all at the very same time. Her presence in the world of the one who loves her is so dominant that he* is not interested in quenching his thirst for delight and freshness with any other woman. The doe of love is the most original woman—both in the sense of origin and in the sense of originality. She is the most first and the most last, or, in other words, both source and resource. The male scripture says about her: **May your source be blessed.**

It is worthwhile to remember that one of the meanings of the word "source" *(mekor)* is "womb"; each time the male lover returns to the womb, he goes back to the most original of sources and closes the circle. The Hebrew word for womb, *reḥem,* has another meaning in Hebrew and Aramaic, "to love." The very same womb the man loves is the womb that envelops him in love, surrounds him with his most existential existence, and returns him temporarily to his most original experience.

The doe of love is the goddess of love! When the loving woman is sick from love and can no longer bear her love, she adjures the daughters of Jerusalem, **I swear to you, daughters of Jerusalem, by the deer and the gazelles of the field, that you should not wake or disturb love till it is time . . . .** Oaths have an effect only when they are yoked to the holy and divine. The deer and gazelles of the field are the love goddesses of the many varied male pantheons of East and West. The doe of love is the doe of dawn, who is Venus, who is Aphrodite, who is Ashtoret, and Ishtar, and Istahar, and Astar, and Esther. They are all variations of the same exalted star whose reflection on the earth is the reflection of feminine erotic divinity.

*It is almost impossible to use inclusive language for this rabbinic love of Torah, a love conceived in thoroughly masculine terms. (Translator's note)

I WILL SURELY HIDE (HASTER ASTIR) MY FACE FROM YOU ON THAT DAY.

The Scroll of Esther *is also known as* megillat hester panim, *(the scroll of the hidden face) because the name of* God *is not mentioned in it at all.* However, *this hidden* God, *the* Esther-Goddess, *appears throughout.* This Esther-Istahar-Ashtoret-Venus-Aphrodite-*doe of dawn-doe-of-love has something that no human woman has.* This *something is the subject of fantasy for many males who always yearn for her and shut her up in the figurative temples of their love.* This *unique characteristic, this doeness or female divineness, is shared by both* Esther *and the* Torah. Ahasuerus *finds in* Esther *what the* talmid ḥakham *finds in his* Torah. What *neither* Ahasuerus *nor the* talmid ḥakham *can find in any human woman.*

A late midrash tells this *aggadah* about Esther:

> **When Hadassah was brought before the King, he looked at her and at a picture of Vashti and was astonished by her beauty and grace, for he had never seen their like in his life, and he said, "You are more gorgeous than any human woman. Your name will no longer be Hadassah, but Esther, for I see your face as the sign of the enchanting star Istahar."**[2]

In an earlier talmudic midrash, we read:

> **Why was Esther compared to a doe? To tell you, just as the doe has a "narrow womb" and is as desired by her mate each time as at the first time, so Esther was desired by Ahasuerus each time as at the first time."**[3]

The difference between these two midrashim is more or less the difference between the children's story we all grew up with and the deeper meanings that emerge from a careful study of the Scroll of Esther.

Esther's beauty was perhaps necessary for arousing Ahasuerus' love, but not sufficient. This Ahasuerus gave instructions to bring to his palace every beautiful virgin girl from the 127 countries in his empire and to spend a whole year preparing them. For six months, each was to be prepared with oil or myrrh and for six months with spices and beauty emollients in anticipation of the one night when the king would examine her wonderful qualities, **In the evening she would go and in the morning she was brought once more to the women's house by Shashgaz, the eunuch in charge of the harem. She would no longer come before the king unless the king wanted her and called her by name.**[4] Esther was one virgin among countless beautiful girls in the lands between India and Ethiopia. Nevertheless, **The king loved Esther more than any other woman and she found more favor with him than the other virgins.**[5] The gazing Ahasuerus found in this divine woman what he would not and could not find in any human woman.

The Scroll of Esther is one of the wildest, most fantastic male fantasies ever written. There is a little Ahasuerus in every man. The Scroll of Esther is also known as *megillat hester panim,* (the scroll of the hidden face) because the name of God is not mentioned overtly—not even once. However, this hidden God, the Esther-goddess, appears throughout. This Esther-Istahar-Ashtoret-Venus-Aphrodite-doe-of-dawn-doe-of-love has something that no human woman has. This something is the subject of fantasy for many males who always yearn for her and shut her up in the figurative temples of their love. This unique characteristic, this doeness or female divine-ness, is shared by both Esther and the Torah. This is their "narrow womb." Ahasuerus finds in Esther what the *talmid ḥakham* (the rabbinic sage) finds in his Torah. What neither

Ahasuerus nor the *talmid ḥakham* can find in any human woman. They find an eternally "narrow womb" that is always as desirable to them as at the first time. Ahasuerus calls his love goddess "Esther." The *talmid ḥakham* calls her "Torah."

There is yet another characteristic the two love goddesses have in common. Esther and the Torah reveal and conceal at the same time. This dialectic between revealing and concealing may be the sweet magical secret of their love cult. We will try to examine it closely.

Esther reveals and shines as ***a star.*** However, Esther is also concealed and conceals:

> **How do we know that Esther is mentioned in the Torah? Because it says, "I will surely hide *(haster astir)* my face from you on that day." (Deut. 31:18)**[6]

and **Why was her name called Esther? Because she concealed all her affairs.**[7] Esther has become the symbol of concealing the face.

Esther also contains the revelation and redemption as well as concealment.

> **Just as the doe of dawn at first light comes little by little and then breaks forth swiftly, so does the redemption brought by Esther to Israel.**[8]

Esther is the light at the end of the tunnel, and she is the darkness. Esther is the Esther at the end of Esther. Esther is open and alluring, but she hides her womb and her charms. The classic picture of Venus.

The Torah is like Esther. She is light. The combination *Torah orah* (The Torah of light/the light of Torah) appears many times. The word "Torah" contains clear connotations of light. In the popular conception, she comes shining with rays, lightning, and thunderbolts. The Torah is the historical, theological redemption. She shows the way. She brings light to darkness. This is the nature of the Torah honored by the many. But the Torah also contains the hidden and mysterious. The secrets of the Torah are sealed and hidden from ordinary people, to be revealed only to exceptional *talmidei ḥakhamim,* the priests and lovers who devote themselves to their love goddess in her temple, the *beit midrash.* This hidden Torah is the learned Torah. She is learned in secret, for the process of learning this Torah is a most intimate process.

In the Song of Songs, we find the lover's fervent description of his beloved's body, **Your stunning thighs are like jewels, the work of a master's hand** (Song of Songs 7:2). About this, the Gemara says, **Why are the words of Torah compared to thighs? To tell you, just as a thigh should be concealed, so too the words of Torah should be in private.**[9] The study of Torah is an intimate matter between the student, the *talmid ḥakham,* and his Torah.

> **Any *[talmid ḥakham]* who studies Torah in front of the common people *(am ha'aretz)* is like someone who makes love to his betrothed in front of it, for it is written, "Moses commanded us the Torah, the heritage of the congregation of Jacob." (Deut. 33:4) Do not read *morashah,* (heritage) but rather *me'orasah,* (betrothed)."**[10]

and, "**Whoever has intercourse with a betrothed woman in his dreams is destined to possess the Torah.**[11]

The learned Torah is always the betrothed. The love of a *talmid ḥakham* for her is like the love of man eternally rejoicing in the love of his betrothed.

The Torah is also described many times as an eternal bride: **When the Blessed Holy One gave the Torah to Israel, they desired her as a bride is desired by her mate.** And therefore:

> **Anyone who speaks the words of Torah and does not make them as delicious to their hearers as a bride is delicious to her husband, it would be better for him not to have said them.**[12]

And therefore also, **Just as a bride is adorned with twenty-four ornaments, so too the *talmid ḥakham* must be fluent in all twenty-four books.**[13]

The Torah that is learned in mystery is the eternal virgin, the eternal betrothed, the eternal bride. Just like Venus. The Torah that is studied in mystery has a "narrow womb," giving her students a delight impossible to achieve in this world, a delight that lets her be the original wife of one's youth and the eternal virgin whom *talmidei ḥakhamim* adore forever.

The Torah of the loving *talmid ḥakham* guarantees eternal youth. Her taste is the taste of more. More without end. **The Torah is as desirable to her students each day as she was on the day that she was given on Mount Sinai."**[14] Every hour she renews herself. Every hour that he learns her, he uncovers her anew. He turns her and turns her and always reveals new faces.

The Olympus that Moses Discovered on High

> **Nine hundred and seventy-four generations before the world was created, the Torah lay in the lap of the Blessed Holy One and sang a song with the ministering angels, as it is written: "I was with him as a ward and I was his delight, daily playing before him." (Avot de Rabbi Natan A 31)**
>
> **Rav Yehudah related from Rav:**
> **At the time that Moses went up on high, he found the Blessed Holy One sitting and tying crowns to the letters.**

He said to Him, "Who is making You do this?" (lit. "Who is hindering You?")
He said to him, "There is a man who is destined to come at the end of many generations, whose name is Akiva ben Yosef. And he will explicate onto every jot heaps and heaps of halakhot."
He said to Him, "Master of the Universe, show him to me."
He said to him, "Walk backwards."
He went and sat eighteen rows back (in Akiva's classroom) and did not know what they (the students) were saying.
He felt faint.
When he (Rabbi Akiva) arrived at a certain matter, his students said to him, "Rabbi, where is this from?"
He answered, "It is a halakhah from Moses on Sinai."
Moses's strength came back.
He went back to stand before the Blessed Holy One.
He said before Him, "Master of the Universe, You have such a man and You give the Torah through me?"
He said to him, "Be quiet! That was my intention."
He said before Him, "Master of the Universe, You have shown me his Torah. Now show me his reward."
He said to him, "Go back."
He went back and saw that they [the Romans] were weighing Akiva's skin on a scale.
He said before Him, "Master of the Universe, this is the Torah and this is its reward?"
He said to him, "Be quiet! That was my intention." (BT Menaḥot 29b)

There are two Torahs. One is revealed, and one is hidden. The revealed Torah is the source of authority. The hidden Torah is the source of inspiration. The revealed Torah commands: She is the reflection of the fundamental male God. The hidden Torah is learned: She is the reflection of the female deity; she is the source of inspiration.

In the beginning there was the learned Torah. God learned her. Before the world existed they were both hidden. Nine hundred and seventy-four generations before the world was created, the learned Torah rested in God's bosom and was his source of inspiration. He would delight in her every day, and she would play before him at all times. The men who learn have hidden these invisible details between the secret lines of the revealed Torah:

> **The Lord created me at the beginning of his reign, before his deeds of yore . . . before the mountains were sunk, before the hills. I was born, before he made the earth, the fields, and the first of the world's**

clumps of clay. When he fixed the horizon on the deep . . . and I was his confidant, a source of delight every day, playing before him at all times. (Prov. 8:22)

After 974 generations, the Holy Blessed One looked into the learned Torah and sank the world into her. In this way the Torah says between her hidden lines, "In the Beginning God created the heaven and the earth," meaning "with/in me God created the heaven and the earth."[15]

Twenty-six generations after the world was created from her, the revealed Torah saw the light of day and descended to the people waiting fearfully at the foot of Mount Sinai. And the learned Torah remained on high and continued to be the hidden darling of God. God continued to rejoice daily with the learned Torah. Of his revealed Torah, on the other hand, he wrote, "The secret things belong to the Lord our God, and the revealed things are ours and our children's forever, to do all the things of this Torah." (Deut. 19:28) The revealed Torah is a Torah that one has to do, to act out. And doing it means obedience to a clear, explicit system of commandments.

The commanding Torah is a reflection of the male God, and her rules are open and threatening. She is decisive and singular in meaning. She doesn't have seventy faces. She has a single face, a single meaning, and a sharp edge. You can't turn her and turn her until you find all in her. She cannot be obfuscated and mystified by debate and discourse. She is direct and clear. She doesn't allow changes and she does not renew herself every day.

The learned Torah remains outside these boundaries. Only God knows her.

Or so it seems.

After many generations, it has become clear that the Torah also has other lovers. They, too, like God, know the hidden Torah and learn her in their innermost rooms and rejoice in her and become devoted to her. Retroactively, it has become clear that these lovers of Torah are made of a special substance—the substance from which gods are made.

When Moses goes on high, he discerns immediately that God is learning a different Torah from the one he is giving him to take down to the people, the *am ha'aretz.* The Torah God is learning is hidden from Moses' eyes and guarded from his perception. With green eyes, he sees how God ties invisible crowns of love for his Torah. But little by little, he senses the presence of other creatures who are joining God in the process of tying hidden crowns. These creatures seem male to him but not quite human. Little by little, he is able to discover that these creatures also love to know this hidden Torah and learn her with great passion. Right before Moses' astonished eyes, the sky fills with myriads of males learning Torah and turns into Olympus.

From this point, the Olympus Moses discovered on high will be called the *beit midrash,* and the gods who study in this Olympus will be called *talmidei ḥakhamim.*

Moses understands nothing of the hidden Torah, and finally tries to bring the revealed Torah to those who remain at the foot of the mountain and will be called from here on in the *am ha'aretz.* To this very day, Moses is trying to bring the revealed Torah down to earth.

In contrast, the *talmidei ḥakhamim* remain in their Olympus. Together with God they keep turning the hidden Torah around. They turn her around and take liberties with her. They explicate heaps and heaps of halakhot onto every jot and every tittle. As their beloved Torah tells them between her hidden lines, **"His head is a pure gold spot and his clusters are intricate." This teaches that we should explicate each jot into heaps and heaps of halakhot."**[16]

Moses is everyone's eternal victim. The victim of the *am ha'aretz* who remains close to the ground and the *talmidei ḥakhamim* who live on high. Moses is Sisyphus. To this very day, he ascends on high to bring down the revealed Torah, comes down with her to the folk and breaks her, goes back up on high to receive the revealed Torah, goes down and breaks her, and goes back up. On high, he gazes with eyes weak from envy at how Rabbi Akiva and God discourse with the Torah and do whatever they want with her. He sees with his eyes but cannot approach. He cannot allow himself to remain to learn. He has to go down. The folk waits for him below.

Moses is the eternal mediator between the *am ha'aretz* and the commanding God. He is the one who fights the battles of the commanding God and does all the menial labor for God. He is the one who conceals from the people the orgiastic debates that are going on in the Olympus of the *beit midrash.* He is a real victim. He bears constantly the complaints, trials, threats, and smell of the campfires of the eternal generation of the wilderness. And all the time he envies Rabbi Akiva and God their delight in the Torah.

The Torah is as desirable every day to those who learn her as on the day she was given at Mount Sinai.[17] Only to those who learn her is she original and desirable. Only to them is she as desirable and delightful as a bride on her wedding day. The *am ha'aretz* has no part in this wedding ceremony. He is fearful of the stand at Sinai, and afraid of the Torah, and scared to draw near the mountain; he waits for Moses to come and mediate between him and her.

Everything a *talmid ḥakham* is likely to find new in the Torah was already given to Moses at Sinai. Everything a *talmid ḥakham* will find new at the end of the generations has already been made new by God 974 generations before the world was created.

Each and every day is 974 generations before the world was created and the end of all the generations. Each and every day the Torah is as desirable to the *talmid ḥakham* who learns her as she was in the first hour. She rests in his bosom and plays before him. An eternal game. In another 974 generations, he will look into her and create the world.

At the beginning of every world, there will be the learning *talmid ḥakham* and the learned Torah.

Pomegranate Nectar

> **As for the one who sees pomegranate slices in a dream: If he is a *talmid ḥakham,* he can expect Torah, as it is written: "I will make you drink spiced wine, nectar of pomegranates." (Song of Songs 8:2) If he is an *am ha'aretz,* he can expect commandments, as it is written: "Your temple is like a slice of pomegranate" (Song of Songs 4:3), which means: Even the most empty among you are as full of commandments as a pomegranate (is full of seeds) . . . . (BT Berakhot 57a)**

There are two Torahs: the Torah of Command and the Torah of Learning. The commanding Torah activates the commanded person, known as the *am ha'aretz.* The learned Torah is activated by the learning person, known as the *talmid ḥakham.*

The alluring treasures of the learned Torah do not speak to the heart of an *am ha'aretz* and do not activate his imagination. To the exact extent, executing the commands of the commanding Torah is difficult for a *talmid ḥakham* and cuts off the intimate dialogue that continually takes place between him and the learned Torah.

Most assuredly, it seems as if the *talmid ḥakham* is accustomed to tying many crowns for the commandments and their fulfillment, just as the *am ha'aretz* always extols the value of the study of Torah. Nevertheless, beneath the surface, matters are not at all so. Fulfilling commandments is essentially foreign to the soul of a *talmid ḥakham,* and the study of Torah is essentially foreign to the soul of an *am ha'aretz.*

The *am ha'aretz* will never be able to discern the substantial conflict between study and fulfillment that rages in the soul of a *talmid ḥakham.* Even more, to this very day, he is convinced that the *talmid ḥakham* studies Torah day and night for the purpose of fulfilling her commandments better. The *am ha'aretz* cannot imagine that learning is a delight.

In fact, it is this not inconsequential gulf which people feel between the act of learning and the experiencing of delight that turns them into *amharatzim.**

* *Am ha'aretz* means, literally, "people of the land, folk" and its proper Hebrew plural is *amei ha'aretz.* When *am ha'aretz* is used by the learned to mean the great unlearned masses, the plural is *amharatzim.* As you might expect, this is not a complimentary term. (Translator's note)

The brilliant minority of men who are privileged to be *talmidei ḥakhamim* knows how to take ultimate advantage of this gap in the world of the *am ha'aratzim.* In this way, the *talmid ḥakham* is able to enjoy both worlds: both to enjoy every second of learning with his beloved Torah and also to be revered and exalted by the *am ha'aretz.* After all, the *am ha'aretz* remains convinced to this very day that the *talmid ḥakham* is his delegate, and he is filled with gratitude. He respects the one who is able to forego the delights of this world for such delegation, and he is willing to subsidize him so that he will engage in Torah day and night, will delve deeply into her commandments, and find beautiful and endearing reasons to help him realize his dream and be worthy of the abundance of commandments.

The *am ha'aretz* is "empty" and is counted among "the empty ones among you." The *talmid ḥakham,* by contrast, is filled to overflowing. The vision of pomegranate slices is a vision of abundance. This dream of abundance, dreamed by a *talmid ḥakham,* testifies to the abundance of Torah awaiting him; dreamed by an *am ha'aretz,* it testifies only to the abundance of commandments.

The commandments are poor people's pleasures. *Talmidei ḥakhamim* are millionaires. The *am ha'aretz* is not able to take advantage of the abundance of the learned Torah. The maximum abundance awaiting him is the abundance of commandments. For this reason, even though the dream visions of the *talmid ḥakham* and the *am ha'aretz* are the same vision—a vision of juicy pomegranate slices—their interpretations will be completely different; one for the *talmid ḥakham* and one for the *am ha'aretz.*

Each of the two dream interpretations relies on a different verse from Song of Songs, which revolves around the sensual pomegranate.

Song of Songs is a dream of dreams. It is an unending reservoir of dream symbols. Each of its fruits, its animals, and its scenes can be interpreted and allegorized without end. They are much more than they are in reality. They are much more than nature designed them to be. This is true of the does that we spoke about in the last chapter, and it is true of the pomegranates. Here, when the poet of poets describes the nudity of woman, he plants in the consciousness of *talmidei ḥakhamim* a delicate impression of a pomegranate orchard:

> **A locked garden is my sister bride.**
> **A locked garden without seal**
> **your limbs are a pomegranate orchard,**
> **with fruits of delight. (Song of Songs 4:13-14)**

And lo, the seed that the poet of poets planted in the *talmidei ḥakhamim* created something wondrous for them. From this moment on, pomegranate orchards underwent a considerable transformation in the minds of men who know how to **learn** Song of Songs. From now on, these men would be forced to acknowledge that the description of a pomegranate orchard in any time or place was much more than innocent scenery. Not to mention the pomegranates in the Song of Songs itself. Every pomegranate that these men might discover in the arena of Song of Songs should be treated almost as a live grenade. One must treat it with creative caution.

For example, the verses:

> **Would that you were like my brother, who suckled the breasts of my mother. If I found you outside and gave you drink, they would not make fun of me. I would bring you to the house of my mother who teaches me and would give you drink from wine spiced with pomegranate nectar. His left hand under my head, with his right hand he embraces me. I adjure you, daughters of Jerusalem: Do not awaken love, do not disturb it until it is ready . . . . (Song of Songs 8:1-4)**

Talmidei ḥakhamim bring much peace to the world. They very cautiously ask themselves:

1. Who is this beloved woman whose head is under his left hand?
2. Who is this lover whose right hand embraces her?
3. What is this pomegranate nectar the beloved gives her lover to drink?
4. What is the taste of this nectar?
5. What is this oath with which she repeatedly adjures the daughters of Jerusalem, and what is this love that should not be awakened or disturbed until it is ready?

Talmidei ḥakhamim answer these questions with even more caution and hide their answers under the surface of all possible learning. Here, for example, is part of the answer that is concealed behind our pomegranate midrash:

1. The one whose head is under his left hand is the Torah.
2. The one whose right hand embraces her is the *talmid ḥakham.*
3. The pomegranate nectar the Torah gives the *talmid ḥakham* to drink is the many portions made spicy with new discoveries and sweeter than honey.
4. The taste of this nectar is the taste of more. More without end. At every hour it is renewed as at the first hour.
5. The beloved Torah (the divine woman) adjures the daughters of Jerusalem (human women) that they should not dare awaken her love until she comes ready, forever. For her "narrow womb" is always tight, and she is desired by the *talmid ḥakham* who learns her, and there will be no end to their love affair which began 974 generations before the world was created.

When a *talmid ḥakham* dreams about a nectar-laden pomegranate slice, he dreams how the loving Torah reveals her heart to him and says, "I will give you to drink wine spiced with pomegranate nectar." When the *am ha'aretz* dreams about a nectar-laden pomegranate slice, he dreams how the Blessed Holy One rejoices in the way that he (together with God's beloved *Knesset Yisrael*)[18] observes the commandments: **"Behold you are beautiful, my beloved, you are beautiful. Your eyes are doves . . . your lips are a scarlet thread . . . Even the emptiest among you are full of commandments like a pomegranate (is full of seeds) . . . ."**

In his Song-of-Song dreams, the *talmid ḥakham* always sees himself as the active subject who loves the beloved Torah. By contrast, the *am ha'aretz* appears in these dreams as part of *Knesset Yisrael*, the perennial passive feminine object beloved by the most active of all subjects, the Blessed Holy One.

The pomegranate represents abundance. In all its appearances in the Song of Songs, it is female abundance. Therefore, whenever the pomegranate appears in the dreams of the *talmid ḥakham*, it is part of the yearned-for Other, and his vision is a vision of taking, of possession. He yearns to drink the pomegranate nectar. By contrast, the pomegranate in the dream of the *am ha'aretz* is part of himself. His vision is a vision of giving, of surrender. He yearns to have the Blessed Holy One drink his nectar-rich commandments.

The *am ha'aretz* gives the commandments to the Blessed Holy One. Commandments, as we know, are a refined substitute for sacrifices. They are intended to satisfy God. Therefore, if an *am ha'aretz* dreams about pomegranates, it is a sign he will be worthy to have the Blessed Holy One drink the nectar of his commandments and good deeds. The god of the *am ha'aretz* likes to take. Earning the continuing ongoing love of this god depends on observing the commandments. By contrast, the deity of the *talmid ḥakham* likes to give, letting him drink Her wine and pomegranate nectar. There is no system of gifts in the love cult between the *talmid ḥakham* and his Torah. Their love for each other is a love independent of all.

The Torah of the *talmid ḥakham* is *Torah lishmah*—Torah study for its own sake. He learns her because she delights him. She is not a means to anything, but the goal of all goals. He has nothing in his world besides her; she has nothing in her world besides him. He is lovesick and always absorbed in her. She is lovesick for him and gives him her pomegranate nectar to drink . . . .

Only love among gods is a love independent of all. Everyone drinks pomegranate nectar night and day; everyone is as desired by all at all times as at the first. Nobody sacrifices anything. Only humans offer sacrifices—not *talmidei ḥakhamim*.

As the *am ha'aretz* experiences her, the Torah is a book of sacrifices he must offer to the Blessed Holy One. It has no meaning as a beloved object in his dream consciousness. When an *am ha'aretz* dares dream dreams in the style of Song of Songs and interpret them, he is not the loving subject but the beloved object of the love of the people's *Kadosh Borukh Hu*, The Holy Blessed One. The *am ha'aretz* is the people Israel to whom the *Kadosh Borukh Hu* has made many enticing promises. The people Israel turns into *Knesset Yisrael,* the Congregation of Israel, the corporate woman beloved by the God of Judgment and Fury, Who is also the God of Righteousness and Progress, Who will certainly redeem her some day, as long as she never stops performing the commandments and doing good deeds. This is what the *talmidei ḥakhamim* meant when they said, **"Your *rakah* (temple) is like pomegranate slices—even the empty-headed *(reikanim)* among you are as full of commandments as the pomegranate is (of seeds).**[19]

The commandments were meant for the *am ha'aretz,* the Torah for the *talmid ḥakham.* That is all. It is the same dream, but its interpretation depends on the dreamer. A nectar-rich pomegranate is a nectar-rich pomegranate, but it has two different and contradictory interpretations—just as there are two different and contradictory interpretations to the Song of Songs, which is the dream of dreams. Two interpretations of divine love redeem two different sorts of people who live in the world of human-love-not-to-come. The interpretation for the *talmid ḥakham* is in the image of the Torah—the redeeming divine woman. The interpretation for the *am ha'aretz* is in the image of the *Kadosh Borukh Hu,* the redemptive male God. There are no other possibilities. There are no other men.

Learning Is Delight

Learning is delight. People who cannot delight in the intellectual process in which they are engaged cannot be learners; they can only be readers or studiers. Reading and studying are both necessary to the delight of learning, but they are not sufficient.

You can't learn during a first reading. You can't learn in a second reading. You have to read and reread and reread again. One who has read a portion one hundred times cannot compare with one who has read that portion 101 times.

The Torah read once is external to the reader. At the moment that the reader decides to read her again, he begins a long continuous process of courtship-like review. He discovers meaning in the Torah and tries to grow close to her. He reads and rereads and tries to narrow the gaps. At each stage of such study, the Torah is still external to the one who studies her.

And then the moment arrives when she becomes new to him. That moment is the transition point between studying and learning, *limud.* It is the moment of symbiosis. At that moment, the happy learner cannot distinguish the boundary between him and the learned Torah. He isn't interested in being able to tell. At that moment, the open, external Torah turns into the Torah learned in private. The reader turns into a *talmid ḥakham.*

In other words: The moment of transition to symbiosis is the same moment in which the learning subject ceases to be separable from the learned object. From that moment until the end of the process of learning, the learned Torah does not exist by herself, and her learner cannot exist by himself. The act of learning creates a metamorphosis in both the learning subject and the learned object. The creation of such a metamorphosis is absolutely necessary to achieve the state of learning. If it isn't created, we do not have the creative act of learning; we have only obsessive study.

The moment of transition from studying to learning creates an individual, personal relationship between the learner and the learned. This is the moment of renewal, which is, you will remember, an absolute prerequisite for love. And the learned Torah, it should be remembered, has limitless potential for renewal. She is desired every hour by those who learn her as she was at the first hour. She is the doe of love.

The progression—reading, studying, learning—is a continually repeating process. And every hour it reaches its conclusion, it is as desirable to the *talmid ḥakham* as it was at the first moment. This daily process the creative individual undergoes is the same process that generations of the people's elite have passed through. There is a very interesting connection between reading–studying–learning and *Mikra* (Scripture, the reading)–*Mishnah* (the re-reading or studying)–Talmud (the learning). The biblical Torah is the Torah that is read. The mishnaic Torah is the studied Torah. Both are Torahs of laws and commandments. Neither is the learned Torah. But the talmudic Torah—the *Gemara*—is the learned Torah that we have been talking about in the last few chapters.

The producers of the biblical Torah and the mishnaic Torah did not see their Torah as an end but rather as a mediating means. They did not intend themselves to be a creative and learning elite, but an elite that leads and mediates. They appointed themselves as mediators between the Israelite *am ha'aretz* and their God. The first such mediators were priests and prophets; the later ones were the Rabbis who are called *tannaim.* The priests and prophets are the mediating elite described in the Bible. They mediate between the Israelite *am ha'aretz* who lives on the land and its God who lives in the Temple. The *am ha'aretz* has an ambivalent relationship with its God. On the one hand, it cannot live without God's dominant presence, but, on the other hand, it isn't able to create a direct link with God. Therefore it needs intermediaries. And the major vehicle these mediators use is the Torah. Without paying much attention to the considerable tension between priest and prophet, and in full knowledge of the lack of precision in this generalization, one can say that the priest raises the *am ha'aretz* to the divine level (through sacrifices), and the prophet brings the divine down to the level of the *am ha'aretz* (through laws and commandments).

The sacrifices are the gift the *am ha'aretz* gives its God in order to get abundance and protection from God. The priests who conduct the ritual of offering sacrifices are the mediating elite of the biblical Torah. They cannot live the life of the common people—they have no inheritance of the land, they have no this-world schedule. That is so they can dedicate themselves to being in the Temple and devote themselves as much as possible to the work of sacrifices—to fill their mission of mediation in the best possible way.

With the destruction of the Temple and the abolition of sacrifices came a threat to the survival of the natural and normal system of relationships between the *am ha'aretz* and its God. This threat automatically carried with it a threat to the continued survival of the people. Indeed, a people that does not keep an orderly daily ritual system in relationship to its concrete god cannot continue to survive as a unique people and will be absorbed by other nations. At this stage the revolution of the Rabbis called *tannaim* enters the picture.

These Rabbis took over the role of the priests and prophets and turned into a new mediating elite between the Israelite *am ha'aretz* and its God. This takeover process continued throughout the period of the formation of the *Mishnah* and its supplements. Its essence was the creation of a new halakhic system, in which the commandments are both the ritual substitute for sacrifices and a prescription for executing the moral demands of the prophets. The Rabbis prepared for the *am ha'aretz* the six orders of the *Mishnah,* arranged a set order of prayer, and organized an intricately detailed daily agenda. In this way, they enabled it to continue to have a lengthy and orderly system of relations with its God.

These Rabbis caused the biblical Torah to undergo a fascinating metamorphosis into the mishnaic Torah, the Torah of halakhah. This transformation often caused them to break the biblical text free of its literal biblical context. Anyone who looks at the *Mishnah* and her counterparts can see this easily. Nevertheless, the Torah of the *tannaim* is essentially a direct continuation of the Torah of the priests and the prophets. The *tannaitic* Torah continues to be a book of rules and a guide to action. This Torah, like its predecessor, continues to be a means—an intermediary between the Israelite *am ha'aretz* and its God.

The most substantial transformation, in my opinion, is not the passage from the biblical Torah to the mishnaic Torah, but the passage from the mishnaic Torah to the Torah of the Talmud. The Torah that many of the creators of the Talmud produced is completely different from any of the Torahs that had been created before. These creators of the Talmud (the "Stammaitic editors") changed their Torah from an intermediate means to an end in itself. They even stopped designating themselves delegated elite mediators. They created an entirely new creation for themselves. They created the idea of Torah for her own sake (*Torah lishmah*), and they made themselves an entirely new category of elite—a creative elite.

This creative elite used a very revealing term, *talmidei ḥakhamim* to refer

TWO COMPLETELY DIFFERENT TORAHS.

There are two Torahs: the Torah that commands and the Torah that is studied.

The first is the source of authority
and reflects the male God.
The second is the source of inspiration
and reflects the female goddess.
The first is directed to the entire people,
the second to the small, exclusive group
of talmidei ḥakhamin *who isolate themselves*
in the Olympus of the beit midrash.
Some of them are perpetually
on the verge of addiction to
their love goddess and
on the verge of
abandoning
their obligation
to the God who commands.

to themselves, to the *tannaim*, the *amoraim* and even to some biblical leaders (like David). They didn't say "sages" as in *Ḥazal* (Our Sages of Blessed Memory), which is the name we give them. Instead, they said *talmidei ḥakhamim*, for the act of learning is their defining characteristic. The term *talmid* (student) is a term of professional status. It is also an apt description of the psychological makeup of the *talmid ḥakham:* He learns all the time. The Torah is always new to him, and even the greatest sage among them thinks of himself as only learning.

The *talmidei ḥakhamim* took the value of learning Torah and made it their highest value. They observed (more or less) the commanding and mediating Torah but devoted all their energy and erotic powers to the learned Torah. These *talmidei ḥakhamim* managed to liberate themselves forever from the problems of mediation and left this task to other rabbis of their own period—the heirs of the priests and the prophets. The *talmidei ḥakhamim* isolated themselves in their *beit midrash*-on-Olympus. They turned themselves into gods, and they appropriated for themselves the Torah that was intended for *am ha'aretz* and turned her into an alluring love goddess.

From this point on there are two completely different Torahs which exist side by side: the Torah for the *am ha'aretz* and the Torah for the *talmid ḥakham*. From this point on, a singular dialectic develops between the mediating Rabbis and the creative *talmidei ḥakhamim*—one reflected in many pages of the Talmud. We can continue to characterize it with the help of the surrealistic story about the meeting between Moshe Rabbenu and Rabbi Akiva presented in the previous chapter. The tension between Moshe and Rabbi Akiva is the tension between a rabbi and a *talmid ḥakham*. Moshe has been crowned with the name Rabbenu. He is the all-time Chief Rabbi of the people Israel. Rabbi Akiva, in contrast, is the greatest *talmid ḥakham* of all time.

The tension between a rabbi and a *talmid ḥakham* is the concrete expression of the universal tension between the two elites present in every society, the mediating elite and the creative elite. Moshe is the archetypal representative of the mediating elite; Rabbi Akiva, the quintessential representative of the creative elite.

We should note immediately that any resemblance between the historical Moses and Rabbi Akiva and the Moshe and Rabbi Akiva who are described in the pages of the Talmud is absolutely coincidental. The historical Moses was, to the extent that he was at all, a prophet-leader who mediated between the people Israel and the God of Israel. He brought the people out of Egypt on a mission from God, brought the Torah down to them, and led them to the Land this God designated for his people. Even though the historical Moshe was not a rabbi, the folk consciousness in all of us knows him as Moshe Rabbenu—Moshe our Rabbi. We will never know how this combination of words—Moshe

Rabbenu, which never appears in the Bible—became the calling card of the prophet of prophets in the consciousness of all generations who succeeded him. In the same way, the little ladybug will never know why this combination of words is also part of her strange name, *parat* Moshe Rabbenu (Moshe our Rabbi's cow). If she has to be considered Moshe's cow, then why not Moshe-our-prophet's-cow? Why should the memory of Moses have become so inextricably linked with the image of the Rabbi?

Similarly, the historical Rabbi Akiva is completely different from the Rabbi Akiva who is so devoted to the learned Torah. The historical Rabbi Akiva was the last person to whom the attributes of withdrawal and isolation could apply. He was a spiritual leader who was completely bound up in the life of the people and who devoted his whole life to restoring this people after the destruction of the Temple by constructing a system of commandments and by intervening most actively in the Bar Kochba rebellion. Somebody who lived in Babylonia many years after the period of the historical Rabbi Akiva (the end of the first century CE and the beginning of the second) took care to turn him into a *talmid ḥakham* who lived on Olympus, in much the same way as he took care to turn Moshe into the people's all-time Chief Rabbi.

These transformations that took root so strongly in the consciousness of the people are impressive testimony to the power of those who fashioned them. Their power is expressed most particularly in their ability to bring to the surface a tension that had been ignored until that point, the tension between the creative elite and the mediating elite. *Talmidei ḥakhamim* are an open and living testimony to the existence of this dialectical tension. They recorded it on every page of the Talmud.

And so, Moshe in this story is the archetype of the mediating elite. He goes on high (far above Mount Sinai) to receive the Torah from God and give her to the *am ha'aretz* who are gathered at the foot of the mountains doing at that time whatever it was doing. The God of the *am ha'aretz* gives His commanding Torah through Moshe. The Torah that Moshe gives to the *am ha'aretz* is a functional, mediating Torah. She is intended to be observed. Whoever knows how to fulfill her commandments will be rewarded. Whoever does not will be punished.

Moshe learns this Torah forty days and forty nights. He knows all her details. He is the prophet of prophets and the mediator of all mediators. No comma in this revealed Torah escapes his attention, and he knows the revealed Torah unto its tiniest point. He knows how to take heaps and heaps of rules and judgments and narrow them to a tiny jot. He knows how to make even the hardest sections clear for the *am ha'aretz* and to disperse the thickest fogs before them. But the Torah that Moshe discovers with God on high is completely opposite from the one he knows in such absolute detail. This is the Torah that complicates even the clearest matter and heaps piles of halakhot on every tittle. In the points and the tittles of the letters the journey begins to the secret areas of T*orah lishmah*—Torah for her own sake. The journey into the inner part of the letters is something like the journey of Alice into the invisible confusions of Wonderland. The Torah of Rabbi Akiva and his students is *Torah lishmah,* the Torah for herself and herself alone. They enter the points of the *yod* not to draw new rules, not to improve society, not to contribute to humankind, and not to bring on the Messiah. Their only motivation to enter the tip of the *yod* is delight. The delight of learning.

The Torah of Rabbi Akiva and his students is the inspiration takeoff field for the infinity of possible and unexpected universes (Alma Dee), in contrast to the Torah of Moshe, which is a landing field into the real world. As we know, there is only one real world, in contrast to the infinity of possible worlds. The Torah that Moshe brings down is supposed to be actualized in the world. She is intended to be a Torah of life, and she announces herself as the prescription for life which is the most effective of all other prescriptions and Torahs. But the Torah of Rabbi Akiva and his students is not interested in remaining in the real, bounded universe. She lifts off from the real world, into which the Torah of Moshe descends, and heads for the infinity of secret universes. With the breath of their mouths, Rabbi Akiva and his students create universes, and with the breath of their mouths they destroy them. The letters and combinations and crowns and points are the materials they use. They are creative deities. They are children, building piles of sand castles and Lego palaces. They take them apart as easily as they put them together. They don't take anybody into consideration. They keep turning their Torah around and around and take liberties with her. They delight in the moment. They do not build their heaps of palaces so that someone can live in them. That would not be building *lishmah,* for its own sake. They build in order to build. They are not only nonfunctional. They are antifunctional.

And poor Moshe sits there and hears them and doesn't understand the connection between the words so familiar to him (the words of the Torah) and the strange and surreal interpretations that Rabbi Akiva and his students are giving her. He sees God sitting among them as a *talmid ḥakham* and participating in tying crowns onto the letters. And he understands that there is a whole rich and wild creative system that he is forbidden to enter and that God's real interest in the Torah is creative learning. He doesn't understand why God chose him to give the Torah rather than Rabbi Akiva and he asks, "You have such a person and you give this Torah through me?" and God simply answers him, "Shut up!"

The Moshe of this story really doesn't understand. He is locked into functional thinking. He is locked into the biblical mentality of reward and punishment. He doesn't understand why God doesn't give Rabbi Akiva the honor of bringing the Torah down to the people. He doesn't understand that the creative God would be totally wasting Rabbi Akiva by turning him into a mediator. God wants Rabbi Akiva next to him in eternal *ḥevruta* (study partnership). He wants Rabbi Akiva next to Him to untie for Him ceaselessly all the crowns that He ties for the Torah.

The Creative God—like every creative *talmid ḥakham*—isn't interested in having anything to do with the ordinary people. For that, He delegates a mediator, someone to do the menial labor. For that, He needs Moshe to be tied to him and eternally responsible for all the mediators to come—prophets, priests, rabbis, judges, *poskim*.

In the final analysis, there are two opposite emotions involved here: the sense of *ashmah* (guilt, responsibility) and the sense of *lishmah*. These two emotions developed into two distinct passions: the desire to have control over oneself and the passionate desire to give oneself over to abandon. A sense of guilt prevents one from concentrating on *lishmah*, for the sense of guilt also involves responsibility for others, a sense of mission and of tradition. It demands that one be aware of one's surroundings and prevents total concentration on the act of learning, which is a state of being carried away in the wake of a creative desire that demands loss of control.

Moshe's lack of understanding of the intoxicating principle of *lishmah* (for her own sake) is revealed even more clearly with his second question, "This is the Torah and this is her reward?" He sees Rabbi Akiva's death and decries the lack of justice and the lack of proportion between the life of this man and his death. Between his deeds and their reward. The question—"This is Torah and this is her reward?"—is a distillation of the biblical and folk understanding of reward and punishment. Everyone who sees the reward or punishment as external to the deed lies along the intermediary axis between *am ha'aretz* and God. Moshe asks the question along this axis. The God who tells him, "Shut up!" is not the God of *am ha'aretz* but the creative God. The only answer that anyone from the creative elite can give to a question that assumes a nonimminent connection between deed and consequence is "Shut up!" The problem with these questions is not that sufficient answers don't exist but that these questions themselves have no right to exist. After all, the question of the righteous sufferer relies on the assumption that there is reward and punishment, the assumption which is the essence of the biblical Torah of: **Be like servants who serve their master in order to get a prize.**[20] Only someone freed of this conception can be a God who learns in the Olympus of the *beit midrash*, who can tie crowns onto the letters and interpret piles and piles of halakhot from each point of a letter, and who can be free. Only such a one can be completely released from any sense of social and moral nexus, mission, or responsibility.

Rabbi Yehoshua ben Levi said:
At the time that Moshe ascended on high, the ministering angels said to Him,
"Master of the Universe, what is this son-of-woman doing among us?"
God said to them, "He has come to receive the Torah."
They said to God, "The hidden one, the desired one, she who has been hidden by you for 974 generations before the creation of the world—are you now going to give her to flesh and blood? What is humanity that you should be mindful of it and the child of Adam that you should pay heed to it?"
The Holy Blessed one said to Moshe, "Respond to them!"
Moses said to God, "O Master of the Universe, I am afraid that they will burn me with the breath of their mouths."
God said to Moses, "Hold on to my Throne of Glory and respond to them!"
Moses said to God, "Master of the Universe—the Torah that you are giving me, what is written in it?
"I am the Lord your God Who took you out of Egypt . . . ."
He said to them, "Did you go down to Egypt? Were you slaves to Pharaoh? Why do you need the Torah? What else is written in it?"
"You shall not have any other gods!"
"Are you living among the heathen nations? What else is written in it?"
"Remember the Sabbath day to keep it holy!"
"Do you do work that you have to cease? What else is written in it?"
"Do not take . . . ."
"Do you give and take? What else is written in it?"
"Honor your father and your mother!"
"Do you have fathers and mothers? What else is written in it?"
"Do not murder! Do not commit adultery! Do not steal!"
"Do you have envy? . . . Do you have an evil impulse?"
They immediately thanked the Holy Blessed One . . . immediately every one became a lover [of Moses] and gave him something, as it is written: "You went on high and brought back.." (BT Shabbat 88a)

This is the story of the conflict between Moses—the chosen man—and the ministering angels who were jealous that he, and not they, was privileged to receive the Torah. Moses comes out of this conflict with the upper hand. The ministering angels finally acknowledge that the Torah was not designed for them but for human beings in the real world, who have fathers and mothers, who work and envy, and who struggle with evil impulses.

The Torah that Moses is privileged to bring down from heaven is the commanding Torah. She is a collection of commandments, which are simply the most efficient set of prescriptions to cope with the problems of this world. Thus, the angels who envy Moses are not worthy of the commanding Torah because they are not able to acknowledge the fact that they can envy. The Torah is appointed for humanity, for human beings are the ones who can acknowledge their weaknesses. Those who see themselves as perfect and cannot acknowledge their weaknesses are angels who are not suited or able to fulfill the commandments of the Torah.

Moses comes out of this conflict the winner, but in the previous story he comes out of the conflict with Rabbi Akiva the loser. The reason is simple: The competition with the angels is over the commanding Torah; the competition with Rabbi Akiva is over the learned Torah.

Philological and material analyses of the story about Moses and Rabbi Akiva and the tale of Moses and the ministering angels suggest that the story about Moses and the angels was written first. The story about Moses and Rabbi Akiva is attributed to Rav Yehudah, the founder of the Yeshivah of Pumbedita and its first Rosh Yeshivah (mid third century CE); it was apparently written several generations afterward (not before the end of the fifth century). The anonymous storyteller behind this story is apparently a Babylonian *talmid ḥakham* who writes from the stronghold of the creative elite, whose preferred Torah is without a doubt *torah lishmah.* This storyteller isn't afraid to present us with an entirely different Moses than the one who lays before the angels an impressive set of unanswerable questions. This storyteller's Moshe finds himself surrounded by an ongoing set of questions and answers from another world. Rabbi Akiva and his students do not direct their Torah to the real world but rather return it to the skies. They give and take with the Holy Blessed One in the academy of the heavens, the *yeshivah shel ma'alah.* He ties crowns for them and they loosen them; nobody speaks about mitzvot at all . . . .

One could say that the first story was written by a storyteller relating to the affairs of the mediator elite, and the second story is a hymn of praise the creative elite sings to the debating *talmid ḥakham* who can pile heaps and heaps of halakhot on every jot and tittle.

The complex dialectic between these two stories is characteristic of the complex interdependency of the mediating Rabbis—those who decide upon halakhah and are responsible for its execution—and the *talmidei ḥakhamim,* who heap piles of halakhot on every jot and tittle. This dialectic stands out on every page of the Talmud and the endless literature that comes after it. One can say (being aware that it is somewhat of a generalization) that from the talmudic revolution on, there has continued to be a complex set of interdependencies between these two elites.

The original issue in the developing relationship between these two elites is the fact that since the talmudic revolution, the mediating elite has seen itself as serving the creative elite. This contrasts completely with the way mediating elites of all other revolutions (that I know about) have related to their creative elites. The priests and prophets of other revolutions have looked down upon the creative elites that have sprouted along with them. They have always been quite sure that the artists, philosophers, and scientists should serve their Torah, should beautify it in the eyes of the folk, and thereby magnify their strength. To the extent that they have been tolerant of the creative elite, it has been a limited tolerance. In general, the mediating elites develop an attitude of impressive terror toward creativity, a terror that expresses itself in various means of censorship.

We can understand the causes of the terror that mediating (governing) elites have exhibited to the creative elites that have sprouted alongside them. After all, anyone who turns Torah—any Torah—from a means to an end, constitutes a palpable threat to the existence of the entire system. Not only does he or she not help in the difficult work of mediation, but he or she takes great liberties with the Torah and thereby might clip the plants or destroy the leadership.

The true creative spirit we are talking about is a danger to society because he or she learns Torah for its own sake, *lishmah.* By not being a court poet and not participating in any form of co-opted art, he or she is essentially nonfunctional. In fact, the true creative spirit we are talking about is antifunctional, completely liberated from any delegated obligations. He or she takes liberty with the material, wrenching it out of context. In so doing, he or she poses a threat to the orderly daily continuum of *am ha'aretz*–commissar–God. For this reason mediating (governing) elites oppress their creative individuals before they can become an organized creative elite.

But that is not true in our case. In our case the mediating elite (communal rabbis) has appointed itself at the service of the creative-learning elite, taking care of all its needs and giving it all appropriate honor and respect. Moreover, the mediating elite never interfered with the creative elite's process of learning. It enabled the *talmidei ḥakhamim* to take liberties with the Torah and find in it anything their heart desired. On one condition: The *talmidei ḥakhamim,* for their part, had to promise not to reveal to the public the sense of freedom and openness that dwells in the Olympus of the *beit midrash.*

In other words, the mediating elite created a complicated social structure that rests on absolute pluralism in everything related to the learned Torah and absolute antipluralism in everything that relates to the commanding Torah.

Indeed, this idyll is the formula for survival that has proved itself more than any other formula. The creative elite does not intervene in the deliberations of the mediating elite. On the contrary, it is happy that the burden of mediation doesn't rest on it. The mediating elite, for its part, doesn't intervene in the process of learning. Even more, it takes care to plant in the heart of the people the sense that the learning of the *talmid ḥakham* is aimed at improving the system of commandments.

The *am ha'aretz* and the *talmid ḥakham* are two different personality types. The *am ha'aretz,* in essence, doesn't enjoy learning for its own sake. His mentality is functional; he will learn only if he has to learn and only if he understands clearly what he gets out of learning. In contrast, the *talmid ḥakham* suffers from any learning that is not *lishmah.* He is actually tortured whenever someone asks or demands that he give a practical application for his learning. When he is asked to indicate an application for his learning, he feels intense pressure. Moreover, even fulfilling the commandments or any other role in the ethical or civil system seems to him a necessary torture, a decree that he cannot always endure.

Of course, these are absolute types. There are two-way passages between the commanding and mediating elites. And there are some (often the most interesting characters) who manage to walk both paths at once. In the final analysis, however, anyone who becomes a rabbi because of economic constraints, a compulsion to serve, or a lust for power and position, is an artist who has been co-opted by the system.

The anxiety that the *talmid ḥakham* has about fulfilling commandments is greater than the anxiety that the *am ha'aretz* has about learning *lishmah.* Performing the commandments of the commanding Torah makes the life of the *talmid ḥakham* hard, and cruelly cuts off the intimate and infinite dialogue that takes place at all times between him and his learned Torah. The very need to perform commandments is alien to the soul of a *talmid ḥakham.* The very need to take part in earthly life is a decree that he cannot endure. The ideals of *Torah lishmah* (Torah study for its own sake and *"talmud torah keneged kulam"* (Torah study preferable to all other pursuits) transform his own spiritual limitations into a power formula for survival. This survival formula rests on a brilliant dialectic which offers solutions—through the same Torah—to the opposing spiritual limitations of *talmidei ḥakhamim* and *amei ha'aretz.*

From this point on, learning Torah, *talmud Torah,* becomes a kind of commandment for the *am ha'aretz.* It is enough for him to declaim every day the *Shema* in order to discharge the obligation of learning Torah. The halakhah only requires him to read one portion from the *Mishnah* and the Torah (saying the blessings of the Torah before and after) in order to discharge the obligation of learning Torah.* This, of course, refers to the commandment to learn Torah. In contrast, see BT Bava Metzia 85a-b: **Why was the land destroyed? Because they didn't bless the Torah at the beginning.** In my opinion, this is a criticism of the *talmidei ḥakhamim*, who are the exact opposite of the *amei ha'aretz.* The *talmidei ḥakhamim* learn all the time, but some of them do not bless before and after learning. They cannot or will not do the minimum required to function in the system of commandments, which is to bless before and after the learning they are doing. As Steinsaltz says, following the Maharal, **And the Torah becomes for him like any secular learning that has no holy meaning.**[21] This criticism refers to those among the *talmidei ḥakhamim* who have lost the ability to be obligated to the normative system or those whose addiction to Torah causes them to forget to say the blessing, which is one of the last threads that connect them to the commanding God.

For the *talmid ḥakham,* learning Torah is not a commandment but an existential compulsion. He cannot refrain from learning. He tries as much as possible to be in the *beit midrash,* and to delight as much as possible in the refinements that will come through his familiar and beloved Torah. He will try to be outside the *beit midrash* as little as possible. Not only because learning Torah in front of *am ha'aretz* is like sleeping with your fiancée in public and the desecration of everything he holds holy and esoteric, but because the more he is buried in learning Torah, the more he frees himself from dealing with the daily life of commandments in the real world.

We should remember that the *am ha'aretz* wants to live in the real world and follow in this world all the rules of the commanding Torah that came down to him from the infinity of possible worlds; the *talmid ḥakham* wants to cut himself off from the real world and be carried on the wings of the learned Torah up to the infinity of secret worlds. The *am ha'aretz* is afraid of being cut off from the one sole real world, and the *talmid ḥakham* is afraid to connect with it.

So the *talmid ḥakham*'s formula is *talmud Torah keneged kulam,* (learning Torah is above all) i.e., fulfilling the commandment of learning Torah is more important than fulfilling all the other commandments.

> **Learning Torah is greater than building the Temple.**
> **Learning Torah is greater than honoring your father and mother.**
> **Learning Torah is greater than saving lives.**[22]

* The blessing before the Study of Torah: "Blessed be You, O Lord, our God, King of the Universe, Who has sanctified us with the commandments and commanded us to occupy ourselves with the words of the Torah." The blessing before the liturgical reading of the Torah: "Blessed be You, O Lord, our God, King of the Universe, Who has chosen us from among the nations and given us Your Torah. Blessed are You, O Lord, Who gives the Torah." The blessing after: "Blessed be You, O Lord, our God, King of the Universe, Who has given us your Torah and sowed eternal life in our midst. Blessed are you O Lord, Who gives the Torah." (Translator's note)

But total release is not possible. Even the most addicted *talmid ḥakham* has to recite the morning *Shema,* keep the Shabbat, say the obligatory prayers, dwell in the *sukkah,* hold *lulav* and *etrog,* burn the *ḥametz,* discharge the obligation of hearing the *Megillah* and fulfill the obligation to light Hanukkah candles. The commandments he cannot escape are, among others, *mitzvot shehazman gramah* (commandments governed by time): the breaking dawn, the calendar of the year, the entering Shabbat, and the departing Shabbat—all of these are messages from the real world so that he should not be totally cut off from it.

The commandments are the *talmid ḥakham*'s ballast weights. They are the lifesaving rings floating on the continuum of real time, preventing him from being dragged away and completely cut off from the real world.

The same system of mitzvot that forces the *am ha'aretz* to rise above the daily grind and to give a measure of meaning to their empty lives, also forces the *talmid ḥakham* to come down to a landing from his daily heavenly ascents. The same recital of the morning *Shema,* the same Shabbat, take the *am ha'aretz* up and bring the *talmid ḥakham* down. The *am ha'aretz* and the *talmid ḥakham* meet through the carrying out of a time-bound commandment: One rises a little from the real world, and the other descends from his fantastic universes. When they finish fulfilling the commandment, they both return to their domains: the *am ha'aretz* to his earthly affairs and the *talmid ḥakham* to his Olympus.

Excursus: The Creative Elite and the Zionist Problem

The test of survival of any torah depends on the ability of the society that holds it to create a synthesis between a creative elite and a mediating elite. The moment that this torah becomes the exclusive property of priests and prophets, it is doomed to destruction. The creators who should have created in it will go to pasture in foreign fields or become frustrated leaders. The litmus test of any society's survival prospects is the degree of absolute freedom of action that it affords its creative spirits.

This is true for the "torah" of any "ism." If we define, for example, the "torah" of humanism as a series of commandments (sacrifices) the ordinary person *(am ha'aretz)* is obligated to sacrifice for its god (humankind), then this torah will endure only if within its framework creative people can develop who will treat this torah as their own and will carry it to absurdity, just as the *talmidei ḥakhamim* do with their torah.

The kibbutz torah is a good example of this principle. The kibbutz movement was smart enough to create a society with an effective apparatus enabling priests and prophets to cooperate with *amei ha'aretz.* But this society was not smart enough to create a place for creative spirits who could be creative with the kibbutz torah and take liberties with it without any sense of guilt.

In general, the perfect success of the Zionist revolution was its greatest failure. It created an exemplary *am ha'aretz.* The salt of the earth. They went out into the fields and offered sacrifices, volunteering for every national and movement-wide task and sacrificing their private lives on the altar of the idea of a homeland and the greatest general good. They volunteered for every task and rejoiced in the sacrifice and the giving without end. Without the altruistic *am ha'aretz* who existed here in the first part of the century, without this justifiably praised "silver salver,"[22a] there would have been no state.

There was also an exemplary intermediary: the *ḥalutzim,* they who inherited with great pride the place of the priests and the Rabbis. They became the new intermediaries between the new *am ha'aretz* and its new gods, the gods of nature and equality and earth. The gods of international labor. The gods of *Am Yisrael ḥai,* the still-surviving-Jewish people. Not to mention the leadership of the *Yishuv,* who despite everything that (correctly and justifiably) has been written about them as part of our shattering of sacred cows, was a mediating elite rare in its quality and power.

The problem, in my opinion, was not in the creation of the new axis: *am ha'aretz*–prophet/priest–god. This was an exemplary axis. The problem was this revolution's absolute lack of ability to produce *talmidei ḥakhamim.* Even worse: This revolution suppressed any sign of *talmidei ḥakhamim* as soon as it sprouted. They suppressed any development of a creative system *lishmah,* for its own sake. They suppressed the fantasy and the wildness that are a necessary condition for the creation of a creative elite. They didn't allow anyone to dare take liberties with <u>their</u> torah.

If you want to be an artist (they said), do so on a functional plain. Be a court poet for the harvest ceremony. Be a court painter and make costumes for the Jubilee. Sacrifice yourself like any *am ha'aretz* on the altar of functionality. Be a link in the wonderful mediating chain on which the state of the *am ha'aretz* Jews rises. Everything is for practicality and against nonfunctionalism. One shouldn't even mention antifunctionalism, which betrays the essence of the faith and clips its plants.

The more a system is secure in its beliefs and commands, the more it allows itself to give rise to creative *batei midrash* whose learners take liberties with the text. The structure of the Zionist revolution in all its parts has still not been smart enough to create such *batei midrash* because it is still not secure in its revolution. It is still much more suspicious of its creative spirits than the rabbinic system is. It still sees them as antifunctional parasites. It still demands reports about those it supports so that it can inform the appointees to report to the board. In short, it lacks a basic assurance about the rightness of its way.

What we need most of all is a group of *ribboni talmidei ḥakhamim. Apikorsim* (heretics). Creative learners whose learning is *lishmah* and who operate within the framework of *ribboni* society.

We have to build creative *batei midrash.* Antifunctional *batei midrash, batei midrash* where *talmidei ḥakhamim* can sit without reporting to anyone, *talmidei ḥakhamim* who treat the text as their own and take liberties with it. Who will not mediate between the gods and the people nor between the "second" Israel and the "first Israel;" nor between the *datti'im* and *ḥilonim* nor between Jews and Arabs, nor between men and women; nor between millionaires and professors. *Talmidei ḥakhamim* who will sit with the text and only with the text and will not have to be examined on it and will not have to hand in papers or any practical application. They will just learn the text with a creative learning *lishmah.* They will learn day and night about *Psyche and Eros* or *The Little Prince* or *Alice in Wonderland* or Bava Metzia. And they will read this same text the whole day and the whole night and they will study it one hundred times and 101 times, until they will begin to learn it and create its way. Not in order to apply it; not in order to file lesson plans in the endless file cabinets of our teaching centers; not in order to find the purpose of existence, or the reason for existence, or our right to the land, or our rights abroad. They will learn it in order to learn. Period. In order to delight. Period. In order to pile heaps of completely fictive *halakhot* on every jot and tittle.

You (all the subsidizers and mediators) will discover that by doing it *lishmah* (for itself) they will come to do it *lo lishmah* (not for itself alone), which means they will manage to solve for our distressed youth the problems of emigration and drugs and futility and apathy, etc., etc., etc. It seems unbelievable, but in the end investing in such *talmidei ḥakhamim* will pay off for you. They will profit our economy, contribute to our society, and "bring back our former glory. . . ."

Reḥumi's Love Triangle

Rav Reḥumi could always be found before Rava in Maḥozah,
and used to go home[23] every Erev Yom Kippur (Yom Kippur Eve).
One day the *shma'ata*[24] (portion of Torah under study) allured him.
His wife was waiting for him:
He's coming now! He's coming now!
He didn't come.
She lost her senses,
a tear fell from her eye.

He was sitting on a roof—
the roof opened underneath him and he died. (BT Ketubot 62b)

The verb *rhm* in Aramaic means "to love." Rav Reḥumi is the name of a lover. The name of a *talmid ḥakham* whose love for the divine female—the Torah—comes at the expense of his love for the human woman. Because of his love for the divine female, he stays in her realm all the days of the year. Once a year—every Erev Yom Kippur—he is accustomed to come to his human wife. This custom was his compelling and obligatory practice: He was wont to go home every Erev Yom Kippur.

The pattern of relations between a man and his God can tempt him to escape from establishing the relationships that he ought to create with other people. Rav Reḥumi's God was not the male God of commands and obligations but rather the Torah—the love goddess who remains continually beloved.

Rav Reḥumi's relation to the Torah of study was not one of obligation but of allure. His relationship to his wife, on the other hand, was one of obligation. Relationships with his wife are part of the pattern of normative behavior that the commanding God imposes on him. The tension between the Torah and the wife is a corollary aspect of the tension between the female goddess and the male God. The wife represents the command of the male God and prevents Reḥumi from completely divorcing himself from earthly attractions and being drawn into an ecstasy from which there is no return.

It is well known that Yom Kippur does not atone for offenses against others until one has placated and appeased the other party. Rav Reḥumi's appearance at his house every Erev Yom Kippur extended his visa for another year. He is accustomed to come to his other once a year—every Erev Yom Kippur—to placate and appease her in order to be able to go through Yom Kippur successfully. The woman who keeps back her tears all year is placated by him every Erev Yom Kippur and lets her tears accrue till the next Yom Kippur.

The woman keeps back her tears all the years in which Rav Reḥumi accustoms himself to appear on Erev Yom Kippur. She teaches herself to bite her lips and persevere. She teaches herself to live from the previous Erev Yom Kippur to this one and from this Erev Yom Kippur to the next one. However, she—unlike him—never gets used to this ritual. She suffers silently, keeping back her tears, and fights the deep depression[25] that threatens to draw her down into the depths of despair.

From Yom Kippur to Yom Kippur, Rav Reḥumi lets a heavy sin accumulate, a serious ongoing sin against his wife and against the commanding God. He should stand judgment for this. But his appearance every Erev Yom Kippur appeases his wife and causes her to delay his punishment for another year. If she did not behave toward him beyond all requirements, the God of Judgment would not forgive his sin and would demand his blood.

Yom Kippur and this woman who acts toward him beyond all requirements are Rav Reḥumi's ballast as he is being drawn tragically skyward. Essentially he prefers the vertical connection between himself and the divine female to the horizontal connection between himself and his other. He is going to die on a roof during his tragic ascent skyward. He is going to die on Erev Yom Kippur—the most significant day between any person and another—a day that brings into seventy-fold relief his inverted priorities and his doom. He is not going to get a visa for another year.

Rav Reḥumi's social context enables him to push to the utmost his devotion to his love goddess and elevates him as an esteemed hero. This is the society that engraved on its flag the slogan: "The study of Torah is above all." This is the social reality that the narrator is protesting.

This story is the tragic application of two important utterances that appear in Bava Metzia 59a in the midst of a *sugya* that deals with humiliation and insult:[26]

1. **All the gates are locked except the gate of tears.**
2. **A man should always be cautious about insulting his wife, for the presence of her tear quickly brings calamitous retribution for the insult (read according to Rashi).**

The *talmidei ḥakhamim* who stand behind these statements are aware of the serious and continuous injury, the mental anguish that they cause their wives when they leave them and devote themselves to their Torah. They are also conscious of the power of the tears of the desperate oppressed, a power much stronger than that of any other kind of prayer. Other prayers do not have the power to open the gates of heaven, but the tears of the oppressed can do so, and can fulfill the petitions and prayers accompanying them. They are very conscious of an iron-clad rule: Whatever is weaker is stronger, and they express this sentiment in many ways. The *talmidei ḥakhamim* lived in perpetual fear of the tears of their wives. They knew that whenever a tear fell, calamity would fall on them. The wives, for their part, tried with all their might to staunch their tears.

A man should always be cautious about insulting his wife, for the presence of her tear quickly brings calamitous retribution. The essence of the art of oppression is embedded in this verse. How can we keep our oppressed so they do not let their tears fall against us and bury us under them? How can we avoid stretching oppression too far? How can we prevent the oppressed from getting too depressed? The art of oppression is an important skill to learn, whether the subject is personal oppression (husbands–wives, parents–children) or national and class oppression. Whoever humiliates another in public, and all other oppressors who inflict mental anguish, are worthy of death, according to the *Gemara*. At the moment of humiliation and oppression, death is decreed for the oppressor. On the other hand, enacting this death sentence depends on the oppressed. The execution of Rav Reḥumi's death sentence depended all these years on his wife; will she let a tear fall, or not?

His wife (she has no name)[27] enables him to cut off contact from the world and give himself over to his Torah. She is the one who enables him to walk the high balance wire. One incautious step on his part, and the tear will fall; his balance will be lost; the wire will snap; calamity will come. All the gates will be opened with lightning speed by an instantaneous, hidden hydraulic mechanism, the mechanism of the tear that she can no longer hold back. The power and swiftness of this single tear are the product of an ever-increasing mass composed of the man's ongoing oppression and the woman's continuing self-restraint.

The *talmid ḥakham* creates this terrible balance, and the woman preserves it. He depends on her ability to withstand suffering. As long as she can suppress her reaction, he can continue to be devoted to his Torah.

The very act of oppression entails the death penalty. The calamitous retribution—the execution of the decree—depends on the strength of the injury and the ability of the victim to tolerate it.

How can we know if our behavior has injured another with a mortal blow? We cannot know. Who can know how many long-suffering victims circulate among us, holding back their tears, choking off their cries, and postponing for us the day of reckoning?

Hallelujah at the Death of God-Accursed Children

Yehudah the son of Rabbi Ḥiyya, the son-in-law of Rabbi Yannai went and lived in the *beit midrash*.
At twilight (every Erev Shabbat,)[28] he would come home.
As he came, they would see in front of him a column of fire.
One day, the *shma'ata*[24] allured him, and he didn't come.
Because they didn't see this sign,
Rabbi Yannai said to them, "overturn his bed, for if Yehudah were alive he would not cancel his marital obligation."[29]
It was like an "error made by a ruler,"[30] and Yehudah died.
(BT Ketubot 62b)

Yehudah knew how to press his love for the Torah to the utmost point, just short of addiction and loss of self-control. He knew how to walk with tragic delight on the tautest of balancing wires. This taut wire was an electric wire capable of producing the clearest and most dangerous tones. Too little tension adulterates the sound; too much tension brings immediate electrocution.

HIS TWO WOMEN AND
HIS COLUMN OF FIRE.

Every Erev Shabbat, there is a battle in his soul between the alluring Torah and his wife. Only his ability to withstand the temptations of Torah—the divine female—in favor of his human wife activates the column of fire and gives the townspeople a precise signal that Shabbat has arrived.

Yehudah squeezes the utmost out of his six days of creativity and the utmost out of his Shabbat. He never leaves his Torah before twilight, he never comes late to his wife. He never makes any direct contact with the world beyond the Torah and beyond his wife. At the hour of his obligatory passage between these two females, the column of fire separates him from the world and protects him from its inhabitants. Every Erev Shabbat at twilight, the column of fire stops time and brings down a curtain between the world and Yehudah, who is going from one woman to the other.

To all appearances, the balance wire on which Yehudah walks Erev Shabbat is very firm. But behind the scenes, his life is in perpetual danger. Every Erev Shabbat, there is a battle in his soul between the alluring Torah and his wife. Only his ability to withstand the temptations of Torah—the divine female—in favor of his human wife activates the column of fire and gives the townspeople a precise signal that Shabbat has arrived.

Yehudah squeezes the utmost out of his six days of creativity and the utmost out of his Shabbat. He never leaves his Torah before twilight; he never comes late to his wife. He never makes any direct contact with the world beyond the Torah and beyond his wife. At the hour of his obligatory passage between these two females, the column of fire separates him from the world and protects him from its inhabitants. Every Erev Shabbat at twilight, the column of fire stops time and brings down a curtain between the world and Yehudah, who is going from one woman to the other. Behind the scenes, Yehudah changes the clock: He goes from weekday standard time to Shabbat time.

The column of fire is the tension wire on which Yehudah walks at twilight. It connects the Torah (one light) and the woman (another light). It is stretched taut and burning, and Yehudah floats above it at a great height. Below, the townspeople shade their eyes and set their clocks. Their town is no ordinary town. The coming of the Shabbat isn't announced by an ordinary trumpet blast. For them, the entry of the Shabbat is marked by a column of fire. In their city lives a holy man. Unique in his generation.[31]

The townspeople have the sense that Yehudah the holy man and the column of fire are among those things that were created Erev Shabbat at twilight, creations whose existence is assured forever.[32] Rabbi Yannai, on the other hand, knows that the life of his son-in-law is constantly in danger. Rabbi Yannai knows that Yehudah can continue to exist <u>only</u> with the most delicate and dangerous balance. He knows very well that any release of this tragic tension will take away Yehudah's desire to live. He knows very well that his son-in-law is playing with the eternal fire that burns for his two loves. He knows very well that the column of fire is in actuality the burning wire on which Yehudah walks from flame to flame. Every Erev Shabbat he closes his eyes with great concentration to accompany his son-in-law, who is walking on fire at a great height.

And on one Erev Shabbat, the inevitable catastrophe occurs. The Torah allures Yehudah with excessive allure and tempts him into transgression. He does not come to his wife and does not welcome the Shabbat. By reciting her day and night, he has lost his ability to control the Torah. Through his fantasies, he has made a fatal error.

The taut wire snaps. Yehudah cannot carry his load. He cannot conquer his desires. Immediately the fiery balance bar stops protecting him. Yehudah, now ungrounded, is instantly electrocuted.

At that very moment the shocked townspeople run to inform Rabbi Yannai that the fiery column has not appeared. Right away, Rabbi Yannai pronounces Yehudah's death. He orders them to turn over his bed. He explains to the astonished townspeople that Yehudah cannot possibly be alive and not fulfill the marital obligation.

During the postmortem examination, it will become apparent that Yehudah was at the height of his existence at the very instant Rabbi Yannai pronounced his nonexistence with such certainty. Why did Rabbi Yannai pronounce his death? Why did he not send the people to the *beit midrash* to see what was keeping Yehudah? Instead, Rabbi Yannai pronounced his death and, in so doing, caused it.

Rabbi Yannai is the rabbi of the community. He cannot allow himself to be an addicted *talmid ḥakham*. He must be a leader who mediates between *am ha'aretz* and its commanding God. He is responsible for the axis that connects the townspeople and their God. For this reason, he cannot allow them to glimpse the tragic truth behind his son-in-law's death. The townspeople must never know that their holy man had been doomed from the start. They must never know that their holy man died for his sin. The official explanation the people receive is that Yehudah died as a direct result of Rabbi Yannai's unfortunately premature pronouncement and that this pronouncement was: "Like an error made by a ruler, and Yehudah died." The townspeople will whisper into each other's ears that Rabbi Yannai opened his mouth for Satan and caused Yehudah's death. Soon this rumor will become the official reason. But inside the story, the true reason for Yehudah's unavoidable death stands out like an open wound: **The shma'ata' allured him.** The Torah tempted Yehudah into transgression; the balancing wire snapped and collapsed beneath his feet.

Rabbi Yannai lets the townspeople sense that Yehudah was taken heavenward in a storm—just like Elijah. That is how holy Yehudah is in their eyes, how close to God. How far from this earthly here-and-now. Rabbi Yannai makes a great effort to erase all traces of Yehudah's transgression. He represents responsibility and balance. A time for Torah, and a time for sex. You cannot conflate the times; you cannot force the seasons. You cannot disregard the mitzvah of Torah study in favor of the mitzvah of marital sex. You cannot disregard the mitzvah of marital sex in favor of the mitzvah of Torah study.

Whoever disturbs the balance will die. Not because of the gravity of the deed—what, after all, did he do?—but because everyone saw how he dared destroy the balance. "A star once dared . . ."[33]

The key sentence for Rabbi Yannai is: "I observe; therefore, I am." Yehudah's key sentence is: "I learn; therefore, I am." Only superficially is there no essential contradiction between these two sentences. Rabbi Yannai and Yehudah are conscious of the contradiction that lies beneath the surface. Yehudah is aware, but he cannot prevent himself from being devoted to the Torah. Rabbi Yannai, on the other hand, cannot allow himself to abandon the *amei ha'aretz* over whom he is appointed. All his days he guards them from discovering the essential contradiction between observance and study.

Rabbi Yannai's fate is bitter. As long as the column of fire divided his son-in-law from the masses, he posed no danger. But the moment the curtain came down,[34] Yehudah became a living peril. The leader, the man of halakhah, cannot allow the masses to look eye-to-eye at the acrobats, the gods, who walk about the heights on a taut wire that produces divine tones. They too might drift skyward, only to plummet like Icarus.[35]

The wire can break. The balance can be destroyed publicly. We should praise God at the death of God-cursed children. Praise God at the death of brilliant but ungrounded children, spaced out from the power of direct contact with God. Hallelujah.

The Father, the Son, and the Goad

Yosef, the son of Rava:
his father sent him to the *beit midrash* before Rav Yosef.
They decreed six years (of study).
When three years had gone by, and Erev Yom Kippur arrived, he said, "I will go and see my home(folk)."
His father heard, grabbed a goad,[36] and went out to meet him:
He said, "Were you thinking about your whore?"[37]
They fought.
Neither one ever concluded.[38]

The two previous tragedies ended with the unavoidable deaths of two Torah scholars—Reḥumi and Yehudah—who couldn't carry their personal burdens and destroyed their precarious balance between the Torah of study and the Torah of command. Their death is described as a resting of their spirits.[39] This tragedy doesn't end in death and has not one iota of spiritual rest. Our tragedy ends in a nightmare frozen in nondeath till eternity. Our tragedy freezes its last line forever: A monument to a father and his son arguing on Erev Yom Kippur.

This story has four symmetrical parts, each containing two lines and each a variation of the central verb of the story *pasak.*

The first part describes the situation at its beginning. Yosef is still a boy. A young bridegroom still under the absolute authority of his father, Rava, who decrees *(posek)* for him that he go to the *beit midrash* of Rav Yosef for six years of study and decrees that economic support be provided for his young wife during these years. Yosef is completely passive. He accepts the decree and doesn't open his mouth.

The second part of the story is optimistic: **"When three years passed and Erev Yom Kippur came, he said, 'I will go and see my home(folk).'"** This is the sweet delusion of a maturing boy who believes his father will accept his new adulthood. He may have been aware that his father might interpret his growing up as rebellion against him. Here we see a decisive young man. He knows what he wants; he trusts his own sincerity, and he believes in the importance of what he is doing. (After all, you need a lot of courage to go against the explicit decree of a father as formidable as the great Rava).

We may permit ourselves to imagine his walking along his way, dividing his time between fantasies about his wife and thoughts about his father. We can also imagine his preparing his growing-up speech to his father—and as is usual in such advance preparations, we can picture all the loving and persuasive words coming easily to his command. The speech comes something like: "For three years I have done as you commanded; now I've reached a turning point. I have decreed for myself *(pasakti)* that I go to my wife, and see you, and show you the Torah that I have learned. I have come to prove to you that I have grown up. Established myself. That I am no longer totally passive. I have come to tell you also that I have my own understanding of the essence of six years of Torah study; they are not six years of total isolation but six years of balancing and fine tuning between the Torah and one's wife."

This decision to see his wife ripened in his heart after the completion of the first three years (exactly half the decreed time). And the decision turned into action the moment it was ripe. When Erev Yom Kippur came he said, "I will go see my home," and on Erev Yom Kippur he went. He thought, and he did.

This decision was made in full awareness that he was interrupting the sequence. He broke *(pasak)* the sequence his father had decreed *(pasak)* for him.

This story involves an essential parallel between two contrary conceptions of the relationship between Torah and wife. The father believes isolation is necessary for the creation of a finely wrought *talmid ḥakham.* He understands the decision that he made for his son as a total package: six years of the Torah of study and six years of separation from his wife. Yosef does not agree that Torah study is inextricably connected to separation from wives. Unpacking the two does not interrupt the process of study; it revitalizes and recharges it. According to his interpretation, an encounter with his wife can renew and enrich his encounter with the Torah.

It is almost certain that he also missed his wife on Erev Yom Kippur of the previous two years and thought about his halakhic and ethical obligations to her. By the third Erev Yom Kippur, he had developed the spiritual strength and moral courage to translate his desires into action. Yosef had grown up. He had reached the stage of understanding that he had to take responsibility for his own actions. On the third Erev Yom Kippur, he came down from the rooftop of the *beit midrash* and went to his wife—the exact opposite of Rav Reḥumi who went up to the roof on Erev Yom Kippur and cut himself off completely from the web of human connections, the cutoff that led to a final disturbance of his equilibrium and to his death.

The third section of the story returns us and Yosef to reality: **"His father heard, took a goad, and went out to meet him, saying, "Were you thinking about your whore?"** All the loving and persuasive arguments fled from his mouth. All the appeasing, placating words fled inward. Yosef stood paralyzed before his father—the great Rava—waving a goad and preventing him from entering his wife's house.

The father leaves no possibility for negotiation. He wants to continue to be the only decision maker for his son. He judges his son guilty without allowing him to open his mouth. What son does he know? Only the pliant submissive boy that he sent to the *beit midrash* three years ago. He isn't interested in getting to know another son, the son who stands before him here and now. He sees in him a sinner of weak character and nothing more. He throws the words at him, "Were you thinking about your whore?"

These are the words that the son hears from his father after a three-year absence. This is the scene: A goad waving in his hands, and his whole body speaking fury. And this is the day: Erev Yom Kippur. Yosef has come to make his wife and father happy on Erev Yom Kippur. He has come to show his father another son—a *talmid ḥakham* devoted to the Torah: adult, independent, aware of his responsibilities. But his father only sees a weak-willed sinner whose lust has driven him to his wife.

In the fourth section, the argument between Rava and Yosef becomes eternal. They fight. **"Neither one ever concluded *(pasak)*."** Unto this very day, father and son head toward each other. Unto this very day, the gate of the son's wife's house stands between them. The last time that they had stood by this gate, nothing interrupted them. Rava was the sole decider who decreed sustenance for the son and his bride and six years of separation. The father and son were of one mind: the mind of the father. Now they have two minds. Yosef has acquired a mind. And of his own mind, he has decided to return home and see his wife. Now there are two decision makers. A whole universe cuts between them.

The father cannot be appeased by his son. He threatens him with the goad, taunting, "Were you thinking of your whore?" All the while the son refuses to turn around. In vain he tries to placate his father and come to his wife. Until this very day, they are standing in the gate of the woman's house and fighting with each other. Neither the father nor the son can ever conclude or reach conclusion *(lo mar ifsik velo mar ifsik).*

With the entry of the Day of Judgment, a new decision maker will come. He will cancel or not cancel the prohibitions and vows. He will accept or not accept the appeasements and pacifications between people. Between a man and his wife. Between a son and his father . . . .

The Father, the Son, and the Goddess

Rabbi Shimon Bar Yoḥai said, "I saw the elite and they are few. If they are a thousand, my son and I are among them; if a hundred, my son and I are among them; and if only two, they are me and my son. (BT Succah 45a)

Rabbi Shimon bar Yoḥai said, "Learn my ethical principles, for my principles are loftier than Rabbi Akiva's highest principles." (BT Gittin 67)

Rabbi Shimon Bar Yoḥai said, "It can be that a man plows at plowing-time, sows at sowing-time, harvests at harvest-time, threshes at threshing-time, and winnows when there is wind, but the Torah—what will happen to her? Instead, when Israel does the will of God—then their work is done by others, as it is written: "Strangers will stand and tend your flocks." (Isa. 61:5) And when Israel doesn't do the will of God—then they have to do their work themselves, as it is written: "You will gather your corn, your wine, and your oil." (Deut. 11:14)[40] And even more, they have to do the work of others, as it is written: "You shall serve your enemy." (Deut. 28, 48) (BT Berachot 35b)

Rabbi Yehuda, Rabbi Yossi, and Rabbi Shimon were sitting, and Rabbi Yehuda ben Gerim sat near them. Rabbi Yehuda opened, saying, "How pleasant are the deeds of this nation! They have made markets, they have set up bridges, they have built bathhouses . . . ." Rabbi Yossi was silent. Rabbi Shimon replied, "Everything they made, they made for their own needs. They made markets, to settle prostitutes there; bathhouses, to make themselves feel good; bridges, to collect tolls." Yehuda ben Gerim went and told what they had said, and the government heard it. They said, "Yehuda who declared us exalted—let him be exalted. Yossi who was silent—let him be exiled to Sepphoris. Shimon who spoke badly of us—let him be killed!"

He and his son went and hid in the *beit midrash.* Every day his wife would bring them bread and a jug of water, and they ate. When the decree got harsher, he said to his son, "Women are light-headed; they may give her grief, and she will then reveal where we are."

They went and hid in a cave. A miracle happened: A carob tree and a spring of water were created. They took off their clothes and sat buried up to their necks in the sand. All day they would study and at prayer-time they would get dressed and wrapped. Then they would take off their clothes to prevent their rotting.

They lived twelve years in the cave. Elijah came and sat in the opening of the cave and said, "Who will tell Bar Yoḥai that Caesar is dead and his decree has been repealed?"

They came out. They saw people plowing and sowing, and they said, "They ignore the life of eternity and busy themselves with the life of this world!" Wherever they cast their eyes immediately burnt up. A heavenly voice came out and said to them, "Have you come out to destroy my world? Go back to your cave." They returned and stayed (in the cave) twelve more months. It is said that the decree for the evil in Gehinnom is twelve months. A heavenly voice came out and said, "Come out of your cave."

They came out. Every place Rabbi Elazar harmed, Rabbi Shimon healed. He said, "My son, you and I are sufficient for the world."

Toward twilight on Erev Shabbat, they saw an old man holding two bunches of myrtles and running. They said to him, "Why do you need these?" He said to them, "For the glory of Shabbat." "One should be enough for you;" "one for 'remember' and one for 'observe.'" He said to his son, "Look how the mitzvot are cherished by the people of Israel," and they calmed down.

His father-in-law,[41] Rabbi Pinḥas ben Yair, heard and came to meet him. He took him to the bathhouse and treated him. When he saw the sores on his body, his streaming tears fell, and (Bar Yoḥai) groaned.

He said to him, "Woe that I have seen you like this . . . ." But (Bar Yoḥai) said to him, "You are fortunate to have seen me like this, for if you had not seen me like this, you would not find me like this." For previously (before the cave), when Rabbi Shimon bar Yoḥai would pose a question, Rabbi Pinḥas ben Yair would give him twelve different responses; afterward, when Rabbi Pinḥas Ben Yair posed a question, Rabbi Shimon Bar Yoḥai would give him twenty-four responses.

He said, "Since a miracle happened to me, I will go and fix something . . . ." He said, "Is there something that needs fixing?" They said to him, "There is a place that is possibly polluted, and priests have the extra burden of going around it." He said, "Does anyone know whether there used to be a presumption of purity here?" A certain old man answered him, "Here Ben Zakkai cut down *lupines*—plants for a *trumah*—offering (which means he considered the place pure)." So he did that too. Every place the ground was hard, he declared pure; wherever the ground was loose, he marked it off.

The old man said, "Bar Yoḥai has declared a graveyard pure . . . ." He said to him, "If you had not been with us or if you had been with us and not voted

with us, then you would be speaking well. Now, that you were with us and voted with us, shall they say, "Prostitutes preen each other—all the more so should *talmidei ḥakhamim*"? He fixed his eyes on him and he died.

He went out to the market. He saw Yehudah ben Gerim and said, "Is this one still in the world?" He fixed his eyes on him and turned him into a heap of bones. (BT Shabbat 33b-34a)

Let us begin with a scene from the middle of the story. If it had been up to me, I would have chosen this fantastic scene as the outer cover of the Talmud, for it encapsulates the essential desires of the devoted *talmid ḥakham.* Here it is:

> **(Bar Yoḥai and his son) hid in a cave. A miracle occurred: A carob tree and a spring of water were created for them. They used to take off all their clothes and sit buried up to their necks in sand. All day they would study. At the hour of prayer they would get dressed, wrap themselves, and pray. Then they would take off their clothes again to prevent their rotting.**
>
> **For twelve years they stayed in their cave.**

What is missing from this picture? We have a father and a son naked in a cave studying Torah and covered up to their necks with sand. Only to fulfill the commandment of prayer do they get dressed (in their undergarments) and wrapped (in their cloaks). Once they have fulfilled the obligation of prayer, they take off their clothes and cover themselves once again with sand.

They didn't spend just one hour in this situation and not just one day. Twelve years! And if Elijah had not appeared at the entrance to the cave, they would be there naked to this very day, and the ever-renewed Torah would continue each hour to be as beloved to them as she was the first hour.

This scene is the absolute opposite of the picture of Rava and his son Yosef, facing each other in mute rage with the goad suspended between them in a revolving flame. A father and son naked in the same cave and with the same love goddess. The prayer that they perform together keeps them, maintains their equilibrium: Together they get dressed; together they wrap up; together they pray, get undressed, and return to study.

They stand for the *Amidah.* They sit for their study session. When they study, they cover their nakedness with sand to their necks; when they stand to pray, the sand covering them falls away, and they cover themselves with clothes. The sand covers them like an amniotic sac. An amniotic sac connected to the carob tree and the spring that give them everything that they need. By means of this incredible envelope, they are cut off from the world of reality and take off inward—to all possible worlds (Alma Dee). The Torah and the cave are the take-off fields of their imaginations. Prayer is their landing field. With every daily prayer, they are born once more into the real world, and with the end of prayer they return to envelop themselves in the cave, which is the totality of all possible worlds that exist before birth and after death.

The male God protects them by means of the prayer they have been commanded to pray to Him. And protects them from their fatal attraction to the treasures of the divine female. And what about the human female common to both of them? It looks as if she plays no part in maintaining their equilibrium. It looks as if they are hiding from her.

If we return for a moment to the previous scene we will see why the father and son are hiding from the mother and wife:

> **He and his son hid in the *beit midrash.***
> **Every day his wife would bring him bread and a jug of water.**
> **When the decree got harsher, he said to his son, "Women are light-headed; if they torture her, she will reveal our hiding place.**

On the surface, this is an absolutely realistic description. Shimon Bar Yoḥai and his son Elazar are fleeing the Romans, who have pronounced a death sentence on them. But at this point we should say a few words about the real historical background of this story (and the real historical background of the other stories that appear here). It is easy to make the error of treating the realistic elements of this story as historical. And in fact many have done so. Nevertheless, this is an error. Our story has several parallels in sources from the Land of Israel, like the Jerusalem Talmud and Bereshit Rabbah.[42] The opening about three *Tannaim* who express three different opinions about Roman rule does not appear in any of these sources from the Land of Israel. Similarly, the story of Yehuda ben Gerim's tale-bearing does not appear in Israel sources, nor does the story of the decree that caused Bar Yoḥai to flee for his life. In all these sources, the story begins, more or less: **"Rabbi Shimon ben Yoḥai hid in a cave 13 years; he and his son ate carobs . . . at the end he went and sat at the entrance to the cave . . . ."**[43] It is the late and distant Babylonian source that enters into details about the sociopolitical reason for Bar Yoḥai and his son's flight. This tendency—to add many details to stories from Israel—is very characteristic of the Babylonian Talmud, and we will have reason to turn again to this issue.

In my opinion, the opening of our story cannot provide any trustworthy historical background. The "Romans" and "Yehudah ben Gerim" may have psychological or dramatic significance. They may also point to the political-historical reality of the Babylonian narrator, but they provide no trustworthy information about the historical-political reality of the world of Israel after the Bar Kochba rebellion—the world of the historical Bar Yoḥai. The Israeli versions of the story show none of the tensions we describe: not the tension between the *talmidei ḥakhamim* and the *amei ha'aretz,* nor the tension between them and their wives. There is no mention of conflict between the life of eternity and the life of the moment and no mention of the conflict between the cave and the market. There is no hint in these sources that Bar Yoḥai and his son learned during the thirteen years they were in the cave and certainly no hint that their preoccupation with the Torah of learning was their entire universe apart from prayer. These facts have far-reaching consequences. For now it is sufficient to note that the tensions indicated by this and other stories are more characteristic of the reality of some of the Babylonian *Amoraim* or even of the *Stamaim,* who put the final touches to the story in the Babylonian Talmud. This later reality has been often projected as the world of the Sages of Israel, particularly the *Tannaim,* whose true universe was different.

To return to our story. At first, Bar Yoḥai and his son hide in the *beit midrash,* and the woman brings them food and water. The *beit midrash* is not the most efficient hiding place. Nor is the woman the best provider. Both the woman and the *beit midrash* are too obvious, and the authorities could fall on them at any moment. The father and son are afraid of the moment when the woman will be caught by the authorities; she will be forced to betray them, for she will not be able to withstand the interrogation. The father understands that they have to find a hiding place that will be hidden even from the eyes of the woman.

The sentence "women are light-headed" is not necessary to understand their motive for moving from the *beit midrash* to the cave. However, it gives a wonderful excuse to fulfill long-held desires. There is a fascinating change of functions: The cave assumes the role of the *beit midrash;* the divine female takes over the role of the human woman; the carob tree takes over for the bread and the spring for the jug of water. This is an absolute return to first principles. Spring water is more natural than jug water, the carob more natural than the bread, the cave than the *beit midrash,* and the primeval goddess than the real woman. Than any real woman. "**All** women are light-headed . . . ."

The *beit midrash* is always a refuge from the outside world. It is as if it announces: "The life of the outside world is vanity of vanities; abandon them and come here." Many *talmidei ḥakhamim* see the *beit midrash* as a place to disconnect from the outside world. For Bar Yoḥai and his son, the *beit midrash* changes from a place to which one flees and becomes the place from which one flees. The *beit midrash,* with all its tensions and its social arrangements, turns into the outside world relative to the cave. The cave is their refuge within a refuge. We find this motif of fleeing from the *beit midrash* (to the roof, for example, or to the garden, the lake, other caves, and so on) in other stories about other *talmidei ḥakhamim.* Apparently, the need to flee from the real world is so strong that even an elaborate stronghold like the *beit midrash* is not enough to satisfy it.

In our story, the cave is explicitly described as an ideal existence. A veritable paradise. A father and son naked, a carob tree, and a spring. A divine female. This is paradise after the fruit of knowledge has been eaten. A paradise of knowledge and study. They have nothing in the world but four cubits of the tree of knowledge. And beyond the tree of knowledge is the revolving and flaming sword of the Romans.

In truth, an essential part of this ideal cave existence is that Bar Yoḥai and his son did not look for it on their own initiative but were forced to hide in it. To choose to hide in a cave is to announce that one has lost one's stability and is running away from responsibility. On the other hand, being forced to hide in a cave removes from the happy hider any pangs of conscience about turning one's back on the world.

What else does a hider need? He has a spring. He has a carob tree. He has the Torah. He has a fixed *ḥevruta,* who is his closest flesh and blood. He doesn't have one iota of daily toil or hourly troubles. He can be devoted to the life of eternity. To study Torah for Torah alone. To interpret every fillip into piles and piles of halakhot. He has to stay in the cave. He has to be hidden from the real world and disconnected from it. The Romans, after all, are looking for him throughout the world. How fortunate for him!

The cave is one of our most complex symbols, and, like any complex symbol, it has various, sometimes contradictory meanings. It is a refuge and an Eden, and—as we will soon see—it can also be hell. It is the womb and the tomb. The acme of being and of nonbeing. "Turn it over and over, for all is contained in it." The cave has a referent in history: It is a place of refuge. This meaning serves as the crucible in which many symbolic meanings are created.

After twelve years of splendid isolation, they come out of the cave and see people plowing and sowing. They are not able to make peace with the wretched sight of people sunk to their necks in the vanities of this world. They begin to burn up the plowers and the sowers. As they burn them up, they murmur in amazement mixed with anger, **"You ignore the life of eternity and are busy only with the life of the world!"** The life of the world is agriculture, commerce,[44] prayer,[45] or any other occupation that isn't the study of Torah. Only those who are never diverted and remain continually in the study of Torah can be counted among the gods, the denizens of the beit midrash who live the life of eternity. Certainly those who spend twelve years in a cave absolutely absorbed in the process of studying Torah.

Rabbi Simeon bar Yoḥai said, "I have seen the elite and they are few. If there are a thousand—I and my son are among them. If there are a hundred—I and my son are among them. If there are two—they are my son and I."

He and his son . . . .

He and his son hover for twelve years in a limitless number of possible worlds. They cease to consider what life is like for people who are buried in the miserable world of actuality. As a result, when they emerge from the cave after twelve years, they look upon any occupation other than Torah study as worse than a waste of time. As corruption and sin. They have an inner sense that nobody who passes up the life of eternity has any right to exist. They have no tolerance for the world as it is, so they burn everything. They find themselves intensively engaged in the destruction of the world.

Like creatures from outer space, they descend into misery, and their eyes beam deadly rays. Every place they glance at burns up. It is true that "*talmidei ḥakhamim* bring peace to the world," but sometimes they lose control over themselves and sow destruction. Sometimes they have to descend into this cold world because of the astonishing heat of Torah study, and they may react with violent anger against those who dare sever them from the umbilical cord that connects them to that marvelous carob and the spring. Just so, babies—were they not born blind and miserable—would burn us up with their eyes because of the violent separation that we impose on them.

At this point, the commanding God feels compelled to intervene, to call an unequivocal halt to the burning. **"A voice came out and said, 'Have you come out to destroy my world? Go back to your cave."** Go back to your cave. Go back to your infinite number of possible worlds. You cannot function in the real world. You cannot even accept its right to exist. You are dangerous to the existence of my world. You might destroy it for me. Go back to your cave.

The commanding God is the God of this world. The God of the people and the land. The God of those who plow and sow and offer sacrifices. When He says "to destroy my world," He means this world. When they say *ḥayyei olam,* (the life of eternity), they mean life in all worlds beyond.

As long as Bar Yoḥai and his son are hidden in their invisible Olympus they pose no threat to the world of the commanding God, but the moment they emerge from their cave, they are a threat to the very existence of the populace. They might destroy the delicate tissue that generations of the populace have woven to connect them to their commanding God. In these circumstances, God has no alternative but to react quickly and return them to their cave.

They spend twelve more months in the cave, like the sentence of the evil in *Gehinnom.* This time, the cave is not paradise, but hell. The road from the paradise of all possible worlds to this world passes through hell. Bar Yoḥai and his son have to learn this with their flesh. Bar Yoḥai learns it. Elazar doesn't. He refuses to internalize this knowledge.

After twelve months, the Heavenly Voice comes out and says, **"Leave your cave!"** Again they go out to those who sow and plow, those who keep the commandments and pray, and to the rest of the populace who live the life of this world. Once more Elazar begins to sow destruction wherever he glances. His father is forced to follow behind him to undo his destructions. **"Every place that Elazar would strike, Bar Yoḥai would repair, saying, 'O my son, you and**

I are sufficient for the world.'" The ordeal of Gehinnom has influenced the father but not the son. He still refuses to accept the right of any world to exist that isn't a world of Torah-study. With great patience, the father walks behind the son and rebuilds what he destroys and tries to convince him: **"You and I are sufficient for the world;** it is enough that the world has two *talmidei ḥakhamim* like us. The two elite. We shouldn't get angry at the limited inhabitants of this world. They are extremely simple and fragile. They do not have the capacity to love the process of studying Torah and to rejoice with the Torah of Study. They cannot be cut off from their daily life. They are lightweights. We have to accept them as they are. We have to behave with caution and restraint. Any careless move of ours could bring catastrophic destruction on them." But Elazar refuses to be convinced. He continues to come down on the innocent guiltless populace.

Until Erev Shabbat at twilight. A charming old man runs by them while holding in his hands two fragrant myrtle branches. Maybe Elazar is getting set to burn him up. Maybe not. His father, at any rate, turns to the old man with a question, and the man responds. Once more the father asks, and the old man answers. By their charming conversation and what follows it, we are enabled to hope for peaceful coexistence between the *talmidei ḥakhamim* who sustain the world and the populace who sustain the *talmidei ḥakhamim.*

> Bar Yoḥai: **What are these myrtle branches for?**
> The old man: **In honor of the Shabbat.**
> Bar Yoḥai: **Wouldn't one be enough for you?**
> The old man: **One for *shamor,* "observe" (Deut. 5:12) and one for *zakhor,* "remember." (Exod. 20:8)**

Immediately after this exchange, Bar Yoḥai says to his son, **"See how much Israel loves the commandments!"** The son is convinced and calms down. He accepts the existence of the populace. Maybe he even learns to love its presence.

The Torah of command says only: "Observe the Sabbath day and sanctify it," and: "Remember the Sabbath day and sanctify it." The intermediary directors, the prophets and the Rabbis, entered with great detail into the question of Shabbat observance. But the old man wasn't satisfied with that. Out of his own personal initiative, he beautifies the mitzvah of Shabbat, adding the charming matter of the myrtle branches. He is not <u>obligated</u> to take two myrtle branches in honor of the Shabbat, he <u>wants</u> to. The mitzvot are dear to him. They are not a burden to the populace. They are a delightful gift. The possibility of rising above the crushing battle for existence. The commanding God gave him the Shabbat to delight in, gave him holidays and festivals for joy, and gave him prayers and sacrifices so that he would cherish both the mitzvah and its beautification.

The circle closes. Daily the Torah is cherished by those who learn her as on the day that she was given on Mount Sinai. And, the mitzvot are cherished by Israel . . . . This is the dream of the pomegranate and its interpretation: **"Whoever sees pieces of pomegranate in a dream, if he is a *talmid ḥakham,* he will merit Torah, and if he is an *am ha'aretz,* he will merit the mitzvot."**

A person who loves what he does fulfills himself. The self-fulfillment of a *talmid ḥakham* is achieved only through the study of Torah. The self-fulfillment of an *am ha'aretz* only through observance of the mitzvot. On Erev Shabbat at twilight, they reach a balance. We have already seen this beautiful and critical time in the story of Yehuda the son of Rabbi Ḥiyya. As long as the Torah of learning didn't pull him too far, his balance wasn't disturbed. He would come down from his Olympus every Erev Shabbat at twilight to fulfill the marital sexual commandment. His wife would rise toward him from her busy everydayness to fulfill the marital sexual commandment. They would meet halfway. At twilight.

This is the longed-for idyll that harmonizes the oppositions between the *talmid ḥakham* and the *am ha'aretz,* between the *talmid ḥakham* and his wife. Sometimes it ends in tragedy and sometimes not. Sometimes the Torah of study pulls the *talmid ḥakham* too hard and tears the delicate balancing wire that connects him to his earthly wife. Sometimes the *talmidei ḥakhamim* settle down and fondly accept the presence of the *amei ha'aretz.* And they say to each other, **"You and I are sufficient for the world."** You and I are sufficient for the world. The world cannot exist without a very large majority of *amei ha'aretz* and a splendid minority of *talmidei ḥakhamim.* Would that we will merit that the populace with whose fate our own is intertwined will live the life of this world to perfection and will beautify the mitzvot. Would that we merit that our actual work be done by them. Let them provide us with the clay and the bricks, and we will provide them with the spirit. They will buffer us as much as possible from abrasive contact with this world; we will buffer them from contact with the worlds beyond. For their own benefit, we will close off the entrances to all the gardens of possibility. We will keep hidden from their eyes the deep into which we dive. We will be their insulation material; they will be ours . . . .

Outside the cave, Bar Yoḥai met Pinḥas ben Yair, his father-in-law, who was dumbstruck at the deterioration of Bar Yoḥai's body. All of Bar Yoḥai's skin was cracked from the sand that had covered him for thirteen years. Pinḥas ben Yair took him to the bathhouse in Tiberias to heal him. During the ministrations, they went back and forth in the battle of Torah. Objecting and resolving. Between the objections and their resolutions, Pinḥas ben Yair looked at Bar Yoḥai's sores and cried and said, **"Woe that I have seen you like this . . . ."**

The tears that fell from his eyes scalded Bar Yoḥai's open sores. Bar Yoḥai groaned from pain and said, **"You are fortunate to have seen me like this, for**

if you had not seen me like this, you would not find me like this." In other words, in his pain, Bar Yoḥai comforts Pinḥas ben Yair and tells him the bodily damage he sustained was the necessary price for the great riches he has now acquired. And what are those riches? There has been a substantial change in Bar Yoḥai's skill at *pilpul* (learning by debating). When the two of them learned together before Bar Yoḥai entered the cave, Bar Yoḥai would pose questions and Pinḥas ben Yair would give twelve resolutions for each and every question. But now, when Pinḥas posed a question, Bar Yoḥai could answer with twenty-four resolutions.

Bar Yoḥai has become a virtuoso of *pilpul.* Before he entered the cave, he was a student questioning his master. In those days Pinḥas Ben Yair easily answered his best questions and found twelve resolutions to each objection. But now, the thirteen years have turned everything around. Bar Yoḥai has risen to the status of the Master who answers. And Pinḥas ben Yair has become the student who asks. Furthermore, the debating power Bar Yoḥai developed in the cave enables him to give twenty-four resolutions to each of Ben Yair's objections.

Pinḥas ben Yair is the litmus paper that registers the impact of the cave on Bar Yoḥai's debating ability. Before Bar Yoḥai emerged from the cave, he had neither the opportunity nor the need to check the intensity of the change. But now, when he learns with Pinḥas ben Yair, he understands immediately the enormous changes. During these thirteen years, Pinḥas ben Yair was outside the cave and had to make do with the *beit midrash.* It is almost certain that he too improved during these years. But his improvement couldn't compare with the change that those same years witnessed in Bar Yoḥai.

When Bar Yoḥai speaks of the miracle that happened to him, it is very possible he means this miracle of *pilpul* rather than the miracle of the carob tree and the spring, or the beams that burn from his eyes, or his powers of recuperation. These latter miracles take place in the provincial domain of the life of this world. A *talmid ḥakham*'s true miracle takes place in the realm of the life of eternity. In the study of his beloved Torah. The true miracle is found in the perfection of Bar Yoḥai's powers of study.

This is the true power of the cave in the Babylonian Talmud. The Babylonian cave is nothing other than the take-off field of the imagination of a *talmid ḥakham* who loves the Torah that enables him to employ all his creative, intellectual potential. And there is no miracle more longed-for by the *talmid ḥakham.* It is very possible that this is the plain sense of the passage: **"He said, 'since a miracle happened to me.'"**

There is yet another possible interpretation. The miracle was the substantial change in Bar Yoḥai's social consciousness. He feels the need to give thanks for this miracle by contributing to society and helping the populace. He inquires if there is something that needs halakhic repair. They send him to the lower market of Tiberias[45a] which had been declared impure because of possible pollution.

The situation in Tiberias is intolerable. The most severe interpreters of the law have gotten the upper hand. These legal authorities have declared the lower market polluted on the suspicion that bodies are buried there. In case of doubt, there is a tendency for most authorities not to take chances and to decide severely. But this decision has made it difficult to pass from place to place, to develop or build anything, and to conduct daily life in Tiberias.

With his mastery of debate and logic, Bar Yoḥai finds a way to remove the suspicion and declares the lower market of Tiberias pure. Ironically, it is Bar Yoḥai—a true *talmid ḥakham* who was able to hide hid in the cave and who once belittled in his heart the *amei ha'aretz* who live the life of this world—it is Bar Yoḥai who goes to help the *amei ha'aretz* and make their life easier. He is the one who finds new ways. The rabbinic authorities who had never isolated themselves from society were afraid to carve new paths and make life easier for the people for whom they were supposed to be the intermediaries to the commanding God.

There is a perilous catch to the isolation of a *talmid ḥakham* in his cave. The more he stays alone, the more his powers of debate and logic grow, and he can then turn the laws of the Torah around and around to make them do what he wants. On the other hand, the more he stays alone, the greater grows his desire for solitude and the removal of all responsibilities.

In this story, Bar Yoḥai avoids the trap. This story is not a tragedy. Its hero does not get ensnared in his own webs. When he comes out, he has the upper hand on all fronts. He expands to the utmost his powers of learning and *pilpul* to become the greatest of all, and he uses this fact to contribute to society.

At this point a new issue begins. The many who declare things impure try to invalidate the decisions of the one who declares them pure. One of them responds to Bar Yoḥai's decision with the sarcastic comment, **"Bar Yoḥai has declared a graveyard pure."** His purification of the market, for this critic, is just a case of "declaring the impure pure in 150 ways." Virtuoso *pilpul* acrobatics cannot change the fact (according to him) that the market is impure. He even calls this market a graveyard.

However, as we have said, our story is not a tragedy. It is a story about a good, all-powerful hero standing up to the evil people who try to make him fail. Bar Yoḥai glances at the critic, and he dies on the spot. But first he takes the time to describe in his own sophisticated manner how *talmidei ḥakhamim* should behave toward each other. He compares their relationships to the interrelations of prostitutes (!) and declares it worse. For prostitutes groom and beautify each other, despite their competition with each other. *Talmidei ḥakhamim,* on the other hand, get in each other's way. Each seeks out the other's weak points in order to humiliate him.

We will have opportunities to consider the tensions and competitions of the world of the *talmidei ḥakhamim.* And to ponder the humiliation that they cause each other. Here we pause only to note that this phenomenon exists.

The Infinite Despair of the Babylonian Ḥoni

One day while Ḥoni was walking along the road,
he saw a man planting a carob tree.
He said to him, "A carob tree first bears fruit after seventy years. Is it clear to you that you will live seventy years to eat from it?"
He said to him, "I found a world with carob trees: As my fathers planted for me, I plant for my son."
Ḥoni sat and ate bread.
A deep trancelike sleep fell on him.
A cave[46] surrounded him and hid him from view.
He was unconscious for seventy years.
When he got up, he saw a man picking a carob pod and eating it.
He said to him, "Do you know who planted this carob tree?"
He said to him, "My father's father."
He saw his donkey that had given birth to many young.
He went home.
He said to them, "Is the son of Ḥoni the circle-drawer home?"
They said to him, "His son is not here, but his grandson is."
He said to them, "I am he."
They didn't believe him.
He went to the *beit midrash,*
He heard the *talmidei ḥakhamim saying,*
"This *shma'ata*[24] is as clear to us as in the days of Ḥoni the circle drawer. When he would come into the *beit midrash,* he would resolve all the difficulties the Sages had . . . ."
He said to them, "I am he!"
They didn't believe him.
They didn't act toward him with the deference due to him.
He despaired.
He asked for mercy;
He found his rest (he died). (BT Ta'anit 23a)

The Babylonian Ḥoni is a tragic *talmid ḥakham* who closes himself up in the four cubits of the *beit midrash,* devotes himself to the Torah of study, and lives the life of eternity. He is the greatest of the *talmidei ḥakhamim* of his generation. On every jot and tittle, he can interpret piles of legal rulings. For every argument, he knows many counterarguments—maybe twenty-four. As long as he is in the *beit midrash,* no question remains unanswered or unclear.

The Babylonian Ḥoni is very different from Israel's Ḥoni, who is an antitragic *tzaddik.* Both fell asleep for seventy years and awoke to a different world. Israel's Ḥoni fell asleep just after the destruction of the First Temple and awoke with the building of the Second Temple; he went into the sacred precinct, illuminated it with his halo, and became a great hero. The Babylonian Ḥoni left the *beit midrash* as a great hero, fell asleep for seventy years, returned miserable and dejected to the same *beit midrash,* and asked to die.

The difference between the Babylonian Ḥoni and the Israeli Ḥoni is substantial, for it reflects two different conceptions of humanity. Here is the full story of the Israeli Ḥoni from the Jerusalem Talmud Ta'anit 3,5,10.[47]

Ḥoni the circle drawer lived just before the destruction of the Temple. He went out to the workers on the Mount. Before he reached it, it began to rain. He entered a cave. After he sat down, he became drowsy and remained asleep for seventy years, until the Temple was destroyed and another built. He awoke after seventy years, emerged from his cave, and saw a changed world—where there had been vineyards, there were olives; where there had been olives, there was grain. He asked for the city. He said to them, "What is this noise in the world?" They said to him, "Don't you know what this noise in the world is?" He said to them, "No." They said to him, "Who are you?" He said to them, "Ḥoni the circle drawer." They said to him, "We heard that he used to enter the sacred precinct and illuminate it . . . ." He went in and illuminated it and quoted about himself, "When God returned us to Zion, we were as dreamers."

The story of the Babylonian Ḥoni is very different. One day he leaves the *beit midrash* and begins to walk along a road. Why he left the *beit midrash* is not clear, nor is it clear to what extent he knew that this expedition would be significant in his life. In any event, on the road he sees an *am ha'aretz* planting a carob tree and poses the following question: **The carob first bears fruit after seventy years—is it clear to you that you will live seventy years to eat from it?**

As we have said, this Ḥoni is the greatest poser of questions in his generation. He is used to the idea that there is no *talmid ḥakham* in the *beit midrash* who does not fear his questions. He is dumbfounded to stand before this healthy lummox of a planter who dares answer his sophistic question with the unequivocal certainty of an *am ha'aretz:* **"I found a world with carob trees. As my fathers planted for me I am planting for my son."**

This answer tears Ḥoni's world apart. He enters a cave and falls into a deep trance that lasts seventy years. He will wake up a completely different Ḥoni. He will wake up into the response of the *am ha'aretz* now become actuality, into a world planted with carob trees. He will not be able to return to the *beit midrash.* The *talmidei ḥakhamim,* his past admirers, will not recognize him and will not acknowledge him. He will ask to die.

We cannot ignore the elements common to the stories of Bar Yoḥai and Ḥoni. Both have a cave that surrounds the *talmid ḥakham,* who is enveloped in it; both have a carob tree, and both have a *beit midrash* with its arguments and counterarguments. Both have a significant meeting between a *talmid ḥakham* and an *am ha'aretz.* Bar Yoḥai and his son meet with people who are plowing and sowing. Ḥoni meets a man planting carob trees. Both these meetings are intersections between the life of eternity and the life of this world. Between the inhabitants of Alma Dee (the perfect world of the imagination) and world *B* (the parallel [real] world). These meetings have dramatic results. They make the *talmidei ḥakhamim* take a completely different look at their own life of eternity and the others' life of this world.

The life of this world is a life of here and now alone. In contrast, the life of eternity happens simultaneously in all possible places and all possible times. The time of the life of eternity is before the creation of the world, after the end of history, and forever. Its place is the yeshivah in the skies and the yeshivah below. Any form of life other than *talmud Torah* (Torah study) lacks this continuity.

This starting point—we may assume—is also Ḥoni's starting point as he leaves the *beit midrash* and walks along the road. Ḥoni is walking on a road. To his right and left people are plowing and sowing and planting. And he—we allow ourselves to imagine—is either belittling them in his heart or pitying them—that they live the life of the moment, the life of this world, and do not know the taste of the everlasting continuum, the taste of the life of eternity.

The man planting the carob tree causes Ḥoni to stop and ponder. New thoughts come to him as he stands before the simple man who labors without expecting to see the fruits of these labors in his lifetime. They do not match his classification of the world into *talmidei ḥakhamim,* who live "for her own sake" (for the sake of Torah) and the *amei ha'aretz* of the Land of the Living, who do not. And so, on the surface, Ḥoni's question to the planter is the question of an astronaut who emerges from the spacecraft of Alma Dee for a quick visit to the parallel world—is it possible that here too, in the real world, living involves considerations beyond the here and now?

But underneath the surface of this question, lies the *talmid ḥakham*'s practical side. Ḥoni's question is the question of someone who knows how to squeeze the maximum out of the moment. It may sound strange, but there is something very functional about the ability of a devotee to turn the present moment into the life of eternity. This practical ability holds much happiness and many disasters, like the disasters of Rav Reḥumi and Ḥoni. As long as a *talmid ḥakham* continues to devote himself to Torah, he continues to live the life of eternity. His devotion enables him to avoid the frightening necessity of situating himself on the time continuum between the past and the future.

As long as Ḥoni is engaged in the act of learning, he lives the life of eternity.

He argues and counterargues with Moses, with Rabbi Akiva, with Abaye, and Rava simultaneously. He is transported beyond space and time. But the moment that he is cut off from his studies, he returns to travel along the space-time continuum.

As long as he is engaged in learning, he doesn't pose questions about life in the real world and the meaning of life in the real world. Whoever learns Torah "for her own sake" avoids dealing with the real world. He sinks into a *sugya* (section) and puts all his creative-intellectual energy into mental gymnastics in and around it. All his problems begin when learning is cut off. This interruption forces him to look at this world, not as a takeoff field to one of the infinite possible worlds, but as a landing area. And the landing is tragic.

He asks the planter, "Why are you planting?" The planter doesn't ask himself such questions. To him it is clear that planting does not depend on eating the fruits. To Ḥoni walking along the road, it is not clear. For Ḥoni on the road doesn't see meaning in any activity whose simultaneous reward is not obvious. Ḥoni has nothing in his world but four cubits of *talmud torah.* As a result, when he is not studying, he has nothing in his world. Ḥoni walks along the road and looks at this world from the outside. The planter experiences this world from the inside. Ḥoni's illusion of being inside can continue only as long as he is immersed in learning.

The planter is anchored in this world. His passages in time are not as abrupt as Ḥoni's. He doesn't switch between total devotion to *lishmah* (for her own sake) and the absolute escape of unconsciousness and catatonia. He is planted in this world but is not devoted only to the here and now. He eats the carobs his fathers planted for him and plants the carob that his sons will eat. He doesn't try to squeeze the past and the future into a single unreal present moment. He doesn't cut off the branches of the past and the future that he sits on.

Ḥoni's reality is completely different. It is a tragic surrealistic pendulum. Everything or nothing. When he is immersed in his *talmud torah,* he has a glorious present, which is the future and the past fused together in a heavenly compound. But when he isn't immersed in Torah, he has nothing in the world. He flees. Flees.

He winds up in a cave. He cannot gaze directly into the reality embedded in the planter's answer; he is not capable of living the simple life. He cannot endure the simple daily tasks which are so utterly different from the fantastic tasks of studying a talmudic *sugya.*

Bar Yoḥai and his son also flee to a cave; they too are wrapped up in one. But their envelopment is embryonic and paradisiac; Ḥoni's produces despair. For Ḥoni meets the carob-tree planter on the way from the *beit midrash* to the cave, while Bar Yoḥai and his son flee directly to the cave. On the way from the *beit midrash* to the cave, Bar Yoḥai and his son make no contact with earth-people *(am ha'aretz).* Ḥoni makes contact. His direct contact with the earthy normality of the *am ha'aretz*-person plants in him seeds of doubt. Bar Yoḥai and his son's presence in the cave contains no doubts. This fact enables them to hover in all possible worlds without sinking into anger or doubt. (The anger comes later, in their encounter with the plowers and sowers).

Bar Yoḥai's carob tree is inseparable from the cave. In Ḥoni's story, the carob remains outside the cave—in the domain of the *am ha'aretz* who eats from it and plants it for his sons. In the cave, Ḥoni will have to make do with bread. Processed food, not primal. He will also not learn Torah in his cave. He will fall asleep for seventy years.

In seventy years, he is destined to wake and go on his way. When he returns to the *beit midrash,* he will no longer be a virtuoso. He will not be able to speak the language of the *talmidei ḥakhamim.* He will lose his ability to live the life of eternity. He will ask to die. In fact, from the moment he meets the carob-tree planter, he loses his virtuoso ability to hover simultaneously among all possible worlds. From that moment on, he cannot rid himself of the dominant presence of this world, the world of plowers and sowers and planters.

In order to be a *talmid ḥakham* and live on the Olympus of the learning gods, it is absolutely necessary to cut oneself off from the life of this world and live only in the life of eternity. One must be able to concentrate entirely on the world that is being studied, to divorce oneself from the world not studied, the world of the earth-people. **"Whoever walks on a road and studies and stops studying to say, 'how beautiful is this tree, how lovely is this plowed field'—Scripture considers him as one who has forfeited his life."** [48]

It is as simple as it sounds. First you go out of the *beit midrash,* then you walk along the road, then you look around you, then you lose the ability to be a *talmid ḥakham* and to live the life of eternity in all possible worlds . . . you forfeit your life.

Ḥoni forfeits his life. He loses his ability to be a *talmid ḥakham.* The only thing that remains for him is to contemplate his own tragedy from the sidelines. This he isn't prepared to do and he asks to die.

The Most Beautiful Man in Pumbedita

> **Rabbi Yoḥanan said, "I alone am left from the beautiful men in Jerusalem."** (BT Bava Metzia 84)
>
> **Rabbi Yoḥanan would go and sit in the doorway of the gate of the *mikvah.* He said, "When the daughters of Israel come up from fulfilling their mitzvah of immersion (after menstruation), let them encounter me, so that they should have children as beautiful as I who can learn Torah as I do." (Ibid.)**

A STORY ABOUT RABBI YOHANAN,
THE MOST BEAUTIFUL MAN IN PUMBEDITA,
AS HE SWIMS NAKED IN THE JORDAN.

A *story about* Rabbi Yoḥanan, *the most beautiful man in* Pumbedita, *as he swims naked in the* Jordan *and is spotted by the desirous eyes of* Resh Lakish. *Resh Lakish is the strongest man in* Pumbedita, *the leader of an armed band of bandits that terrorizes everyone. When he sees* Rabbi Yoḥanan, *he doesn't hesitate: he removes his weapon, takes off his clothes, and jumps into the raging* Jordan. (*The* Jordan *river that flows through the* Babylonian Talmud *is more furious than the* Euphrates *and wider than the* Tigris. *From one of its banks you cannot see the other.*)

Rabbi Yoḥanan's *attendants*—talmidei ḥakhamim—*stand on one bank, and* Resh Lakish's *attendants—armed bandits—stand on the other. Their leaders approach each other, heading towards their unseen confrontation in the midst of the great river.*

Rabbi Yoḥanan *breaks the silence first and says admiringly,*
"May your strength be for Torah*."*
Resh Lakish *answers him,*
"May your beauty be for women."...

Rabbi Yoḥanan's member was like a jug that is ten liters long. And some say, six liters. (Ibid.)

One day, Rabbi Yoḥanan was swimming in the Jordan.
Resh Lakish saw him and jumped into the Jordan after him.
He said to him, "May your strength be for Torah."
He said to him, "May your beauty be for women."
He said to him, "If you turn aside from your ways, I will give you my sister, who is more beautiful than I."
He accepted the offer. He tried to turn back and get his clothes. He couldn't turn back.
He read him the readings *(Miqra')*, he studied the studies *(Mishnah)* with him and made him a mighty man of Torah.
One day they were disputing in the *beit midrash:*
The rapier, the dagger, the stiletto, the spear, the handsaw, and the sickle—at what point can they become impure?
At the moment their fashioning is complete.
What is the moment that their fashioning is complete?
Rabbi Yoḥanan said, "When they are refined in the furnace."
Resh Lakish said, "When they are polished in water."
He said to him, "The bandit knows his banditry."
He said to him, "What good have you done me?—There they called me Rabbi, and here they call me Rabbi."
He said to him, "The good that I did for you is that I brought you under the wings of the *Shekhinah*."
Rabbi Yoḥanan despaired; Resh Lakish became ill.
His sister came and cried. She said to him, "Do it for my sons."
He said to her, "I will provide sustenance for your orphans."
She said to him, "Do it for my widowhood."
He said to her, "Your widows will depend on me."
Resh Lakish died, and Rabbi Yoḥanan grieved greatly.
The *talmidei ḥakhamim* said, "Who will go and revive him? Let Elazar ben Pedat go, whose *shma'atas* are so sharp.
He went and sat before him. To everything that Rabbi Yoḥanan would say, he would say, "Here is a tannaitic passage that supports you."
He said to him, "You are (supposed to be) like Ben Lakish?! Ben Lakish, whenever I said anything, would pose twenty-four questions, and I would give him twenty-four responses and the *shma'ata* would expand. You answer, 'Here is a tannaitic passage that supports you.' Don't I know that I am speaking well?"

> **He would walk tearing his clothes, crying, and saying, "Where are you, Ben Lakish? Where are you, Ben Lakish?"**
> **He cried until he lost his mind.**
> **The *talmidei ḥakhamim* asked mercy for him:**
> **He found his rest (he died). (Ibid.)**

Rabbi Yoḥanan was the most beautiful man in Pumbedita and the greatest *talmid ḥakham* of his generation.[49] The beauty of Rabbi Yoḥanan was incomprehensible and attempts to describe it in words futile:

> **Whoever wants to see the beauty of Rabbi Yoḥanan should take a silver goblet as it emerges from the crucible, fill it with red pomegranate seeds, top it with a rose circle, and place it between sunlight and shadow. Its lustrous glow is but a hint of the beauty of Rabbi Yoḥanan.**[50]

Rabbi Yoḥanan was in the habit of learning Torah facing the gate of the *mikvah* of Pumbedita. As the daughters of Israel came out pure and permitted after bathing, the features of Rabbi Yoḥanan would be engraved upon their hearts. At night as they lay upon their beds, they would see him. He encouraged their fantasies, for he would say explicitly, **"When they emerge from ritual immersion and come upon me they bring into the world children as beautiful as I, and as good at studying Torah as I."**

There is something beyond imagining about the beauty of Rabbi Yoḥanan as he swims naked in the Jordan and is spotted by the desirous eyes of Resh Lakish. Resh Lakish is the strongest man in Pumbedita, the leader of an armed band of bandits that terrorizes everyone. When he sees Rabbi Yoḥanan, he doesn't hesitate: He removes his weapon, takes off his clothes, and jumps into the raging Jordan. (The Jordan river that flows through the Babylonian Talmud is more furious than the Euphrates and wider than the Tigris. From one of its banks you cannot see the other.) Rabbi Yoḥanan's attendants—*talmidei ḥakhamim*—stand on one bank, and Resh Lakish's attendants—armed bandits—stand on the other. Their leaders approach each other, heading toward their unseen confrontation in the midst of the great river.

Rabbi Yoḥanan breaks the silence first and says admiringly, **"May your strength be for Torah."** Resh Lakish answers him, **"May your beauty be for women."** Each envies the other's treasure. Each regrets its screaming waste. Resh Lakish sorrows over the awesome beauty being wasted in the study of Torah and not used for the conquest of all the women in the world; Rabbi Yoḥanan is pained by the awesome might being wasted in banditry and not used for the conquest of all the passages in the Torah.

. **Simon**
Dept. of CTL
r St. West
ario M5S 1V6
nada

	Author	List Price	Our Price	Total
(350-1-5)	Ari Elon, Tikva Frymer-Kensky	27.95	25.16	25.16

Books Total	25.16
Shipping	5.95
Order Total	31.11
Paid via Visa	31.11

on.com, and please come again!

1 million titles, consistently low prices

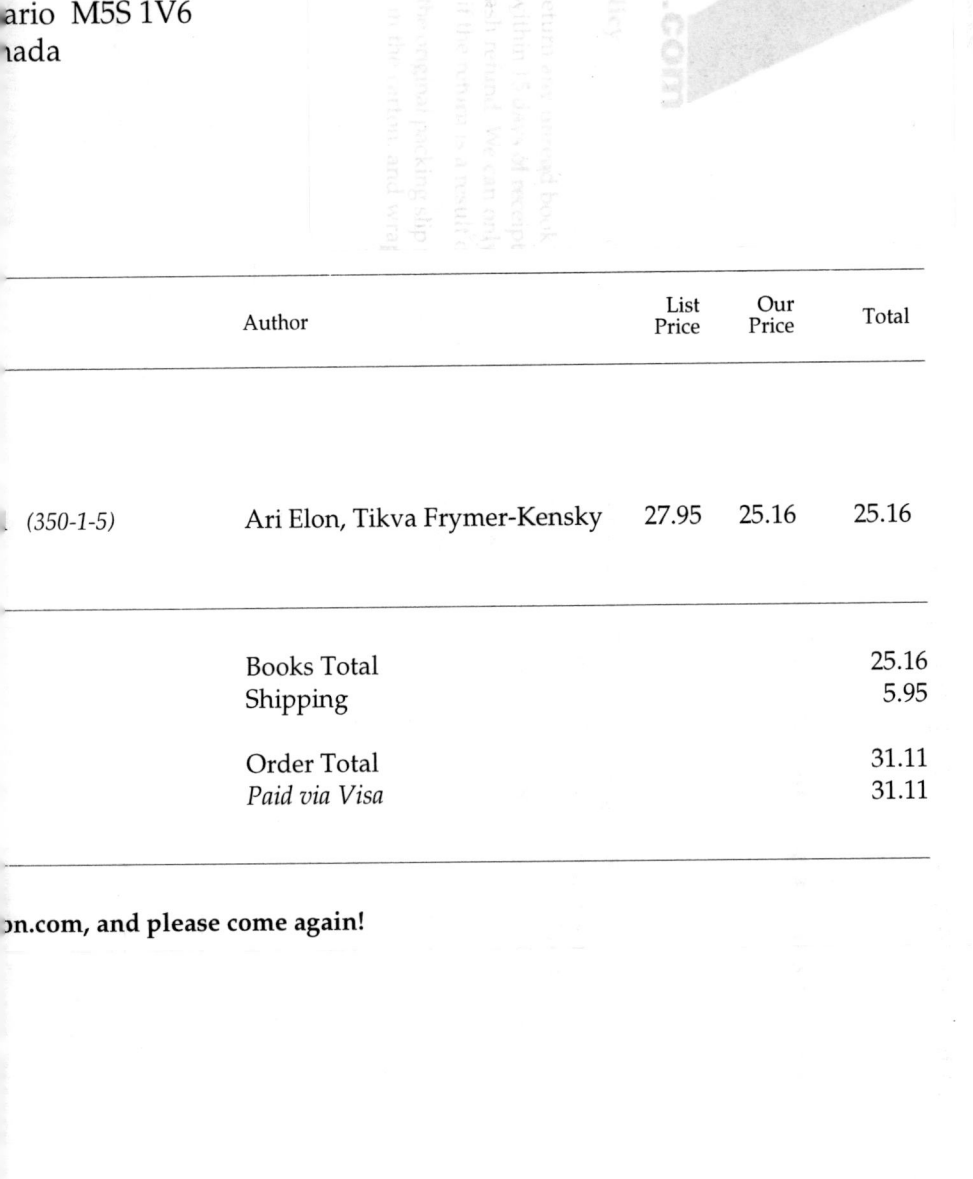

amazon.com

http://www.amazon.com
orders@amazon.com

Roger
OISE/UT -
252 Bloc
Toronto, On
Ca

Amazon.com Books
2250 First Avenue S.
Seattle, WA 98134
USA

Toll-Free: (800) 201-7575
Voice: +1 (206) 622-2335
FAX: +1 (206) 622-2405

Your order of October 30, 1996 (Order ID 7592-6738488-761885)

Quantity	Title
	Shipped Today
1	From Jerusalem to the Edge of Heaven : Meditations on the Soul of Israe

Thanks for shopping at Amaz

312477/1b/1t/2516/std-intl/416-923-6641

With all his strength, Rabbi Yoḥanan wants this might at his side. He can already see in his imagination how the presence of Resh Lakish will give new power to the Torah of learning.[51] He wants him at his side and invests all his charm and his brilliance in arranging Resh Lakish's transformation from a man of might to a mighty man *(gavrah rabbah)*, a *talmid ḥakham.* He tells him, **"If you turn your life around, I will give you my sister, who is more beautiful than I."** Resh Lakish is ready to turn his life around. He agrees to occupy the benches of the *beit midrash.* He is led astray by the possible beauty of one who is more beautiful than the most beautiful. With his last remaining strength, he tries to turn around and return to the far-off bank in order to bring his clothes and equipment. In vain. His might is gone.

Torah uses up human might. Even the strongest man loses his strength when Rabbi Yoḥanan introduces him to the Torah, the most desirable but exhausting object of love that we can imagine.

How does Rabbi Yoḥanan make Resh Lakish fall in love with the Torah? He promises him somebody more alluring and beautiful than he. He calls her my sister. This fantasy of an as-yet-unseen woman causes Resh Lakish to fall in love at last (for the who knows how many-eth time!) Rabbi Yoḥanan knows how to reach the heart of Resh Lakish and understands what compels his heart. He senses strongly that in the river next to him rages a most energetic man who is still looking for lasting salvation through a woman. For this reason he tempts him with language familiar to him, out of his strong conviction that *mitokh shelo lishmah yavo lishmah*—that by being attracted to a human female, Resh Lakish will come to be attracted to the divine female, the Torah. There, in the Jordan, on one foot, Rabbi Yoḥanan teaches the whole Torah to Resh Lakish. At first he "reads" Miqra' (the readings), then he "studies" Mishnah (the study), and finally he "learns" Talmud (the learning). Rabbi Yoḥanan teaches Resh Lakish how to be a *talmid ḥakham.* He reveals to him the secret of pursuing Torah: First you read; then you study; then you learn.[52]

Rabbi Yoḥanan's dream comes to fruition. Over the years, Resh Lakish brings new energy to the *beit midrash* and becomes Rabbi Yoḥanan's star pupil. For everyone who is privileged to see Resh Lakish during his studies, it is like seeing a giant uproot mountains and grind them one against the other.[53] He turns all his power and potency to the Torah. When Rabbi Yoḥanan said to him, **"May your strength be for Torah,"** he saw him in his mind's eye as that Samson who uprooted the two big mountains Ṣor'ah and Eshta'ol and ground them against each other.[54] Resh Lakish grinds the mountains into tiny projectiles that he casts at Rabbi Yoḥanan through the eye of a needle. Rabbi Yoḥanan ripostes. Resh Lakish presents twenty-four objections to everything Rabbi Yoḥanan says during their joint studies and meets a defense of twenty-four answers. Their Torah expands and becomes for them like the entrance to a palace. And as their palace of love expands, their analytical skills become as sharp as an otherworldly razor. Eternal joy takes root in them, and nothing remains in their world but four square cubits of *talmud Torah.*

The content of the *shma'ata* (the study portion) they study is ultimately only a backdrop, a pretext for *pilpul.* A takeoff field for objections and responses. They train themselves to think twenty-four moves ahead. Rabbi Yoḥanan opens with the first gambit. Resh Lakish immediately is able to see a loophole and present an objection. Rabbi Yoḥanan sees this objection and counters with a solution to the problem before it is asked. Resh Lakish sees the solution before it is offered and prepares a parry in the form of arguments against the solution to the argument—even before the question has been asked. Rabbi Yoḥanan can predict even these later arguments which will be offered as solutions to the arguments to the solutions to the first question before it is even asked.

And so it goes. Twenty-four moves in advance before even one argument has been cast into the *beit midrash.* All in thought stored in their heads. Before anything has been done. The true contest between them will happen on the twenty-fifth move and be the telepathy of grand masters whose wisdom is a legendary combination of might and beauty.

Resh Lakish and Rabbi Yoḥanan never separate. Not in their lives and not in their deaths. Rabbi Yoḥanan's beautiful sister becomes Resh Lakish's wife. The Torah of Rabbi Yoḥanan becomes Resh Lakish's daily rations and the focus of his reveries. Resh Lakish finds his total salvation. He finds in the Torah what he had searched for in vain in human women. He becomes one of the greatest lovers of the Torah of all time. She is his saving love goddess, and he expresses love for her day and night and always revels in her love.

He explains the verse, **"The adulterer has no heart"** (Prov. 6:32): **This refers to the one who learns Torah occasionally.**[55] So much is Resh Lakish zealous of his beloved Torah that he depicts as an adulterer anyone who apportions specific time for the Torah and doesn't devote all his being to her. He even desecrates the Shabbat out of his love for the Torah: **Resh Lakish would walk beyond the Shabbat boundaries while he was reciting Torah without noticing, fulfilling what is written: "In her love he revels constantly."** (Prov. 5:18)[56] The Torah of learning entices him to trespass the rules of the Torah of command. Every Shabbat he walks past the Shabbat boundary, returning as he left, totally unaware that he is desecrating the Shabbat.

The *talmid ḥakham* finds in the Torah everything that the bandit couldn't find in the women he conquered. He calls her "delight;" he revels in her day and night. The outlaw becomes a blunderer. The one who had controlled a pack of bandits and had purposely broken the law now loses his ability to control himself and blunders all the time during his revels in the Torah. He has lost all malice. His divine beloved has changed all his evil intentions to blunders.

He doesn't love his children, and he doesn't love himself. He doesn't love his wife, and he doesn't love Rabbi Yoḥanan. Only the Torah.

Rabbi Yoḥanan becomes upset at the power of Resh Lakish's love for the Torah. Fear mixed with rage begins to fill him. The occupants of the *beit midrash* start worrying. Resh Lakish ignores the anger and ignores the worry. He continues to learn in *ḥevruta* with Rabbi Yoḥanan every day. For each study session, he reads and rereads and arranges his lesson forty times and only then does he enter to study with Rabbi Yoḥanan.[57]

Many years pass and he continues the same schedule and is diligent in courting the Torah of learning. He reads and repeats forty times. He comes completely prepared to his study session with Rabbi Yoḥanan, and for every matter of Torah Rabbi Yoḥanan speaks, he responds with twenty-four arguments and Rabbi Yoḥanan parries with twenty-four counter-arguments, and the joy of learning covers up his fear and repression. But Rabbi Yoḥanan shows signs of ever-increasing worry. He becomes ever more threatened by Resh Lakish.

And Resh Lakish never senses it. He continues to devote his whole being to the Torah of learning. He continues to uproot mountains with blinded eyes and take delight in the arguments and solutions and new arguments. And the less attention he pays, the more Rabbi Yoḥanan becomes angry—not only because Resh Lakish loves the Torah more than he loves him, but also because he invests all his power and might in her. It is growing hard for Rabbi Yoḥanan to counter Resh Lakish's arguments, and still Resh Lakish attacks. For the first time in the history of the *beit midrash,* there are signs that Rabbi Yoḥanan's undisputed preeminence can be overturned. Cracks appear in his beauty. He is afraid of the monster he himself has created. He has a deathly fear of the bandit-gang's chief who once leaped into the Jordan after him and stilled the waves and breakers of the most raging river in the world. He is suspicious of his objections and suspicious of his counterarguments and afraid of every point on which Resh Lakish can pile heaps and heaps of halakhot.

Resh Lakish continues to learn Torah *lishmah* (for her own sake). He pays no attention to the changes in Rabbi Yoḥanan's behavior. They never speak openly about the tension between them. In many respects, they have reached an exceptional quality of communication. Each can read the other's thoughts many steps in advance. For every point of Torah that Rabbi Yoḥanan teaches, Resh Lakish poses twenty-four objections, and Rabbi Yoḥanan has twenty-four responses. The trouble is, they have fascinating communication only about matters between person and Torah. They avoid person-to-person issues as *biṭul torah* (a waste of time that could better be spent in learning Torah). They never speak directly about the relationships between them—about their fears, their jealousies, and their mutual desires. All these matters are part of our real world, which is, as we know, the only world outside the boundaries of learning Torah. On the surface, they have wondrous lines of communication between them; underneath, there is a total lack thereof.

Outwardly, the order of each day remains unchanged. It begins with Rabbi Yoḥanan's daily lesson and continues with Resh Lakish's lesson, which expands on Rabbi Yoḥanan's.[58] After that, the *talmidei ḥakhamim* in the *beit midrash* hang around till the next day, either singly or in *ḥevruta*. In the previous years, they have spent much time learning the law of purities. Many days they deal with the purity or impurity of vessels: of ovens and kettles, adornments and shoes, spices and perfumes, baskets and pots, tents and cloths. Every study session begins with identifying the cases that everyone deems pure and the cases that everyone considers impure. Little by little they approach those cloudy areas in which all the exciting doubts lie.

The cloudy areas between pure and impure are the transitional points between raw material and finished product. Raw materials cannot become impure. Only after they are turned into manufactured items can they receive impurity. A person in a state of impurity can touch a giant heap of unworked clay without contaminating it. But the moment that same person touches a small clay spoon, the touched spoon stops being pure, becomes contaminated, and is forbidden to touch. Preliminary drafts do not become contaminated. They are always pure. Only something that moves from potential to actuality can become impure.

The question is, what is the moment of transition from potential to actual? What is the exact moment that a substance's raw-material nature metamorphoses so that it becomes a manufactured object? Is it the moment that it is fashioned in the mind of its creator? Or perhaps the first minute that it can be used? Perhaps when it is sold? Or when it leaves the assembly line? It is hard to imagine a more meaningful question or one that crosses more disciplines. And it may be that this is the fundamental question that underlies all of Seder Ṭaharot[59] and especially Masekhet Keilim.[60]

In any event, a substantial part of the cloudy areas between pure and impure are the cloudy areas between raw material and finished items. And these cloudy areas give us a good example of the essence of the Torah of learning as an inspirational take-off field for *pilpul* or for the infinity of possible worlds irrelevant to the real world. After all, none of the questions of purity and impurity have any relevance in the days when there is no Temple. And it is in such days that the *talmidei ḥakhamim* occupy themselves with the Torah of learning. In other words: Regarding matters of purity (apart from menstruation), no *talmidei ḥakhamim pilpul* has any relevant halakhic impact. That doesn't weaken the hands of those who engage in *pilpul.* On the contrary, it increases the learning *torah lishmah* aspect of their learning and magnifies their delightful flight to their infinity of possible universes.

From these cloudy areas, infinite arrays spread out, the battlegrounds of the Torah. One *talmid ḥakham* will always declare the doubtful object pure. Opposing him there will always be a *talmid ḥakham* who declares it impure. All the rest will choose sides behind each leader. When the sign is given, they begin to throw missiles at each other. Thrusts and parries and parries and thrusts until the battle is over.

One day the following question is cast in the *beit midrash:* **The rapier, the dagger, the stiletto, the spear, handsaw, and sickle—from what point can they become impure?** After long hours of thrusts and parries, they all reach an agreement: **From the time they are fashioned.** In other words, everyone accepts the idea that the weapons can become impure only after they are fully fashioned. Now they have to define the exact point at which they are finished being fashioned. They ask, **When is their fashioning complete?** And here begins the split. Rabbi Yoḥanan says, **From the time they are refined by fire.** Resh Lakish says, **From the time they are polished in water.** Rabbi Yoḥanan holds that placing the weapon in the furnace marks the end of its manufacture. Resh Lakish holds that one must wait one more stage, the stage at which the rapier, the dagger, and the stiletto are taken from the furnace and polished in water. This split between Rabbi Yoḥanan and Resh Lakish is the sign that yet another dispute is beginning in the *beit midrash* on the subject of the purity or impurity of vessels. All the *talmidei ḥakhamim* arrange themselves behind the heads of the two camps and begin to fight with each other.

Resh Lakish attacks Rabbi Yoḥanan; Rabbi Yoḥanan counterattacks. Their attendants hasten to bring support from all possible passages. Rabbi Yoḥanan is able most wondrously to pose and answer questions. So is Resh Lakish. On this day, Rabbi Yoḥanan and Resh Lakish pose every question in the world and answer with all the responses in the world. The battle is undecided. Everyone is exhausted and tense. The two giants fortify themselves behind their opening positions. Rabbi Yoḥanan continues to claim: The rapier and the dagger and the stiletto, and the spear can become impure from the moment the artisan places them in the fiery furnace. Resh Lakish insists: The rapier and the dagger and the stiletto and the spear can become impure only from the moment the artisan takes them out of the furnace and polishes them in water.

At this point, Rabbi Yoḥanan loses control over himself and shouts into the *beit midrash:*

> **"The Bandit knows his banditry."**

The cry: "The bandit knows his banditry" echoes to this very day. The *beit midrash* has never recovered from the trauma. The sentence never leaves us but has become the paradigmatic example of humiliation. Rabbi Yoḥanan has brought upon the body and spirit of Resh Lakish that about which we are taught: **Anyone who humiliates his comrade (lit. makes his comrade's face go white) in public is like one who spills blood.** With dagger and sword, he humiliates Resh Lakish. With dagger and sword, he spills his blood. The Babylonian *talmidei ḥakhamim* developed this comparison between public humiliation and spilling blood. It is given figurative expression by the sentence attributed to Rav Naḥman bar Yitzḥak: **Anyone who humiliates his comrade in public is like a murderer, (for) we all see how the blood leaves the face (of the injured party), and whiteness takes over.**[61] First you bring blood to your colleague's face—you cause him to blush, and you know that he knows that everyone knows that you are going to insult him unforgettably for the *n*th time. There is a tension in the air. The delightful sense of a sacrifice about to be made. Your colleague is bound on the altar, the knife is in your hand, and you brandish it with great festivity. And then, with one wave, you distill a poisoned sentence that totally humiliates him. This well-chosen sentence is short and pithy. And it is true. A truth forged in fire and polished in water. One who humiliates his colleague in public isn't slandering him; there isn't a shred of falsehood in what he says. That is the power of his statement.

Humiliation is an art. The art of the black truth. The absolute opposite of the art of the white lie. The great artists of the cult of humiliation know how to plan many steps in advance. The *beit midrash* can be an incubator for them. In the *beit midrash, talmidei ḥakhamim* are always defeating each other, fighting each other in their eternal battle of Torah. *Talmidei ḥakhamim* like to describe themselves with the metaphors of warriors, in part because they cannot attack each other with real knife and sword. They don't even know how to hold them. They do not injure each other physically and certainly do not spill real blood. The spoken word is their main weapon.

For this reason, the might of the spoken word is much greater in a society of *talmidei ḥakhamim* than in a society of bandits. The spoken word is almost the exclusive element in the world of the *talmid ḥakham.* Even the erotic delight that he takes in his Torah of learning can only be expressed by speech. After all, the greatest *talmid ḥakham,* God, created the world by speech. Even the physical acts contained in the performance of mitzvot are foreign to the *talmid ḥakham,* and he performs them like someone pursued by a demon. It shouldn't be surprising, therefore, that his violence is also expressed in words, that he distills the fear and frustration his *ḥevruta* is causing him and squeezes it into one pithy poisoned sentence that can spill blood: **The bandit knows his banditry.** The bandit knows his banditry!

Resh Lakish appears to rally first. He responds to Rabbi Yoḥanan with a terrible blow beneath the belt: **"What good have you done me; there they called me 'Rabbi' and here they call me 'Rabbi'?"** He has never forgotten the trade of banditry. He is good at grasping rapiers and stilettos and spears, and he is good at delivering mortal blows beneath the belt. "There I was a leader, and here I am a leader. There the world is violent, and here the world is violent. In a situation like this, there is no difference between the world of bandits and the world of *talmidei ḥakhamim.* There and here, people clash and wound each other. There and here, people make evil use of rapiers and daggers, stilettos, and spears . . . ."

After the fact, it is clear that all these years, burning lava has been flowing beneath the surface and has kept alive the unending tension between the there of Resh Lakish and the here of Rabbi Yoḥanan. On the surface, "there" is a violent world, and "here" is a cultivated one. The Jordan, we may say, is a kind of bridge between "there" and "here." But when they approach the question of the rapier, the dagger, the stiletto, and the spear, the issue bursts forth. It is as if Rabbi Yoḥanan is asking, "What is he doing here?" and Resh Lakish is wondering, "Why am I not there?"

It turns out that swordplay is the major issue between Rabbi Yoḥanan and Resh Lakish. Rabbi Yoḥanan has taken a marvelous rapier and transported it from the fencing arena of "there" to the fencing arena of "here." He said to him, "Your strength should be for the battles of Torah and not for the fights of bands." He saw in him a perfect training partner. It turns out that he was too good a training partner. Rabbi Yoḥanan has no alternative but to say the last word and invalidate him. He answers the question, **"What good have you done me?"** with the winning answer, **"The good I did you is that I brought you under the wings of the *Shekhinah*."**

That is how you win the battle of Torah: You say the last word. The one who poses a question that has no response or counters with a parry that cannot be answered is the victor. Back when he first met Resh Lakish in the Jordan, Rabbi Yoḥanan had already put him in his place. Resh Lakish may have jumped first, but Rabbi Yoḥanan was the one who opened the verbal confrontation and the one who ended it. Rabbi Yoḥanan said, **"May your strength be for Torah,"** and Resh Lakish answered, **"May your beauty be for women,"** but Rabbi Yoḥanan ended by saying, **"If you turn (your life) around, I will give you my sister who is more beautiful than I," and Resh Lakish capitulated.**[62] Ever since then, Resh Lakish, besotted with love, hasn't cared who has the last word. His Torah is Torah *lishmah.* His redemption comes through the abnegation of his desire to win. From then until now, Resh Lakish has been posing innumerable questions, and Rabbi Yoḥanan has been giving innumerable responses. And despite the fact that he doesn't win, or because of the fact that he doesn't win, nobody is happier than he—for he has found the divine woman with whom every hour is fresh and endearing.

Rabbi Yoḥanan knows this very well and takes advantage of this knowledge to defeat Resh Lakish in the cruel and violent battle that now takes place in the *beit midrash.* He opens by saying, **"A bandit knows his banditry."** Resh Lakish answers like a wounded bear, **"What good have you done me; there they called me 'Rabbi,' and here they call me 'Rabbi?'"** But Rabbi Yoḥanan ends the argument by saying what Resh Lakish has always known, very, very well: **"The good I have done you is that I brought you under the wings of the *Shekhinah.*"** Resh Lakish has never been jealous of Rabbi Yoḥanan's superiority or of his beauty. He is just grateful that he rescued him from his obsessive conquest of human women and brought him under the wings of the alluring *Shekhinah.*

But Rabbi Yoḥanan has been jealous. Jealous of the Torah because Resh Lakish preferred her to him. He has been hurt to the depths of his soul that Resh Lakish isn't interested in defeating him and isn't really interested in him. He has resented it and been full of envy. And underneath the envy and the beauty, Rabbi Yoḥanan's true face has appeared, the face of a vengeful god. His desire for revenge has been driving him out of his mind and weakening his senses. He loses control over himself and careens without brakes toward Resh Lakish.

Immediately, Resh Lakish is mortally wounded. He loses consciousness and is carried out of the *beit midrash* on a stretcher. And immediately thereafter, Rabbi Yoḥanan is himself carried out of the *beit midrash* in the grip of an attack of madness.

None of the *talmidei ḥakhamim* dares approach him. Only his sister—the one more beautiful than he—comes and pleads with him to come to Resh Lakish's bedside and avert the evil decree. Rabbi Yoḥanan refuses. She tries every possible way to convince him to cancel the death sentence that he has passed on Resh Lakish. In vain. She doesn't stop trying. **"Do it for my sons,"** she cries loudly. **"Do it for their sake, if not for yours, and for the sake of your *ḥevruta.*"**

Rabbi Yoḥanan is steadfast in his refusal. He murmurs a verse from Jeremiah, **"I will sustain your orphans."** (Jer. 49:11) I will take care of them. She doesn't give up. "Do it for my widowhood—do it for your sister prettier than you—whom you gave to the one mightier than you so that he would agree to be your training partner in the murderous battle of Torah." He continues to cruelly murmur the rest of the verse from Jeremiah, **"And your widows will depend on me."** I take the responsibility of your widowhood on me. Resh Lakish is still alive, but Rabbi Yoḥanan is already speaking about his children as orphans and his wife as a widow.

In just a few minutes, Resh Lakish dies. Immediately, Rabbi Yoḥanan mourns him with enormous sorrow. He locks himself in his room and refuses to come to the *beit midrash.* His condition keeps getting worse. The *talmidei ḥakhamim* who remain in the *beit midrash* try to avert another tragedy. They know that learning Torah in *ḥevruta* is the only chance they have to save Rabbi Yoḥanan and bring him back to his senses. They understand the urgent need to send him their greatest *talmid ḥakham.* One who will try to sweep him into debate. They choose Elazar ben Pedat, who doesn't overturn mountains like Resh Lakish, but is the sharpest of those who remain.

Rabbi Elazar ben Pedat comes to Rabbi Yoḥanan and questions him about purities and impurities. Rabbi Yoḥanan tells him what is pure and what is impure. For every response that Rabbi Yoḥanan gives, Rabbi Elazar offers supporting evidence from explicit texts and saying, "There is a text that supports you . . . you are right . . . ."

And with each proof that Rabbi Elazar brings his support, Rabbi Yoḥanan increasingly realizes the finality of Resh Lakish's absence. The more Elazar continues to support Rabbi Yoḥanan's opinions, the more Rabbi Yoḥanan's mind—which is already weak—deteriorates. He stares at the supporting Elazar, and through his great frustration comes to understand how much he is addicted to the questions and provocations of the bandit who was in love with the Torah.

Elazar ben Pedat continues to murmur supportive comments, and Rabbi Yoḥanan continues to weep over the loss of his rival. At a certain moment, he can't contain himself any longer and bursts out at Rabbi Elazar, **"Are you (supposed to be) like Ben Lakish?! Ben Lakish who would answer any issue with twenty-four questions, and I would respond with twenty-four responses, and the passage would expand from it?! And you say to me, 'the text supports you?' Don't I know that I speak well? . . . ."**

He completely loses control over himself. His mind leaves him. The well-intentioned attempt by the *talmidei ḥakhamim* to restore Rabbi Yoḥanan to his full strength has gone awry. Rabbi Yoḥanan has turned the spigot the wrong way, and his already weakened mind weakens further. He goes out into the public spaces, tears his clothes, and cries out in anguish, **"Where are you, Ben Lakish? Where are you Ben Lakish?! . . . ."** All the *talmidei ḥakhamim* follow him from the *beit midrash* and are afraid to approach him. All the daughters of Israel coming out of the bathhouse cover their eyes and flee from him in terror. He continues to tear his clothes and cry, **"Where are you, Ben Lakish? Where are you, Ben Lakish?!"**

Everyone, without exception, feels sorry for him. And everyone, without exception, wishes him dead.

And he dies.

The Broken Threads of the Shabbat Boundary

> **While he was studying Torah, Resh Lakish would step beyond the Shabbat boundary and not realize it, thus fulfilling what has been written: (She is a doe of love, a charming gazelle; may her breasts always satisfy you) and always revel in her love . . . .(JT Berakhot 5:6)**

The commanding Torah explicitly forbids us to go past the Shabbat boundary. She bounds our settlement within a border that one is forbidden to cross on Shabbat but may cross the six days of the week. The Torah of learning, on the other hand, never encloses her learner within boundaries of time and space. The learner always behaves toward her with love and learns her day and night—when he lies down and when he rises, when he sits in his house, and when he goes on his way.

The learner of this Torah cannot tear his mind from her, cannot even bear the thought that one could learn her in intermittent portions. Whoever learns the Torah intermittently is an "unwitting adulterer."[63] **Whoever walks along the way with her and stops in the middle of his studies and says, "How beautiful is this tree and how beautiful is this furrow?"—he has forfeited his life.**[64] It is as it says: how can anyone pay attention to the existence of trees and furrows during study? How can anyone pay attention to the existence of a Shabbat boundary?

So Resh Lakish would walk and study and get involved, and traverse unheeded distances, and walk out of the permitted area, and enter the forbidden area, and lose the ability to distinguish between holy and ordinary. The ordinary week left his mind and was swallowed up by the limitless lengths of Shabbat. The life of eternity took root in him; temporal life was plucked out.

Temporal life is bounded life. Eternal life has no bounds. The Torah of command defines for her observers each and every minute of their temporal lives. The Torah of learning provides her learners with eternal life. The commanding Torah deals essentially with the minuteness of every possible minutiae of the here and the now. The learned Torah bears her learners on the wings of inspiration and carries them to the heights far above the here and the now. The commandments of the commanding Torah are the inspirational takeoff field of the learned Torah. On his unwitting way to the limitless beyond Resh Lakish learns the full extent of his limits. He learns the boundaries and transgresses them in the very act of studying them. To this day, he goes past the Shabbat boundary, returns during Shabbat, and isn't even aware that he is desecrating the Shabbat. To this day, his Torah is renewed for him each hour as at the first hour. To this day, he lives the life of eternity and is always ardently in love with her.

An eternal miracle happens to him each hour: His ardent acts, though they become inadvertently wrong acts,[65] nevertheless, are transformed into mitzvot. In his learning, he cancels the possibility of observing the mitzvah of the Shabbat boundary, but by canceling the mitzvah of the Shabbat boundary he carries out the mitzvah of "always revel in her love." Only when his ardent actions bring totally inadvertent misdeeds devoid of any awareness, only then is he able to carry out the best part of the mitzvah "always revel in her love." In truth,

Resh Lakish's jump into the Jordan was several years earlier than Kierkegaard's leap over the same raging pure absurd.

Resh Lakish was not the only *talmid ḥakham* whom the learned Torah succeeded in seducing into transgression and caused to destroy the strings of the Shabbat boundaries in their excessive love. There are many such, and one of them was Neḥemiah ben Hanilai. He also passed the Shabbat boundary because he was drawn by the Torah of learning. But he, unlike Resh Lakish, realized what was happening while he was still outside the boundary. Some of his friends also realized it and one of them—Rav Ḥisda—came to Rav Naḥman and said to him, **"Neḥemiah, your student, is sunk in sorrow."** Rav Naḥman and his students took counsel and found a halakhic solution to help Neḥemiah escape from the snare in which he was trapped.[66] They delivered him with devotion and sacrifice from the minefield, and he never moved till they finished their halakhic rescue.

Neḥemiah ben Hanilai's situation is much worse than Resh Lakish's. He suddenly becomes aware of his own unawareness. Like Ḥoni, he suddenly finds himself entrapped by the laws of the real world. He cannot continue to allow his devotion to reach the point of addiction. His surrender rises into self-aware consciousness.[67] Resh Lakish's surrender, on the other hand, was entirely unconscious. Lucky for him.

Rabbi Meir is the third *talmid ḥakham* whose excessive attraction to the Torah of learning prevents him from discerning the existence of a Shabbat boundary. If his Rabbi, Elisha ben Avuya, had not been with him, he too would have desecrated the Shabbat inadvertently.

> **A story about Other (Elisha ben Avuya), who was riding his horse on Shabbat, and Rabbi Meir, was walking behind him learning Torah from him. When they reached the Shabbat boundary, Elisha said, "Meir, turn back; I have figured out from my horse's paces that we have reached the Shabbat boundary." He said to him, "You turn back, too." But (Elisha) said to him, "Haven't I told you, that I have already heard from behind the celestial curtain, 'Turn back, oh wandering sons, except for Other.'" (BT Haggigah 15a)**

Elisha ben Avuya also desecrated the Shabbat on that occasion, but he—as opposed to his student Rabbi Meir—did so out of conscious choice and not through inadvertent fervor. As is known, Elisha ben Avuya was one of the four *talmidei ḥakhamim* who entered the *pardes*.[68] The other three were Ben Zoma, ben Azzai, and Rabbi Akiva. The *pardes* is everything the revealed Torah wants to keep outside the boundaries of contemplation of those who keep the commandments. The Holy Blessed One not only bounds the commandment-keepers on the physical level (by Shabbat boundaries, or by the time limits

A STORY ABOUT ELISHA
WHO WAS RIDING HIS HORSE
ON SHABBAT.

A *Story about* Elisha *Who* Was *Riding* His *Horse on Shabbat and* Rabbi Meir *was walking behind him learning* Torah *from him.* When *they reached the* Shabbat *boundary,* Elisha *said,* "Meir, *turn back;* I *have figured out from my horse's paces that we have reached the* Shabbat *boundary."*

Maybe he means to say to him, "Don't *cross the boundary inadvertently but rather in clear consciousness.* Wait *till you have reached the level of denial* lishmah..." Or maybe, "Don't *make the terrible mistake* I *made by taking this terrible step into the abyss of denial from which there is no return."* Maybe *he just wants to gallop his horse on the* Shabbat *and free himself from the suffocating desire for study, from the spiritual burden that his student loads on him, and from the hateful and fearful glances of the* amharatzim *who observe the mitzvot.* And *from the whole steaming and confining air of the* Shabbat *enclosure.*

placed on saying the morning prayers) but also on the contemplative level. For those who observe commandments, the contemplative world of the revealed Torah is bounded and sealed by two boundaries in space—above and below—and by two boundaries in time—before and after. One must not ask or inquire, **"What is above and what is below; what is before and what is after."** And certainly one must not dare answer.

In fact, there is a revealed Torah, the source of authority, and there is a learned Torah, the source of inspiration. The first, as is known, was given to the *amharatzim,* and the second to *talmidei ḥakhamim.* And indeed, never did any *am ha'aretz* dare enter the *pardes.* Never even dared approach it. The four who dared permit themselves to enter the *pardes* were exemplary *talmidei ḥakhamim.* And even they were taking a very substantial risk. As the result shows:

Ben Zoma looked and was wounded. Ben Azzai: looked and died. Only two remained whole in body and spirit: Rabbi Akiva and Elisha ben Avuya. Furthermore, even though Rabbi Akiva returned to the *beit midrash,* Elisha ben Avuya never returned. Another difference: Rabbi Akiva continued to see himself obligated to the revealed Torah's entire system of commandments, and Elisha ben Avuya stopped.

In effect, the only one of the four who was able to change and stay whole in his body and spirit was Elisha ben Avuya. The Rabbi Akiva who went in was the Rabbi Akiva who came out. All the answers he found to the questions of "what is above, what is below, what is before, what is after," never made him undergo a metamorphosis. Elisha ben Avuya didn't allow himself to stay the same. This may be why Akiva continued to be called Akiva and Elisha ben Avuya merited the new name: "Other."

We could argue until the end of time whether the metamorphosis Elisha underwent caused him to be somebody else, or whether it caused him finally to become the person he really was. One thing is clear: The temptation to deny the authority of the revealed Torah exists deep inside the essence of every *talmid ḥakham.* By his very essence, an *am ha'aretz* cannot deny this authority. Only one who allows himself to learn the Torah can deny her authority. The ones who read, the ones who study, and the ones who declaim (each according to his or her species) will never learn and will never deny.

Let us learn from this: A person's spiritual ability to be a *talmid ḥakham* is a necessary condition for becoming an *apikores* (a denier) but is not sufficient.

The great and eternal disagreement between Akiva and Elisha concerns how they regard actualizing the sufficient cause. According to Akiva, one is obligated to suppress any revelation of this denial. According to Elisha, such suppression is forbidden. The two of them are very conscious of the garden *(pardes)* of denial planted deep in their hearts. Rabbi Akiva believes that every *talmid ḥakham* has an obligation to cut off the plants so that the revealed

Torah can remain whole and the *am ha'aretz* can continue to function. Elisha ben Avuya holds that one has to cut off the growths of the commanding Torah and remove her sting of authority.

Is Elisha ben Avuya a wicked egotist who is interested only in self-actualization, even at the expense of forcing all the *amharatzim* to make this terrible denial? Very possibly. It is also possible that Elisha believes in the ability of the *am ha'aretz* to change. It is hard to believe that a *talmid ḥakham* like Elisha, who sees so many steps ahead, can really believe this is possible, but stranger things have happened.

At any rate, Elisha rides his horse on Shabbat in front of all the *amei ha'aretz* and in front of all the *talmidei ḥakhamim*. Behind him walks his student Rabbi Meir, who is learning Torah from him. Why is Rabbi Meir walking behind his master as he desecrates the Shabbat, learning Torah from him in front of the *am ha'aretz?* He has to. He can't do otherwise. He is totally addicted to the Torah of learning, and to Elisha's Torah in particular. **This is the Torah Moshe placed before the children of Israel—do not read "placed" *(śam)* but "drug" *(sam).*** It may very well be that he is not even conscious of the fact that he is in public and never notices the glances of those who pass by. He also doesn't discern the Shabbat boundary. If Elisha were not with him, he would go outside the boundary, would go and get lost in the garden of denial, and lose his way home to the pomegranate garden of his beloved Torah.

But Elisha is there and stops him, saying, "Turn back!" Maybe he means to say to him, "Don't cross the boundary inadvertently but rather in clear consciousness. Wait till you have reached the level of denial *lishmah* . . . ." Or maybe, "Don't make the terrible mistake I made by taking this terrible step into the abyss of denial from which there is no return." Maybe he just wants to gallop his horse on the Shabbat, freeing himself from the suffocating desire for study, from the spiritual burden his student loads on him, and from the hateful and fearful glances of the *amharatzim* who observe the mitzvot. And from the whole steaming and confining air of the Shabbat enclosure.

Today in the Ravine

To this very day, many rabbinic efforts are expended to enable the *amharatzim* to function. Many are interesting variations on the original midrash: "What is above and what is below." This is still the most forbidden question of all times. One may not look at what-is-above-what-is-below-what-is-before-what-is-after. One cannot explain what-is-above-what-is-below-what-is-before-what-is-after. One cannot ask what-is-above-what-is-below-what-is-before-what-is-after.

The rabbis who warn against all concern with these matters are usually the very ones who could not withstand temptation and asked what-is-above-what-is-below in their youth. As a direct result, they were orphaned from their God. They took an overdose and dared to stare directly at the real world, dared look into what was beyond their understanding, and dared ask the most penetrating questions. Until they reached the inevitable and traumatic conclusion that there is no God in their real world.

After they recovered from this shock, they hoped to prevent their flocks from going through the same trauma. They devoted their entire lives to rejecting the fact that God does not exist in the real world of the congregations of their *amei ha'aretz.* From then on it has been important for these paternalistic rabbis to give their innocent believing *amharatzim* the sense that the world is constructed in the almost closed form of the letter *bet,* that it is a kind of brilliant little terrarium created by the hand of God out of chaos. To this day, it is important for them to ensure that the *amharatzim* running back and forth in the terrarium do not stop casting their eyes up with prayers and petitions so that their God will regard them well and will occasionally open for them the glass cover of heaven, will throw crumbs of bread at them, and bring them the rains in their season.

From then till now these rabbis, orphaned from their God, make sure that their *amharatzim* will remain on the ground and will not dare approach the marked boundaries of the *bet* world. They surround the *bet* world with fences upon fences to prevent the *amharatzim* from taking off for Alma Dee.

To this day these God-bereft rabbis have no faith in the spiritual ability of the *amharatzim* to fly from the *bet* world to Alma Dee and return safely. They fly up for them to the most tempting and hidden parts of Alma Dee, and bring back decisive testimonies and explicit statements about the existence of miracles and angels and the finger of God in the *bet* world. From then till now these God-bereft rabbis keep turning their *amharatzim* into dreamers whose dreams abide.

Alma Dee is the land of dreams; the *bet* world is the land of waking. All the miracles and the signs and the wonders take place in Alma Dee. A grown man who goes around the *bet* world and never ceases to see the finger of God, the hand of God, and the outstretched arm is just a dreamer whose dreams abide. He cannot become an autonomous person, a *ribboni.* A *ribboni* is a grown person who is aware of his passages from the dream to the waking world. Most of the rabbis who fly up to Alma Dee are *ribboni* people, and they land safely in our *bet* world. Among themselves, they know full well which is the world that has miracles and in which world the laws of nature apply. Their decision not to let the *amei ha'aretz* know that God does not exist in the *bet* world is a principled decision that stems from their ethical deliberations (even if often accompanied by considerations of power).

The true revolution does not lie in the discovery that God is dead. In every generation, God has died in the world of quite a few individuals. The Babylonian Talmud is the most convincing proof of the death of God in the world of many *talmidei ḥakhamim.* The true revolution lies in the publicity given to this matter; the true revolution lies in the democratic-egalitarian belief in the right of each and every person to be *ribboni.* The dubious delight of being in a de-theologized world is no longer the exclusive property of the exceptional person. One should turn it into a collective delight. Even a slave girl on the Sea can be *ribboni.* Why not? She also deserves to see with no-longer-despairing eyes that there is no God in the *Bet* world.

Far too many leaders have believed in the ability of too many people to enter the *pardes* and leave it safely. Too many singular individuals have allowed too many masses to ascend to Alma Dee and return to the *bet* world. They believed, apparently, in the essential right of each person to ask what-is-above-what-is-below-what-is-before-what-is-after. It is very possible, and has become clearer with hindsight, that this egalitarian faith is a most dangerous and naive perspective. It is very possible, and has become clearer with hindsight, that this faith has brought into the world terrible masses of *ḥiloni* (secular) *amharatzim.*

Ḥiloni amharatzim, just like *datti amharatzim,* cannot cut themselves off from the *bet* world. They do not dare ask what-is-above-what-is-below, and even more, do not dare explain, look, listen, and know. And so, just as the *datti amharatzim* are convinced that Alma Dee is an inseparable part of the *bet* world, they, the *ḥiloni amharatzim* deny the very existence of Alma Dee. In short, *datti amharatzim* are those whose dreams abide; *ḥiloni amharatzim* cannot abide dreams.

With hindsight, it may well become clear that *ḥiloni amharatzim* who cannot abide dreams can create a terror that is much worse than the simple naïveté of the *datti amharatzim* with their abiding dreams. This dread is practicality. Only that which is functional in the *bet* world is real, and anyone who sees the *bet* world as a means to Alma Dee is fundamentally naive, totally lost in space, and a social disaster. These *ḥiloni amharatzim* understand that one should use creativity for advertising, and for marketing and so make a profit. But creativity for the sake of creativity? For spiritual uplift? Don't make them laugh!

Sha'ar Ha'ashpot:
The Dung Gate

And the Gate of God has turned into the Dung Gate

—H.N.Bialik

The Diary of a Beautifully Tender Soul

The following pages reflect scenes of suffering and anguish. These scenes reflect a beautiful image of my soul. I will present emotional heart-wrenching descriptions, so that everyone—even the most miserable refugee children who run around Gaza—everyone will know how beautiful I am.

Tuesday Afternoon. Reporting time

I arrived here two hours ago, and I still haven't gotten out of the car parked at the edge of the improvised army camp that overlooks Gaza. I am still worried about my determination not to declare myself a conscientious objector. I am afraid I will not be able to maintain it.

On the back seat of my car, my army outfit is laid out: pants, shirt, helmet, high boots, billy clubs, rubbers, equipment belt, rifle, compass, dog tags, woolen socks, a magazine of rubber bullets, four magazines of live bullets, field glasses, bandages, gas grenade. In a little while, I have to go with everyone to an officers' briefing and an orientation tour of the sector. I postpone as long as possible the ritual of changing clothes.

Gaza—a gigantic city—is stretched out at my feet. Never-ending. Even with a telescope, I cannot see its end. Ten meters from me is an intricate wire fence. Ten meters beyond the wire, children are trying to fly a kite. They run downhill with great speed, but the kite refuses to fly and gets snagged on a hut with blue shutters. A girl in a red dress is chasing after a white goat that almost gets caught in the wire. The children extract the kite from the shutter and climb the hill again in order to slide down it. They cannot climb to the very top of the hill because the army camp has been erected there. They begin to slide from the height of the wire and fail again. If a little wind had been blowing, their kite would have ascended to the skies, but the air is still, and the sun is beginning to set.

Dudik, the battalion's millionaire, is parked next to me in his Volvo. He parks himself in the rear seat and talks to everyone by car phone. He hasn't changed clothes either. Behind us are gathering many men from the greater Tel Aviv area (Gushdan) who haven't seen each other for almost half a year, everybody already in uniform—all set up and ready for the officers' briefing. They punch each other on the shoulder and exchange smiles, steaming mugs of coffee in their hands, and their thundering voices drown out the joyous shouts of the playing children. It is already seven-thirty. Gentle breezes are cooling the air a little. Jeeps come in and out of camp without a break.

Ten minutes later, the whine of a generator rises from the other side of the camp, and immediately after, dozens of security lights go on along the whole length of the wire fence. In an instant, the children at my feet are plunged into darkness and turn into happy, little, dark shadows skipping after their kite that has finally managed to ascend.

At this hour, many kites are hovering over the skies of Gaza, shining like stars. I count them. When I get to the fifty-eighth kite, the voice of a far-off *muezzin* can be heard, delicately trilling, *"Allah hu akbar."* In just a few seconds, he is joined by hundreds of *muezzins* who cause all Gaza to tremble with their hundreds of trilled, *"Allah hu akbar."*

I open the windows of the car and listen to the intricate melodies. Afterward, I close my eyes and sway for a long time with the evening prayer of the *muezzins* who cause the times to change and arrange the stars in their watches in the heavens.

When I open my eyes again, the soldiers of the troop we are replacing are standing behind us, all set for their last night patrol. They are wrapped in coats, and pack the armored jeeps with their helmets, shields, and nightsticks, just like knights of old. Like policemen dispersing the demonstrations of students in the late 1960s. With great skill, they load their jeeps with boxes of gas grenades, rubber bullets, first aid kits, searchlights, and night-vision instruments. Afterward, they check the fuel in their tanks and the air in their tires; then they activate their radios calling, "Roger, out" to headquarters, "Final communications check."

Finally, their commander stands facing them and begins for the thirtieth time to call out the daily instructions about opening fire:

> Return fire only if they fire upon you.
> If they are fleeing, fire into the air . . . .
> If they continue to run away, you may aim at their legs . . . .
> Never aim at the head.
> Never shoot at children.
> Don't go near the women . . . .
> Don't go near the mosques.

Two hours later. Tuesday—10:30 P.M.

A giant city under curfew. No one comes in or out. The curfew started half an hour ago and will continue until 3 A.M. I pass through the curfewed city as a part of the officers' briefing. During the night, each officer from the new troop joins his counterpart in the previous troop. I, the most junior officer, join the commander of a jeep in the Sajaiah quarter.

The armored jeep travels with measured slowness through the alleys of the quarter. A plastic face-shield comes down from the helmet on my head and shades my eyes. A hardwood billy club dangles at my waist. At every sudden stop, it jabs me in the ribs.

An open sewer runs in the middle of the alleys. In the middle of the flowing sewer are garbage cans lying on their sides and islands of garbage. The blinding searchlight I hold reveals many cats and dogs. Every once in a while, swift rats cross the alley. Not a single human being can be seen in the area. Everyone is shut up in their houses. For months now, the people of Gaza have been shut up in their houses from 10 P.M. until three in the morning. Only rats, cats, dogs, and soldiers are permitted to roam freely during the hours of curfew.

At 11 P.M., we park at the central square of the quarter. We join the jeep already parked there. Everyone gets out of their vehicles and exchanges cries of *"Ahalan,"* "What's up? and "How's it going?" After that they begin a raucous discussion about that afternoon's semifinal soccer match in Ramat Gan. There are a lot of dwellings around us. Thousands of families with lots of children are confined in them. Dim lights escape through the drawn shutters, and occasionally one can make out the shadow of an imprisoned soul behind a closed curtain.

The loud discussion wakes the babies, and their parents rush to quiet them. Only babies allow themselves to cry when they wake from their sleep. Gaza children who are three years old have already learned to stifle the sounds of their tears in the night. All the inhabitants of Gaza have learned to accept silently the noisy conversations that the men of Gushdan carry on beneath their bedroom windows in the middle of the night. Every once in a while you can see how one of the confined inhabitants tries to black out a blue or violet slit of light that seeps through the curtain. Even Gaza's most hardened fathers have taught themselves how to be model prisoners, while the fathers of Gushdan waken their babies with loud discussions about soccer. Tens of thousands of Gazaites have learned to contain themselves so impressively that the men of Gushdan have learned to ignore them completely during the curfew hours. One could easily think we were standing in the central square of an abandoned ghost town.

Only dreamers with great imaginations can measure the strength of the restrained hostility directed toward the ten noisy men in the square at 11 P.M. Only such dreamers can count the windows around the square and multiply the number by four (a guess as to the average number in a room) to arrive at an estimate of the hostile tens of thousands: hostile babies, hostile old people, hostile boys, hostile girls, hostile mothers, hostile dogs, hostile goats, hostile sheep, hostile kites, hostile *muezzins.*

The strength of this restrained hostility makes me recoil at the realization that for the next thirty days I have to take command of this jeep, these alleys, and these people. An irresistible sadness spreads through my body. Before it can overpower me, I shoot up two full doses of Alma Dee. In an instant, this quarter stops being the Sajaia quarter and becomes Nehardia. Then the Nehardia paths begin to glow as paths in the sky,[1] and my inevitable sadness assumes a beauty which is not of this world.

I maneuver the stars in their courses as a *muezzin* his trills. The velvet club in my hand traces the Divine name on each and every star in the sky of Nehardia. Quiveringly, it etches the Ineffable Name on countless stars, stars that are none other than kites held by the dream cords of countless Gaza children. I count the stars—187,456—the number of Gaza children who are sleeping, and clutching in their little fists 187,456 invisible ends of star strings. When the children of Gaza awaken, their stars will become invisible kites flying above the skies. When they go to school, they will tie the invisible strings to their bookbags, and the invisible kites will accompany them through the alleys, and guard them from every trouble and injury, and keep them from burning tires and erecting barricades and casting stones at the men of Gushdan. At the end of their studies, the children will run through the narrow alleys to the few open spaces still left for them and release the invisible strings and bring their kites down through the seven heavens to the field of human vision at the bottom of the lowest heaven.

Every once in a while, a star falls from one of the distant quarters. The stars of Gaza fall when her children wake from their sleep and throw out their arms in a dream and call for help. I hurry to the children who are crying and quiet them. Afterward I delicately close their fists and do not let go until their star steadies itself in the sky.

The first six stars, I catch quickly while they are falling, but on my way to the seventh, three giant dogs with covered faces spring at me. I grab the wooden club hanging from my belt, but it is too heavy, and I cannot wave it. I fall under it and the dogs fall on me. I try to shoot them, but the outgoing commander grabs me with both hands and smiles apologetically.

He is sorry to wake me, but I almost fell out of the moving jeep. "Besides, it's 1 A.M. In a little while the night patrol will be over and you still don't know your sector."

In the morning, I enter the assistant battalion commander's *(samgad)* tent and ask that I not have to leave the base during my turn at reserve duty. I am prepared to have guard duty or KP, just so as not to go on patrols of Gaza. He emphatically refuses.

I try to convince him this is not a political matter, that from a professional standpoint there isn't a chance I will be able to function on such expeditions. It is even more certain that I won't be able to command them.

He is sorry, but he has no choice. As it is, the battalion suffers from a worrisome lack of junior officers. It turns out a large part of the noncoms and second lieutenants of the battalion have evaded this reserve tour of duty in all kinds of ways (nobody in the battalion refused as a conscientious objector), and in light of this shortage he can not dispense with me as a patrol officer. (In the summer of 1969, I had completed a course for platoon leaders. Since then I have remained the most junior officer in the Israeli army. It turns out they cannot do without my good services as such a junior commander.)

While he is speaking, salvation comes from an unexpected place. Dudik breaks into the tent and asks the *samgad* to release him from the terrible penalty that is called lookout. "You can die from the boredom. Fourteen hours to be imprisoned on the roof and to be responsible for Yehudah and Reuven and Amsalem . . . . They never raise their heads from their cards. I have no one to talk to there. And the *muezzins* pound my head with their *Allah-hu-akbar.* One more day, and I'll jump off the roof . . . . I need movement; I need action. In short, I urgently need to transfer to one of the patrols . . . . I won't even mention the economic losses that this miserable observation duty can cause me. Do you know what it means to be on this roof for a solid month? It means complete isolation from the business world . . . . I have to be able to reach my car phone during the day. I have to speak at least twice a day with my broker and my importer. I didn't ask for a hearing (to excuse me from this tour of duty) because I was relying on the car phone and papers that I have in the Volvo. I cannot allow myself to be separated from them."

Before the *samgad* is able to answer, he points at me and adds, "Moreover, I am sure this spaceman will be happy to switch with me. Lookouts are just right for him. I have known him for twenty years."

I agree enthusiastically. I have always loved lookouts. I always prefer lookouts to patrols. Immediately afterward, I regret my obvious enthusiasm and think to myself that I should have given someone like Dudik the impression this deal was not so terrific for me. It wouldn't hurt for him to feel that he owes me one. But I can't do that, and Dudik, as always, comes out ahead. For his part, the *samgad* says he doesn't care. He just supervises the work. If we agree, he has no objection to the switch.

A heavy stone lifts from my heart. I have been freed from the nightmare of patrols. Starting tomorrow, I am going to take command of the observation post overlooking Palestine Square. In my fancy, I decide to change the name of the square to Pumbedita Square, and I begin to get enthusiastic at the prospect of the appealing symbolic realm that lies beyond what one can actually see from a high roof overlooking Pumbedita Square.

Starting tomorrow, I will have all the time in the world at my command. On observation duty, you can read and get a tan and write. Occasionally you can even join in the poker game of Reuven and Judah and Amsalem. Nobody chases after you on observation duty. And most important: nobody has to be chased by you.

Angels in the Skies over Gaza

Pumbedita Square is one of the big central squares of Gaza. At dawn, I come down from my heights to the roof of the Hotel Semiramis that overlooks the square. And from there, I observe the tens of thousands who pass back and forth below me.

The abandoned Hotel Semiramis is the tallest building in the square. Only the mosque is taller. All the windows of the hotel have been shattered, and all its floors are strewn with shards of glass and tin cans. A strong smell of urine arises from its hundreds of rooms, and rats live in them. From sunup to sundown, I live on its giant roof and observe the square with my perpetual telescope.

The sight of me carries authority, and many are afraid to lift their eyes up to my roof. Only the boys and girls are not afraid. They laugh in my direction, and make the "V" sign with their fingers.

I sit on a box of ammunition and record the fascinating faces of the despairing. If a black cloud ascends between me and the horizon, I stop my recording for a moment, report to headquarters the exact location of the burning tire, and return to my note-taking.

This note-taking is my holy mission. I have made myself an observer in order to bear witness to the sorrow and the cruelty, in order to show the world my own beauty. Behind the mask of an army mission, I record my holy notes. My army mission is to keep guard over clean skies. So that thick black clouds won't ascend skyward, and the smell of burning tires will not befoul the air.

Behind the mask of my holy recording, I prevent Gaza from stopping its clocks and make it possible for the daily routine to continue to go on at any cost. In this way, traffic continues to move; traders continue to sell; women continue to buy. In this way, the children continue to play permitted games—they don't burn tires and they don't throw rocks.

Most important: In this way the men of Gaza continue to build buildings in

JEWISH SOLDIERS
PLAYING CARDS
ON A HIGH ROOF
THAT LIES BETWEEN ALLAH
AND HIS MUEZZINS.

All the muezzins of Gaza are trilling their intricate melody to Allah, *and the* Jewish *observers from* Gushdan *are playing cards on a high roof that lies between* Allah *and* His *muezzins.*

The Jews *of* Gushdan *are not fiddlers.* They *aren't fiddling on the roof. The* Jews *of* Gushdan *take cards and field glasses up to the roof.* They *have perhaps heard about* Tevye *the dairyman who played intricate folk melodies on the roofs of the shtetl.* But *none of them has heard of* Alma Dee's *rooftops of delight which rise high above the roofs of* Pumbedita.

Gushdan (greater Tel Aviv). They go out in the dark before sunrise, and they return in the dark after sunset. Between the dark and the dark, they build houses. The men of Gushdan keep a short rein on the men of Gaza. They send them to build houses in Gushdan before dawn and return them quickly to Gaza after sunset, maneuvering them efficiently past many obstacles so that the men of Gaza will be able to reach their homes before curfew, so that they will be able to sleep well, and so that they will not fall asleep the next day on the scaffolds of Gushdan. The men of Gaza do not guard themselves at night. The men of Gushdan guard them. They protect them from the masked curfew-breakers who use any means to prevent the workers of Gaza from leaving for Gushdan every morning before dawn.

The men of Gushdan are willing to serve in Gaza for thirty consecutive days and nights; they are even prepared to assume a certain risk, so the men of Gaza will continue to build houses for them in the treasure cities where they live.

The buildings of Gaza, on the other hand, are not finished. Gaza is a perpetually unfinished city. Countless rusty iron poles stick out of countless concrete blocks. Countless temporary roofs are attached with temporary materials and temporary bricks. Like an unsuccessful rough draft. If you didn't hear the tumult of people and cars, you could easily imagine that Gaza had been abandoned in the middle of her construction. But the ceaseless tumult underscores the fact that as of now Gaza is the most densely populated city in the world. Denser than Hong Kong.

It is also the most observed city in the world. Most of its high roofs have been commandeered as observation-posts. On her commandeered roofs, soldiers play cards and backgammon. Only angel-soldiers don't play—they write or sunbathe. They write to take care of the beauty of their souls or sunbathe to take care of the beauty of their bodies.

I rub suntan oil on my body. It is only 7 A.M., and the sun is already blazing. Thousands of girls are going to school in a singular uniform: white kerchiefs, gray dresses, blue trousers under the gray dresses. The *beigele* vendors are already set up at our feet. Across from them are the stalls for cloth, for children's clothes and women's clothes. In the alley of the market, on the other side, traders are setting up stands of beans, spices, flour, oil, rice, and watches. Beyond them spreads a very broad area of fruit stalls: apples, grapes, pears, peaches, bananas, plums. Most of the stalls are already set up; the rest are being erected at this hour. The gray girls continue to walk in larger and larger groups toward the school. The lookout next to us is reporting two Palestinian flags hanging from the electric wire in the alley across from them. The patrol reports over the radio that it is going there to take care of the problem. That means to stop the first two men who pass by, to take their identity cards, and return them only after the flags have been taken down.

From all the streets, countless lines of automobiles crawl in the direction of

Pumbedita Square. There are no traffic lights in Gaza. Cars creep forward by blaring their horns. Children tug their schoolbags between the creeping cars, women with baskets on their heads cross noisy bottlenecks without looking right or left. Donkeys tied to pushcarts overtake crawling cars.

The stalls have not been permanently erected. Nothing here is permanently erected. The whole bustling turmoil at my feet was a flat night plain hours ago. Every morning they erect anew the scenery of Pumbedita. Thousands of vendors, stage-hands, and drivers set it up anew every morning. At dawn, when we reach the observation post, there are still no stalls in the square. In this quiet hour, the square is occupied by thousands of taxis whose drivers continually call out dozens of destinations in Gushdan: Rishon Letzion, Holon, Ramat-Aviv, Petah-Tikva, Netanya, Ramat-Gan.

A few minutes after curfew ends—in the absolute darkness of 3 A.M.—workers are already congregating in the square. One hour later, when the dawn breaks, the square is noisy and bustling. There is no other square in the world as noisy at dawn as Pumbedita Square. Dozens fall on every taxi or van that isn't already completely crowded. The lucky ones crowd out at dawn, their bags on their knees. For more than two hours, tens of thousands of lucky ones crowd their way northward; by seven in the morning, they will already be on the scaffolding of Gushdan. At that hour, Pumbedita Square fills with hundreds of colorful stalls set up by traders. They start arriving at six with their donkeys and spread out their wares: clothes, *beigeles,* fruits, lots of fruits.

We too arrive at the observation post on Hotel Semiramis at dawn, before the shop vendors. Every dawn, we set out our supplies on the roof: a field radio, telescope, suntan oil, belts, rifles, gas grenades, rubber bullets, food rations, gas burners, two packs of cards, and a giant transistor radio. Until dark we are stuck on the roof. After dark—after the traders break up their stalls—we pick up our supplies and return to the base. Between dawn and dark, we are stuck on the roof. We play cards and sunbathe.

All the women go veiled in public and barefaced in secret. All the men go veiled in secret and barefaced in public. All the women leave a slit for their eyes, and I look in their eyes with the 20×120 telescope.

A pretty woman with a lined face is carrying two babies in her arms and a basket on her head. She looks straight ahead, and her eyes are calm and full of self-assurance and nobility.

I bore into her eyes. She crosses eight lanes of traffic jammed with cars, wagons, donkeys, and army jeeps. She looks neither right nor left. As if she were walking through air. She also doesn't look up. She stands perfectly erect the whole time, looking straight ahead, a giant basket on her head and two children in her arms. I smile at the children bundled in her colorful scarf. They notice me and return my smile. They acknowledge my existence. Only children acknowledge my existence. For the adults, I see, and I am not seen. It is, of course, true that they are afraid in my presence, but they don't acknowledge me as the children do. They are convinced I am a flesh-and-blood soldier and for this reason they fear me and are afraid of the sight of me. For this reason they hate me. I forgive them and continue to write.

I wander with my telescope to the cemetery at the edge of the square. Seven boys are running between the tombstones, trying to fly a kite. They run very quickly down the slope. But the kite refuses to fly and falls on one of the graves. In another corner of the cemetery, girls are jumping rope. They chant while they jump. The girls' lips move, but their voices cannot be heard because of the tumult and the distance. I can read their lips with my telescope, and I write down the prayer that keeps repeating over and over forever: "Apple, grapes, pear; apple, grapes, pear." The boys continue to run among the tombstones and manage to fly the kite to a height of twenty meters. It starts to spin and lose altitude, and they implore it not to fall. In vain. On the third try, the kite accelerates and lifts over the cemetery. The children dance below it and encourage it with loud cries.

Every day I count the kites in the skies above Gaza. The kite the cemetery boys manage to fly is number thirty-eight.

The sun begins to set, and the wind blows the kites westward. Thirty-eight kites sail above the setting sun, and the chant, *"Allah-hu-akbar"* trills from the northern mosque. It is still trilling, when it is joined by two western mosques. Not a minute passes, and all the muezzins of Gaza are trilling *"Allah-hu-akbar"* from all possible mosques. All the muezzins of Gaza are trilling their intricate melody to Allah, and the Jewish observers from Gushdan are playing cards on a high roof that lies between Allah and His muezzins.

The Jews of Gushdan are not fiddlers. They aren't fiddling on the roof. The Jews of Gushdan take cards and field glasses up to the roof. They have perhaps heard about Tevye the dairyman who played intricate folk melodies on the roofs of the shtetl. But none of them has heard of Alma Dee's rooftops of delight, which rise high above the roofs of Pumbedita. None of them knows the almost-unfinished melody that is played without stop on the rooftop of delights of Rav Reḥumi and his beloved Love-with-the-Narrow-Womb.

Rav Reḥumi is one of those mysterious men of Pumbedita who couldn't hold out and preferred the rooftops of delights in Alma Dee to the rooftops of economic livelihood in Gushdan. He fled from this world and ascended to his Beloved. And left below—among the alleys—his veiled wife and his children.

The "narrow womb" of his beloved made Rav Reḥumi lose his mind. He tasted the eternal taste of the first time and the eternal taste of more, more without end. He erected no fence around his roof; he was beside himself from the sweetness and bliss. If not for the eyes of his wife, Rav Reḥumi would not have come down from the roof.

Every day, Rav Reḥumi's wife was careful not to endanger this world and careful not to reveal herself before it. She walked in the world veiled from her head to her toes. Only her eyes remained visible, and she took care not to look at this world directly so as not to turn it into heaps of ruins. In times of emergency, she turned her eyes to other worlds to make this world better.

In short, Rav Reḥumi could not escape from his wife's eyes. He had nothing in the world but the narrow womb of his beloved and the big eyes of his wife.

One day his wife lost her control over herself. A tear fell from her eyes and destroyed the rooftops of delights. Rav Reḥumi flew up in the air like a kite. At first he flew heavenward in a whirlwind. But after forty or fifty seconds, he lost height, began to spin around, and rose up into the cemetery between whose tombstones children still fly dozens of colorful kites that first gain height, then lose it, and spin down onto the tombstones.

What Should a Samgad Know about a Mosque (misgad)?

Friday at noon. The Mosque-Watch.

The prayers are at their height. Tension is at its height. The prayers have been going on for more than an hour. And for more than an hour, the patrols from Gushdan have spread through Pumbedita Quarter. Many other patrols are spread over the other squares in Gaza. Many transmitters whisper into the crowded air. Battalion commanders and assistant battalion commanders *(samgadim)* give their last commands, "Improve your positions!". . . . Take cover! . . . . Report every suspicious movement!" At the same time, the intricate melodies of the many muezzins ascend into the blazing skies. Even though no official curfew has been declared, not a single local dares walk the streets of Gaza. Everyone not in the mosques is buried deep in the houses. Taking no chances.

It is hot in Gaza. Blazing. I drink a lot, look through my telescope, and take notes. There are no children or women in the streets, so I track the sweating faces of the men of Gushdan, who are waving their clubs back and forth and listening to the commanders' instructions blended with the muezzins' trilling. Two Piper Cubs patrol without stop over the mosques and try to block the trills as they ascend to heaven. In vain.

Little by little, the sad and biting melodies of the muezzins fade away. Little by little, they segue into the tone of command. They give long instructions to the tens of thousands of their faithful. The battalion commanders and assistant battalion commanders also give their commands greater dramatic force. "Improve your positions! Don't fire plastic bullets without orders! . . . . Don't aim at the head! . . . . Don't throw gas grenades into the mosque courtyards! . . . . *Allah hu Akbar!* Nobody on the roof understands the classical Arabic of the mosques. Nobody knows if the muezzins are inciting unrest or restraining it. Sometimes their speech sounds inflammatory and sometimes like a futile attempt to pacify. Sometimes we get the impression that the muezzins are arguing with each other through the loudspeakers of Gaza. It's impossible to tell. What, after all, do the men on the roof know about the mosque facing them?

The *samgad* asks Dudik over the radio, "Have they come out of your mosque yet?" "From my mosque they don't come out so quickly," arrogantly answers Dudik. But masked kids are assembling in the mosque courtyard. Do I have permission for a gas grenade? . . . ." (When the five-year-old kids of Gaza want to look as big as fifteen-year-olds, they put scarves over their faces and wave their fingers in the "V" sign.)

"Don't you dare get near those kids," cries the *samgad.* "I am ordering you to distance your men from the area of the mosque . . . . Do you read me?" I write down their conversation and make a note to myself with paternalistic satisfaction that there are indeed righteous people in Sodom. Who knows what tender soul is hidden in the heart of the gruff *samgad.* Ultimately, what does a *samgad* know about a mosque? What does the *samgad* from Gushdan know about the mosque of Pumbedita? What explanation is there for the strong holy trembling that causes him to forbid his soldiers to throw gas grenades into the mosque courtyards?

All of Gaza is one big mosque. An open temple. The voice of God walks about the city. It is impossible not to join in the prayer of the muezzins. It is impossible not to sway and bow down and fall on one's face. The prayers are an inseparable part of the daily experience of the secular conquering army from Gushdan, whose soldiers have a distinct fear of God, incipient and completely undeveloped. The conquerors from Gushdan stand in awe beneath the mosques, their helmets over their hearts, and their eyes moist, like the eyes of those who conquered the Western Wall.

My eyes already hurt me. I ask one of the card players to keep watch for a while in my place. "I can't," he says. "I'm losing . . . ." I ask the second one. "I won't let him," says the first one. "He has my money . . . ." I take off my uniform, spread suntan oil all over my body, plug into my Walkman, and stretch out on an army mattress. They continue to play.

Suddenly the *samgadim* in the distant quarters report the end of prayer in their mosques. At once, black clouds of smoke ascend over those distant quarters, and the dim echoes of shots are heard without cease. In Pumbedita Square, there is still a tense quiet. On the airwaves, a whole war is taking place. All the lookouts are warning the patrols about kids lying in ambush throwing stones. Patrol 44 shoots a gas grenade at a group of children, and the wind carries the gas to observation post 57. In a strangled voice, the commander of observation post 57 curses the commander of patrol 44. The commander of patrol 44 apologizes.

I am lying in my underpants in a corner of the roof, suntan oil spread over my body, totally given over to the sun, listening to the war on the radio. An officer from the other battalion drives into an ambush of children. "One hundred children are stoning me," he reports in high hysteria. "If reinforcements don't arrive, there will be a catastrophe here." Another gas grenade explodes, and with closed eyes I listen to Arik Einstein's music over *Galei Tzahal,* the popular Army radio station. The smell of the suntan oil my body has absorbed hides the stench of burning tires, and I lift my eyes to the blackening skies.

In Tire Square, a row of five obstacles, one after the other. In Policemen Square, many Palestinian flags are flying; in the Faris Market, two tires are burning; in Fishermen Square, there is a suspicious vehicle—emergency vans are getting ready. In the girls' high school there is a great tumult—and above all of these, on the roof closest to the sky of Gaza, I am lying with closed eyes, giving myself over to the sun.

Come My Beloved to Meet the Bride

Late Friday afternoon.

A time of great mercy. All week at this hour, the inhabitants of Gaza gather their strength from the noontime shock of the battle of the mosques. Slowly but surely, Pumbedita Square fills with the spirit of life. Families walk around its alleys, boys and girls spread out in their multitudes over the giant cemetery, which is the most open space and, therefore, the only playground of the giant quarter. Girls are jumping rope. Boys are flying kites.

Men in white *galabiyas* are strolling at leisure in the alleys. All the other days of the week, they run about like industrious ants with plastic bags, but tomorrow is Shabbat—they don't work in Gushdan—there is no need to wake up in the dark. No need to rush. There are still more than two hours till curfew and God is great. *Allah hu akbar* . . . .

Until curfew, they will walk about like kings in their mighty heaven. Their beautiful wives will walk at their sides, and their children will run before them. Until curfew, they will neither fail nor be defeated. They will be neither subjugated nor dismayed. They will only walk around, proudly at rest in their white *galabiyas,* and roll their colorful beads. Over their heads waves a multicolored royal chariot drawn by kites.

The kites of Gaza's Erev Shabbats are as many as the sands of the sea. Like numberless colorful sperm, they swim the skies to welcome the Bride. Like infinite one-eyed tadpoles, they penetrate the dusk of the wondrous honeypot who crowns her master.

Come, my beloved to welcome the bride. Every hour she is as dear to you as a well-praised virgin, as a doe. At each and every hour, Pumbedita is rebuilt upon her ruins. A great hour of mercy. Come, my beloved, to welcome the bride.

Sura III

Where did Rabbi Akiva's twenty-four thousand students go during the Intifada? To the detention camps of Sura![2] One of these detention camps—Sura III—lies on the western shore of Gaza, and nuzzles the army camp where we lodge nights from lookout to lookout. It is fenced with intricate chains of wire, crowned with rows of red geraniums, surrounded by dozens of guard towers, and lit all night with strong searchlights so Rabbi Akiva's students will not abandon their Torah study for even one moment.

They study in tents and send intricate melodies toward the sea but cannot touch it. The roar of the waves blends with the noise of their studies, and their study overalls are blue.

They make do with the least of the least. They eat bread and salt, drink a small measure of water, and sleep on the ground. They wrap themselves six in one tallit and study Torah. Every day they kill themselves in the tent of the Torah. They attack at dawn, deploy their troops, return stormy fire till the small hours of the morning, sleep a sweet fleeting sleep, and return to attack with the dawn.

Every Erev Shabbat at twilight, Rabbi Akiva comes to visit them and deliver his weekly lesson. Oh, then they are silent, crowded six to an armspan, drinking his words thirstily.

Rabbi Akiva finishes his lesson at midnight and rises from his place. At that very instant, everyone stands up without moving and shows him honor beyond this world. Only after he leaves, do they allow themselves to move their bodies, and a cloud of stardust rises from their blue overalls giving light to the whole world. At that time, they say in the farthest refugee camps, "In Sura III the thousands of Rabbi Akiva's students have stood up. The lesson is over."

At that same moment, twenty-four thousand wives shade their eyes from the blinding light and count the days and the months and the years they still have to wait. On the next day, they come veiled to the market of Pumbedita Square and choose their *beigeles* and spices, their children in their arms, and their fruit baskets on their heads. By their veils, every merchant in the market can tell who are the wives of the detainees at Sura and who are the wives of the workers of Gushdan.

All the vendors of Pumbedita are afraid to argue with the wives of the sages.

The fear of Rabbi Akiva hovers over them. They take whatever coins the women place in their palms, and sometimes they refuse any payment at all.

The whole week long, Rabbi Akiva moves back and forth in the doorway of his abandoned *beit midrash* and studies. Nobody dares cut his studies short. Even the patrols are afraid to go near him. Occasionally, he gets up and walks about the stalls, while he thrusts and parries with himself in the battle of Torah. Everyone who passes clears the way for him. The bravest of them steal glances at him, but nobody dares stare directly at him.

Only once a week, at twilight on Erev Shabbat, does he leave the great Square of Pumbedita behind and walk toward the thousands of his students who are waiting for him in the Sura camp. A pillar of fire goes before him, and all the muezzins of Pumbedita announce the entry of the Shabbat through their loudspeakers.

How awesome is the pillar of fire, how awesome the sight of Rabbi Akiva who never stops his studies and continues to murmur. He crosses Gaza and passes the tens of thousands of her inhabitants. Nobody dares look at him. All lower their heads and bow down.

When he passes below my hotel, I look at him carefully through my telescope. I am not afraid of him. After all, I am a rebel. I have denied the most significant and the least significant, and I am not afraid to look directly at saints through my 20×120 telescope.

His White Donkey

In the traces of the Messiah, effrontery will grow . . .
the people of the border will go around from city to city without mercy . . .
young men will humiliate old men . . . . (BT Sota 49b)

What is his (the Messiah's) sign?—he sits among the afflicted poor in the gates of Rome. All of them loosen (their bandages) together and retie them together. He loosens and reties one at a time, saying, "So that I will not delay." (BT Sanhedrin 98a)

(The Messiah) is poor and rides a donkey. (Ibid.)

On the other side of Pumbedita Square, on the Umar al Mukhtar Hill, between the municipality building and the abandoned *beit midrash* stretches the wholesale market of Gaza. Between it and me waves a row of flowering poinciana trees, whose red flowers are intoxicating these days. It is now nine o'clock in the morning, and the market is alive, crowded, and colorful. Not one among the hundreds of merchants crowded there was present last night at the officers' briefing, and, therefore, nobody knows what I know: In exactly one hour, a jeep with a loudspeaker will pass through this tumult and announce the immediate closing of the market.

The decision to close the market was prompted by a desire to demonstrate the might of the occupying powers. Yesterday and the day before, the market had been closed by an order from high in the command of the Intifada. Yesterday and the day before, the conquering powers tried to force the merchants and farmers to conduct an ordinary market day. They came up empty-handed. Against the background of these events, the decision was reached yesterday at the highest levels to punish the local inhabitants by suddenly closing their market. The local inhabitants have to decide whom they want to obey—the occupying forces or the directors of the Intifada. If they obey the leaders of the Intifada and stop work, then the army will close their market on the remaining days.

It is my job to observe the process of closing and to report to headquarters every irregular event. That is why I survey the market exclusively and do not explore the side alleys and deserted rooftops with my telescope.

In the center of the square are the farmers' stalls. In general, each stall is loaded with one fruit or vegetable—stalls of tomatoes, eggplants, potatoes, apricots, melons, squash, onions, garlic, watermelon, peppers. Across from the farmers' stalls are the stalls for beans and spices and *beigeles,* and many stalls for grains. Across from them are the stalls for meat, fish, and fowl. All the stalls are tethered to donkeys, and every once in a while one of the stalls moves behind its donkey.

Thousands of women pass between the stalls and choose whatever comes to hand. For them it is the first market day of the week, and there is great commotion. Through my telescope, I constantly see merchants weighing and filling baskets, and many women milling around their stalls. Meat is hanging from hooks in various corners of the market, and women are showing the meat merchants where to cut. They cut and weigh skillfully and fill the women's baskets. In another corner there is a heap of ground meat, and it too is being sold very rapidly.

It is also the hour for beggars. Every morning at nine, dozens of afflicted beggars enter the market. They arrive with the last of the merchants and arrange themselves for their market days. With my telescope, I follow their repeated setting-up process throughout the day. At the first stage, they skillfully and rapidly loosen the many bandages wrapping their sores. Afterward they spread them on the sidewalk like arrays of merchandise and present their sores for inspection. Immediately after, they take a tin box from their patched overalls and put a few coins into it. Then they begin the ritual of scratching their sores. Every once in a while they stop scratching, shake the box, and mutter, "Charity saves from death . . . charity saves from death." Between the shakes, they wave green flies off their sores. Toward evening, when the last of the merchants load their donkeys with empty crates, the beggars empty their tin boxes and slip their day's earnings into their big pockets. Then, they wrap all their bandages on their bodies and tie them tightly. A moment later, they hobble off into the alleys of the quarter and are swallowed up.

One beggar, whose dark sunglasses cover his face, stands out among all the afflicted beggars. This beggar is sorely afflicted, bandaged from his head to his toes. His appearance casts dread on the throngs who check out the Pumbedita market every day, and they are careful not to intrude on his four cubits of space. Even I was afraid at first to approach him through my telescope, but little by little I conquered my fear and began to record him.

Every morning at the same time, he comes to the market riding on a white donkey (all the other beggars come on foot). He doesn't tie up his donkey when he reaches his set place, and the donkey roams free among the fruit and vegetable stands. The donkey returns late in the afternoon and stands before his master, and they disappear together into the alleys.

The whole day long, the afflicted beggar never removes a single bandage and doesn't reveal his sores for inspection. If he loosens a bandage in order to scratch, he makes sure to tie it up immediately after. Even at noon, when the sun burns his sores, he is careful not to leave even one sore open. On the hottest day, he loosens, scratches, and refastens without pause. Even then he continues to follow everything with a tense watchfulness. From morning till evening, he maintains the highest readiness for a sudden emergency assignment of the most secret nature. From morning until evening, he unties, scratches, and reties, keeping an eye on every possible direction.

He is alertly tense and given constantly to observing the passersby. An empty tin box sits at his head. Every once in a while I look into it and ascertain that it is indeed empty. Nobody dares to get close enough to leave a coin in it, and nobody dares throw a coin from afar.

The whole day, his donkey roams over the huge square and grazes at will. Its unfettered presence agitates the hundreds of merchants' donkeys who are constantly tethered to their stalls. The awful beggar pays no attention to his white donkey and allows it to wander as much as he wants. He knows that at the end of the market day, his faithful donkey will take its place before him, and he feels no need to keep an eye on it. Especially since he is perpetually occupied with untying and retying his bandages and watching everyone who passes by.

The white donkey roams ceaselessly among the stalls. It stops for a long minute next to a corn stall and selects a few ears. From there it goes to the watermelon stall, knocks a few down to the ground, chomps on them, and continues on its way. No merchant dares chase it away. All the merchants of Gaza know who the white donkey belongs to, and they don't bother it. It chews and chews in great bliss.

Suddenly, something suspicious occurs in another corner of the market. Several energetic merchants are bending down and searching feverishly under the wheels. A woman and a girl are standing near them. Through my telescope I see one of the merchants pounce on something out of sight, maybe a Molotov cocktail, and I get set to report this to headquarters. But after a minute he stands up, waves a little yellow chick in his hands, and gives it to the little girl. Two other merchants continue to chase two more chicks and catch them. The girl smiles happily.

It is ten o'clock. From headquarters, they notify me that the jeep with the loudspeaker is headed toward me. The colorful commotion is still at its height. The muezzins' trills blend with the chants of merchants announcing their wares. The smells of mint and savory ascend skyward. Every minute, hundreds of additional women enter the area and scatter among the stalls. They have straw baskets on their heads and black veils over their faces like bridal veils of death. Reuven, Yehudah, and Amsalem continue to concentrate on their card game in the shade of a brightly colored beach umbrella. They have nothing in their world except four cubits of poker. Nobody besides me knows what is about to happen any moment.

I conduct it all from the roof and count backwards. I feel so sorry about the glorious sight that will disappear in a minute. I feel so sad about the unending material for observation and inspiration that is going to disappear before my eyes. So, too (I feel the need to point this out to myself with satisfaction,) my heart aches for the fate of the multitudes at my feet. The market was closed yesterday and the day before. I feel so bad about the suffering this new closing will cause them. They still don't know the market will close, and they are still making so many plans for this wonderful day. Really wonderful. Such a pity to cut it off at its peak.

I know what the most seasoned merchant doesn't know. My rooftop knowledge could have substantial economic benefits. If I only had the energy, I could go down to the market and reveal my secret to several seasoned merchants for a not inconsequential price. But I don't have the energy. I am just a Greek chorus composed of one observer. So I stay on the roof and give myself over to the wonderful noisy tumult that will be cut off at its height in just a minute. I am set up and prepared to witness it and make it everlasting.

At the top of the Umar Al Muktar Hill, there is a row of blooming poinciana trees. Along this boulevard, an unseen procession of four jeeps is coming slowly and ceremoniously. At the head of the column comes the jeep with the loudspeaker. I follow it with my telescope. One hundred meters before the entrance to the market, it activates two very loud sirens. Below me, everyone abruptly cuts off all exchange and stands motionless as at a memorial siren. After the siren, over the loudspeakers, comes a dramatic instruction in radio Arabic. Immediately afterward, an unearthly tumult begins.

Merchants rush to load their last crates. Farmers hurry to get rid of their produce. Women begin to rush around between the stalls. Prices suddenly plummet. Everybody tries to delay following the edict as much as possible. Each extra moment is worth money. Two jeeps drive among the stalls and urge the merchants and women to stop their transactions. Another jeep sets itself up at the entrance to the market and tries to stop the entering stream. The trembling voice of an unfamiliar commander commands the process. I observe the commander's jeep and ascertain that Dudik is not there. Every day between nine and ten, Dudik shuts himself up in his Volvo and contacts his brokers. Last night he asked the *samgad* to postpone the closing of the market by fifteen minutes. The *samgad* passed along his request to his superiors, but it was not accepted. The decision was made that the operation would begin without Dudik, and he would join it the moment he broke free from his business affairs.

I do not recognize the officer replacing Dudik. Apparently, he has been temporarily attached from another unit. He is not able to take control of the market-closing operation. He is especially unable to stop the stream of women who continue to crowd around the stalls. They hadn't known about the strike and had been waiting three days for this market day. They had come early in order to have enough time to prepare lunch for their older children who come home from school and supper for the husband and the grown children who went out to the scaffolds of Gushdan at four in the morning. And what do they see? The market is closed. Just like yesterday and the day before.

A young mother is standing near the substitute commander and two of his soldiers—a one-year-old girl in her arms and a four-year-old holding on to her robe. Suddenly the girl takes her hand off her mother's skirt, points to a wagon loaded with vegetables, and runs past the soldiers to the wagon. The mother starts and runs after her; the girl stops next to the wagon and grabs everything at hand—corns, tomatoes, eggplants, squash, and puts them on the scale. Neither the merchant, the mother, nor the new commander reacts, and the girl continues to pile up produce and put it into the baskets her mother is holding.

Suddenly, many women come, surround the wagon, grab everything they can, pay quickly, and disappear. The new commander doesn't react. The two soldiers behind him try to intervene. He doesn't let them. They leave him alone and go to stop the purchases at a fish stall. The women who have not yet managed to buy fish are begging them to let them finish. The soldiers ignore the women and continue to stand between them and the stall. And suggest to the merchant that he get out of there quickly. The merchant breaks up his stall while the women are still pleading. The soldiers continue to walk between the merchant and the women. While they walk, they twirl their clubs on their fingers as if the clubs were tennis rackets.

A rush of purchases is also taking place at the meat stalls. The new commander hurries to the merchants and tries to convince them to leave the spot. He is very indecisive, almost apologetic, and the merchants take advantage of this. They plead with him about their merchandise. They have already opened and cut the meat and they will have to throw it out. Wouldn't that be a pity?

He listens to them through the commotion and tries to convince them that he has no alternative; he has orders from above. They ask for only ten more minutes. Everything has been so sudden—if they had only been told from the beginning, they would not have cut open so much meat and spread it out in the sun.

Suddenly, I see him approach his communications gear in the jeep and ask headquarters for permission to postpone the closing by fifteen minutes in order to close the market in a pleasant fashion. He actually said those words in combination, "in a pleasant fashion"; on the other side of the radiotelephone there was a long silence.

Suddenly, I can hear there is Dudik's well-known voice on the radio, "Pay attention, new commander, don't be a softie. Stay firm; I'm on my way to you. I'll be there in five minutes." Dudik's voice is very decisive and as convincing as the voice of a general barking metallic commands during the storming of a well-fortified target.

Meanwhile, the merchants see that they are dealing with a softie commander, and they continue to bargain. Merchants know how to bargain—that is their business. They take utmost advantage of the fact that they are dealing with a teacher or with a literature student who doesn't understand market language. The softie signals them to wait. He walks over to his communications gear again and asks headquarters once more if he has permission to delay the closing of the market by fifteen minutes. Once again Dudik intervenes, makes a dismissive comment, and advises the softie to stand firm and concentrate on self-defense until Dudik arrives. "Listen: I'll be there in two minutes. When I arrive, I will invite you to a free practical demonstration. The name of the performance: 'How to close a market in three minutes.' Over and out."

Once again the airways are silent. Nobody on the radio reacts. Not even the *samgad.* I wait tensely and observe through the telescope the hill from which Dudik's jeep will appear. In the meantime, many women are arriving, and the jeep set up at the entrance to the market is not able to take control of them. The other jeep tries to help. In vain. Hundreds of women walk around them and spread out quickly among the stalls. The softie commander's jeep cannot move in the throngs, and those who sit in it get ready to defend themselves. I cover the jeep out of the corner of my eye; though it is clear to me that none of the milling women plans to attack it. They have one well-defined target—the stalls. The merchants take the risk and continue to sell. A few of them slowly fold their umbrellas to show compliance with the closing order, but most of them are selling feverishly, despite their ever-increasing awareness of the risks that they are taking. The women pay quickly and run with their baskets to other stalls. They don't count their change. And the merchants don't weigh carefully. Many fruits and vegetables fall to the ground, and nobody bothers to pick them up. The hurried weighing continues. Another kilo and another. Another crate and another. I have no chance to keep up with the rhythm. I record only highlights in my notebook.

In all the commotion, the dozens of beggars rush to bind up their sores and empty their boxes into their big pockets. One by one, without anyone seeing them, they are swallowed up by the alleys. Far from the seething crowds. Only the most awful beggar stays rooted on his spot and doesn't stop following everything that happens from behind his sunglasses. Meanwhile, he binds up and loosens his bandages with great rapidity. Despite the tumult and the over-crowding, everyone is careful not to enter his four cubits of space.

And his white donkey continues to chew with gusto and roam peacefully among the wealth of fruits and vegetables that roll on the ground. The unending abundance excites it. It chews and chews and stares straight ahead, listening inwardly with wide open eyes.

Suddenly he trembles at the sound of a mighty explosion. So do I.

I look around quickly and spot Dudik's jeep stationed in the middle of the market. Dudik himself is standing on the hood, throwing dummy grenades at everyone who passes by. Before I can even focus my glasses on him, he raises his weapon and fires a clip of live ammo into the sky.

Dudik's fatigue shirt falls over his tight trousers. His belt and helmet are thrown on the back seat, and his hair is flying. In an instant, the market empties out, and the two jeeps stationed at the entrance barely extricate themselves. Twenty seconds later, Dudik begins to drive toward a line of stalls while standing easily. The stalls are pushing each other, and the donkeys tethered to them begin to move in all directions. Their merchants rush after them, hurrying to grab their leads and steer them outside. At the same time, they try to look after their falling crates.

In an instant, the line of stalls disappears, and Dudik finds himself next to the meat stalls. He stands on the driver's seat and strikes a calf hanging from a hook with his club. The hook falls to the ground with the calf and pulls down a great bowl of ground meat along with it. The ground meat spills on the tire of his jeep as it continues to move forward slowly. Holding the steering wheel in one hand, Dudik continues to hit all the other hooks lined up in that row with his club. Parts of calves and lambs are strewn on the ground like broken statues.

At the end of the meat row, he finds a small pen of chickens for slaughter and topples it to the ground. Flapping their wings, the chickens jump up over the heads of the fleeing women, and one of them lands on the back of the white donkey, which continues to dream with wide open eyes.

Then Dudik steps on the gas and drives among the women still in the area, chasing them away. There still remain clusters of stalls in the far corners of the market. Dudik drives his jeep into one of the clusters, and the merchants scatter in all directions. Here and there, you can see stalls moving without their merchants. Dudik continues, driving his jeep into a group of spice merchants—their dispersion is too slow for his taste. He takes away the identity cards of the spice merchants. At once, all the merchants who had still dared remain in the far corners of the market run away.

The market is empty. Three minutes haven't passed, and Dudik is driving through it as fast as you could go on a closed race track. A gold chain on his neck, and hair flying in the wind. Meanwhile, he is calling the *samgad* and reporting that the market is shut tight and the mission completed. The *samgad* asks him if any of the local inhabitants were wounded.

"Absolutely negative," answers Dudik, "no local was even grazed."

"Nice," says the *samgad*, "A clean job."

After the report, he parks in a far corner of the market square, puts his parachutist boots on the wheel, and begins the ritual of handing out documents. The spice merchants stand in a line, and Dudik looks for a long time at their identification papers. In a whisper, he calls out a name and address. An old merchant comes toward Dudik with a bent-over gait, careful not to enter Dudik's four cubits of space. Dudik motions with his club to come forward two more steps. The old man approaches with trembling knees. Then Dudik throws his papers on the ground. The old man bends down fearfully, picks up his papers, and moves three steps back without turning his back on Dudik. The next merchant takes his place, and the ceremony begins again.

Only after Dudik has given the fourth merchant back his documents does he notice the presence of the horrible beggar sitting in the middle of the market square. He throws the rest of the papers in the air and rushes with his jeep toward the beggar. Four cubits from him, he stops, brakes squealing and almost overturns. The beggar doesn't move. Dudik steps on the gas and prepares for another attack. But the beggar lifts his sunglasses for an instant. Dudik immediately kills the engine, gets down from the jeep, and leaves the market with measured steps backward, not daring to turn his back on the horrible beggar.

The moment Dudik walks backwards is the very same moment the white donkey begins to bray a song. Blessed are those who are privileged to hear how his song resounds from one end of the world to the other and how all the agitated donkeys of Gaza join him with sorrowful longing brays.

After the last of the donkeys grows quiet, an unearthly silence falls under the blazing sun. Echoes of the dummy grenades still thunder in my ears, and colors swim in my eyes. I pull off my shirt—how can I wear it? I take off my boots, take off my socks, tie my elastic cuffs around my shoes, take off my pants and am left in my underpants. I drink a full canteen of water, I rinse my face and wet down my hair, and I smear suntan oil all over my body. I stretch out on the roof and meditate ten minutes in the Alexander position—knees bent and energy streaming through the spinal column, and a great peace comes over the row of poinciana trees on the Umar al Mukhtar Hill as you come to Pumbedita Square, which is Palestine Square.

Like the Beauty of the Word Intifada

> **To the singer for the doe of dawn a psalm of David—at night—even though it is night—there is moonlight and stars and constellations. And when is it dark? At dawn! The moon goes in, and the stars go in, and the constellations leave; at that hour, there is no darkness greater than that. And at that hour, the Holy Blessed One responds to the whole world and brings the dawn up out of the darkness and brings light to the world. (Midrash Shoḥer Tov 22)**
>
> **A story about the great Rabbi Ḥiyya and Rabbi Shimon ben Ḥalafta who were walking at dawn in the Arbel valley and saw the doe of dawn as her light was cracking. Said the great Rabbi Ḥiyya to Rabbi Shimon, I declare, Rabbi, just so is the redemption of Israel: At first bit by bit, and then as it continues, it continues to grow greater. (JT Berakhot 1:5)**

4 A.M.

At this hour, no intersections in the world are as noisy as the crossroads of Gaza. An endless snake of automobile headlights creeps northward; thousands of laborers crowd on their bags in the dark. Like a column of battle units on the way to an attack due to start at dawn. Like 600,000 dwarfs blinking toward Snow White.

Workers who wake the dawn have some sort of extra soul. In their existential desire to creep forcefully from their starting place in darkest dark and to storm the doe of dawn whose light breaks forth and rises, there is an extra soul in their existential longing for redemption.

All the men of Gaza get up while it is dark and see the doe of dawn whose light is cracking, and they say to each other, "Just so is the redemption of Palestine . . . ." and the doe is as guarded and as beautiful as the beauty of the word Intifada.

The men of Gushdan, on the other hand, have gotten used to getting up in clear strong light. They no longer await the new day in the bend beyond the darkness. New days grab the men of Gushdan in the heat of their dreams and dazzle them in their sleep. And when do the men of Gushdan wake the dawn? On their tour of reserve duty. Serving on reserve duty is one of their points of inspiration. Reserve duty is their great escape from routine. During this service, they are more collegial, more relaxed, are drawn out of themselves a little, concern themselves more with other people, are less materialistic, less acquisitive, more open, and more openhearted. They read more, and they even write. They have a lot of time to be by themselves, to think, to ponder, to discuss. In general, during one month of reserve duty, the average man from Gushdan sees a lot more sunrises than he does all year. The men of Gaza, on the other hand, see all the sunrises.

The great victory will come with the dawn. The people who knows best how to wake the dawn will win out in the end over the people who governs it and makes the conquered people get up in the dark and build buildings for it. But the people who walks in darkness will once again see a great light, will win once again over the people that walks in light, and will once again make it wake up at night to build its buildings. The conquered will always conquer the conquerors and will then neglect the sight of the rising dawn. They will never learn.

Only *talmidei ḥakhamim* will learn for ever and ever and ever. Only *talmidei ḥakhamim* will always wake the doe of dawn. And will live forever in a world that has redemption but no victory. The great attraction of the doe of dawn will be for them an unending source of inspiration. She will always be as beloved to them as at the first time. Every hour they will wake her and stir her until she is ready . . . .

Fifteen years ago, an astounding sunrise lit the Sinai desert at the end of battle maneuvers that had begun at sunset and lasted all night. Dudik was arranging ammunition boxes inside the half-track, and I was cleaning the machine gun on the deck, and I said to him, "Dudik, leave the boxes, and come see a beautiful sunrise."

He didn't react and continued gathering empty packs and stuffing them in the boxes.

"You're missing out, Dudik; you don't see sunrises like this every day."

"You're the one who is missing out," Dudik answers, "I always win—I grasped the principle of sunrises long ago."

To this very day, I keep missing out. To this very day, I refuse to grasp the principle and still hope to see all sunrises with my naked eye. The crack of orange continues to move me to tears. And I continue to hide my tears behind my telescope, and a tear moistens the lens and the whole world seems to cry because it can't contain the beauty. I will yet be a kite tied to an invisible string, and a little child will lead me and guide me through the hidden pathways of the sky.

I will yet rise up into God's strong heavens. I will yet walk in God's temple and sing, "Holy, Holy, Holy." Thousands of muezzins will brim over in me, and I will brim over and ride up in a whirlwind to heaven, pay a visit to

I STAY
NEXT TO
MY FATHER
UNTIL
THE END
OF
ADON OLAM.

Another Friday. Once again, the mosques are in service. Boys and girls are playing "red light, green light" in the mosque's courtyard. Their fathers are praying inside.

I can't join them because I have been strongly forbidden to play during prayer-time.

I look at their game with a jealousy mixed with contempt and stay next to my father until the end of Adon Olam.

Michael and Uriel, and then land at my lookout post when day has fully come to my abandoned hotel.

H(agar) P(arpar) T(aleh) R(aḥel) H(agar)[3]

Another Friday. Another Mosque-Watch.

Once again, the mosques are in service. Boys and girls are playing "red light, green light" in the mosque's courtyard. Their fathers are praying inside. I can't join them because I have been strongly forbidden to play during prayer-time. I look at their game with a jealousy mixed with contempt and stay next to my father until the end of Adon Olam.

In most of the mosques of Gaza, prayer has already ended. In the mosque facing me, it will continue for a long while yet. Today there are two bridegrooms and a bar mitzvah and all are being honored with a festive *aliyah* to the Torah. So the lucky boys continue to play "red light green light" outside, and inside, the Torah reading has been going on for more than an hour.

A hot Sabbath sun is blazing on the hotel's roof. The card players hide in the shade. Trills of *Allah hu akbar* ascend through the melting gates of heaven.

The *samgad* calls me on the radio.

"Ruth avor," I answer him ("Roger, over.")

"What is happening with your mosque? Why haven't you reported the end of prayer? Over"

"The prayer in my mosque hasn't ended yet. It will go on for another hour. Over."

"Did you say an hour? Over"

"Affirmative. Over"

"How do you know? Over"

"They've just finished the haftarah. Over."

"They finished what?! Over."

"The haftarah. Over."

"Again?!"

"Haftarah-Out-Haftarah H(agar) P(arpar) T(aleh) R(aḥel) H(agar). Do you copy? Over."

"Pay attention. We can't hear you clearly. Do you copy?"

"Ruth, Ruth ("Copy, Copy"). I'm paying attention: I am not clearly heard."

An hour later, I report the ending of prayers to the *samgad.* Instantly, the children stop playing "red light green light" and start to curse us and throw rocks at us. Most of the rocks do not reach our roof and fall into the lower floors of the hotel through shattered windows. Only one boy, around ten years old, is able to aim his slingshot at me and force me to find cover behind the parapet.

When the children see me hiding, they shout and curse, "Maniac . . . *Al Yahud* . . . maniac . . . *Al Yahud.*"

The boy with the slingshot draws encouragement and continues to snipe at me. The *samgad* asks if everything is in order, and I ask him to send one of the patrols to disperse the children. He tells me to make do with my own forces, for all the patrols are busy right now with other targets. While he is talking, a stone hits Yehudah and makes him drop his cards.

Yehudah runs to one of the dilapidated walls of an inner room of the hotel and kicks it with all his might. He picks up one of the larger fragments, runs toward the parapet, and throws it down. All the children run away; the boy with the slingshot takes cover and continues to hurl at us. Yehudah comes back with another big rock, shakes it at him, and mutters, "I'm gonna kill him . . . . I'm gonna kill him." I try to stop Yehudah but understand that there is no way to stop him. The hit and the curses have humiliated him. He throws the rock on the sidewalk and runs to the dilapidated wall to bring more rocks. I move away from the parapet, afraid to see large rocks falling on children from the sixth story, and hope the rescue patrol will arrive before a tragedy occurs.

It has been a few hours that Yehudah hasn't played cards, and he wants to kill the boy with the slingshot barehanded. It has been a few hours that the boy has been passing through the alley below us, driving him crazy, crying, "Maniac . . . *Al Yahud* . . . maniac . . . *Al Yahud.*" Afterward he hides behind make-shift barricades and fires at us with his slingshot. Smooth stones fly toward us and force us to stretch out on the tarred roof. Yehudah walks around our penthouse in a gray undershirt and prepares a heap of large rocks. The whole time he keeps muttering, "I'm gonna kill him . . . . I'm gonna kill him . . . ."

"You <u>are</u> going to kill him," I tell him, "If you hit him with this rock, you are going to kill him."

"It's my responsibility", he tells me, "You left-winger you."

Yehudah doesn't know that I have known this boy for a long time. He has drawn my attention from the moment I arrived at the Hotel Semiramis, and I often follow him with my telescope. I know almost everything about his family and his house and the school in which he studies. Every morning I accompany him to school with my telescope and see him home again. The only thing I don't know is his name.

He lives in an unfinished house at the southern edge of the alley, and he has three little curly-haired sisters. Even his mother is curly-haired. Every day she hangs out the wash and hides behind the dripping sheets. Through the telescope, I see her hands above the sheet, as if behind the screen in a shadow theater. After she hangs the wash, she takes all the mattresses out through the window and cleans the house. When she goes out to the market, she wears black and wraps in black and covers her face with a black veil. While she walks, I follow her eyes. She looks around and knows that she is being followed. On her head is a basket of apricots and bananas. She walks erect. She has no way to curtain her eyes but she stares straight ahead. She is arrogantly oblivious. Her three curly-haired daughters run in front of her.

On his way back from school, the boy leads a gang of slingshot boys, six- to eight-years-old. Every day they fill their schoolbags with smooth stones and load their slingshots. Afterward, he teaches them how to aim at cats and dogs. The children respect him and follow him through the alleys until evening. Once, one of the patrols was waiting for them in a side alley, and when the boys saw them they disappeared in all directions and left behind their heavy schoolbags loaded with smooth stones. The fighters in the patrol loaded the looted ammunition in their jeep and gave headquarters a report about the eight schoolbags loaded with slingshot stones.

I don't know where his father is. Maybe he is shut in with the students of Rabbi Akiva; maybe he stayed overnight in one of the industrial areas of Gush-dan. Maybe he's dead. It's impossible to tell.

I feel a strange responsibility for the boy. I am afraid to fall asleep at my lookout. A picture of a large rock falling from the sixth floor keeps repeating itself in my vision. Reuven, Amsalem, and I are not happy that Yehudah has stopped playing cards. Reuven and Amsalem cannot play two-handed poker, and I cannot concentrate on observing and recording.

I have known Yehudah for many years. Everybody in the battalion knows his good nature. To be sure, from time to time he explodes angrily, but these explosions are extremely brief. Today, it's true, this explosion has lasted more than three hours, but I know it has to subside. In the meantime, he commandeers my telescope to look for the boy through it. While he searches, he never stops muttering, "I'm gonna kill him . . . . I'm gonna kill him."

It is almost evening before he calms down, and everything returns peacefully to the way it was.

Just Like Savta Sarah's Siddur

Saturday night.

I am praying the evening service with thousands of Rabbi Akiva's students in the detention camp at Sura III. Many floodlights surround the chain link fence and illuminate the camp as bright as day. Watchtowers are scattered among the floodlights, and reservists from another battalion are observing from them. Between the towers and the chain link are rusted bronze angles stuck at a height of two meters, and burlap is stretched along the length of the bronze angles, preventing me from seeing inside. I can only distinguish their shadows

SHEMA ISRAEL: ALLAH HU AKBAR.

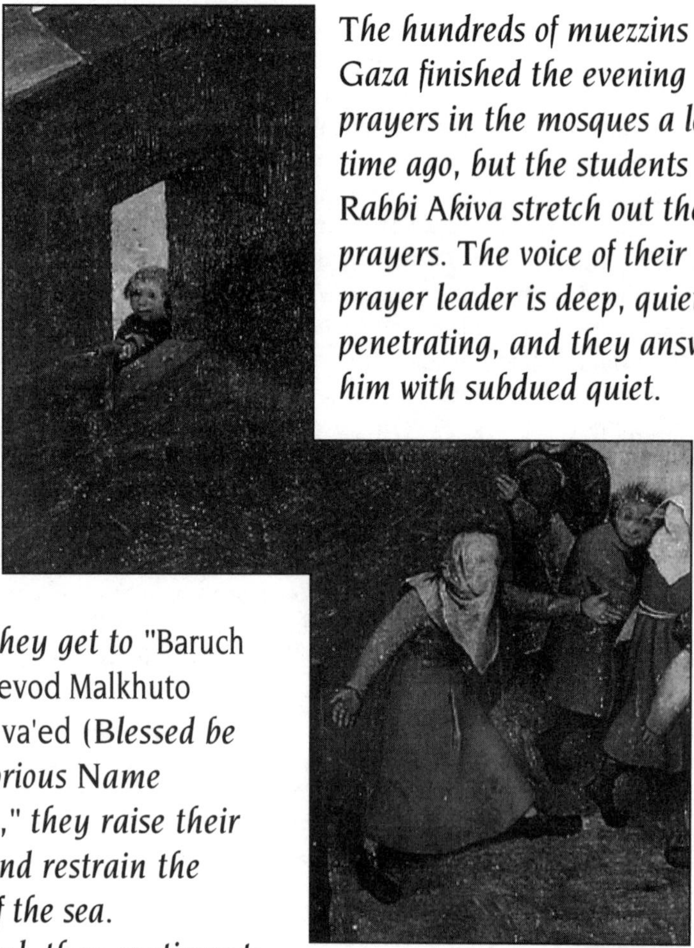

The hundreds of muezzins of Gaza finished the evening prayers in the mosques a long time ago, but the students of Rabbi Akiva stretch out their prayers. The voice of their prayer leader is deep, quiet, and penetrating, and they answer him with subdued quiet.

When they get to "Baruch Shem Kevod Malkhuto le-olam va'ed (*Blessed be His Glorious Name forever*)," *they raise their voices and restrain the waves of the sea. Afterward, they continue to sing their intricate melodies quietly and penetratingly. They pronounce each syllable distinctly.* At "Shema, Yisrael, Adoni Eloheynu, Adoni Ehad" (*Hear, O Israel, the Lord is Our God; The Lord Is One*) *they protract the* "Ehad." At "Allah hu akbar," (*God is Great*) *they extend the Allah. And I join them from the other side of the burlap* meḥitzah (*partition*), *like a woman in the women's section. My lips move, but my voice is not heard, and my notebook is pressed to my chest as my Grandma Sarah's siddur was pressed to hers.*

and hear their prayers. Little by little, I accustom my eyes to see through the burlap, and I can make out their blue overalls and their prayer movements.

The hundreds of muezzins of Gaza finished the evening prayers in the mosques a long time ago, but the students of Rabbi Akiva stretch out their prayers. The voice of their prayer leader is deep, quiet, and penetrating, and they answer him with subdued quiet. When they get to *"Baruch Shem Kevod Malkhuto le-olam va'ed* (Blessed be His Glorious Name forever)," they raise their voices and restrain the waves of the sea. Afterward, they continue to sing their intricate melodies quietly and penetratingly. They pronounce each syllable distinctly. At *"Shema, Yisrael, Adonai Eloheynu, Adonai Ehad"* (Hear, O Israel, the Lord is Our God; The Lord Is One) they protract the "One." At *"Allah hu akbar,"* they extend the Allah.

And I join them from the other side of the burlap *meḥitzah* (partition), like a woman in the women's section. My lips move, but my voice is not heard, and my notebook is pressed to my chest as my Grandma Sarah's siddur was pressed to hers. Like the *Korban Minḥah.* When they bend their knees and fall on their faces, I don't join them because I am embarrassed in front of the observers at the lookout posts.

Every time I reach this point, I am observed by the lookouts. They already know I am not a suspicious character. I am a dreamer in their eyes, maybe a painter who records in his notebook the variety of orange-pink-violet-red-purple-lilac which darkens every second, until the dark-blue horizon of the sea is completely swallowed up by the dark-hued horizon of the sky. Until the last of the kites turns into a star.

In the spreading darkness, I close the notebook like Savta Sarah used to close her *siddur.* Afterward, I walk three steps backward, my face to the sea, the sea a giant holy ark whose violet curtain is darkening. Then I hang my assault rifle on my shoulder and slip away quietly, as far as possible from the lookouts. The last sounds of prayer change into the melodies of learning. Rabbi Akiva's students are returning to the give and take of the battle of Torah, and I return to the base.

In the Shekem Club, everyone crowds together around a flickering black and white screen. The sportscaster Nissim Qiviti is describing for the God-knows-what time the goals scored in the first two games of the European championships. Everyone present in the club is a soccer commentator; everyone is arguing enthusiastically about the goal scored by Spain's Butregenio (the Vulture): Was it or was it not off-side?

The floor of the club is carpeted in sunflower seed hulls, a thick smoke rises from dozens of make-shift ashtrays made from empty cans of Coca-Cola. All are raising their voices in the excitement of the argument, and you can't hear Nissim Qiviti over the din. You can only see his lips move.

They Will No Longer Be Beautiful

During the night, veiled men threw a Molotov cocktail at patrol 49, wounding the *samgad* and the softie commander moderately. They had burns on their faces and arms, and a helicopter took them to Tel Hashomer Hospital. The doctor who admitted them declared on the spot, "We don't anticipate any danger to their lives, but they will no longer be beautiful."

An hour after the attack, an official jeep drove along the alleys of the quarter, its loudspeaker announcing a total curfew until further notice. From now until further notice, all the families of Pumbedita will be imprisoned in their homes. The children won't go to school, the fathers won't climb the scaffolds of Gushdan, and the mothers won't go to the market. From now until further notice, I have to help the patrols enforce the curfew. I have to observe carefully from my rooftop and report to headquarters about every child who disregards curfew and dares to set foot outside his doorway. From now until further notice, I have to put into effect a very collective punishment. So the children will hear and be afraid. So they won't throw Molotov cocktails when they grow up.

I follow the families trapped in their houses. Curfew is, among other things, an invitation to family unity. All the family members have to stay in each other's area. Nobody can get away. No father has to get up at three A.M. to reach the scaffolds of Ramat Aviv by six in the morning. All the fathers can stay in bed until late, and all the shut-in children can climb into their father's bed at eight in the morning.

One father is lying on his back, making his child fly like an airplane atop his extended foot. The boy is shouting in noisy happiness, and three of his younger brothers are waiting in line at the foot of the wide bed, waiting with happy patience for the moment when they will take off. Their amused mother is looking on from the side. I too, renowned humanitarian that I am, peer into their idyll with my telescope and rejoice at their joy.

I see a great idyll through my glasses. An idyll stolen behind the mask of collective punishment. "From doing it not *lishmah,* many families come to do it *lishmah.*" They achieve unity through the good offices of Satan.

Nevertheless, at the same time, I note with a certain uneasiness that I am much more relaxed during the curfew. After all, the curfew is good for my personal safety. When activity streams below us, I have a very justified fear that some brave freedom fighter will steal onto our hotel roof and throw Molotov cocktails. After all, I don't treat guarding our lives as seriously as I do writing. If only the crowds below me knew that up on the roof men are sunbathing and playing cards, they would have marked it a long time ago as a good target for terrorism, but they don't know because they cannot see us. I, on the other hand, know how vulnerable we are, and, therefore, I am filled with anxiety. But now, as I said, I am much calmer. Now I know that there is no living being beneath us. Now I can devote myself to writing and calmly and contemptuously denounce the suffering caused by the curfew, the evil craziness involved in incarcerating hundreds of thousands of children.

Between recording and self-flagellation, I traverse the rooftops of the city with my telescope. On a curfew day you can make out many more observation posts on the rooftops. At a time like this, all the inhabitants of Gaza shut their shutters and draw their curtains in the face of the heavy heat. Far worse is the condition of those whose rooftops have been taken over as observation posts. Men in uniform go up and down their stairwells like a terrible dream. They go up at dawn, and their voices penetrate into the bedrooms of children who are frightened by their own crying.

On days like these, the women of Gaza postpone hanging out the wash as long as possible. Only when they have no other alternative do they go up veiled to their roofs and squint fearfully at their observer who stands opposite them and checks their dripping laundry with a 20×120 telescope.

Sometimes they forget to go up veiled. And sometimes one of them will grab onto the idea that all is seen in Gaza but free will is granted, and she will go up to hang sheets in a transparent nightgown. Almost like Bathsheba. And I, almost like David the sweet singer of Israel, concentrate on her black eyes that can be glimpsed over the hanging sheet.

Red Light, Green Light—One Two Three

Midday. The heat of the day, the second day of the curfew

The main street of Gaza is like a melting wax museum. Everything stands blazing and steaming. No car honks its horn; no merchant announces his wares. No taxi driver implores passersby to come with him to Rafia, to El-Halil (Hebron).

I am beginning to long for the sights and sounds of the lively observation days. For the smells of dill and spices. For the braying of the donkeys. For the fascinating and tortured faces of the masses who are seen and cannot see. I begin to restore the tumult of the market to its blazing silence. But from the houses, many voices break through. The voices of tens of thousands of confined children who cannot bear up any more in their crowded burning houses.

At a certain stage, they decide to take the risk and play with fire with me. With an amusing furtiveness, they open the doors of their houses and venture a foot outside. I purposely ignore it. After a long moment they put out their other foot. I continue to ignore it. Little by little, they get nearer to me. The brave ones have already crossed a distance of twenty meters.

I feel like Gary Cooper, chewing on a match in the corner of my mouth and turning my back to them.

When the first of the children reaches thirty meters, I scream, "Hands up" and turn the telescope toward him with a sharp movement. In a second, all the children disappear into their houses with shouts of *"Al Yahud"* accompanying their disappearance.

Ten minutes later, it starts all over again. This time, many more children join the game. Girls too. Each time we play, more children join. Each time we play, I allow them to advance another couple of meters. Sometimes I shout, "Hands up" while making a sharp turn. Sometimes I shout, "Red light, green light—one two three." They, on the other hand, shout only *"Al Yahud."*

"Hands up" is a risky game. "Red light, green light," on the other hand, is more exciting. "Hands up" is a quick-draw contest that only boys play. "Red light, green light" is pantomime choreography for both boys and girls.

From hour to hour, we get better at it. By evening, I and all the children of Pumbedita quarter are playing the most perfect version of "red light, green light." I lean my head on the parapet and count like in "hide and go seek"—one thousand and one, one thousand and two, one thousand and three. Sometimes I count up to one thousand and twenty. Sometimes, I even approach one thousand one hundred. Suddenly, I turn my head around and call out, "Red light green light—one two three." At once, hundreds of children stop their motion and stand like statues. I study them very carefully through my telescope as they try very hard not to move and not to say a word. Whoever cannot stay immobile returns to the starting place at the edge of the alley.

The victor will be the one who manages to reach the doorway of the Hotel Semiramis without my catching him in motion.

From game to game, I teach myself to turn around with sharp unanticipated movements. From game to game, they too improve their powers of abrupt stopping. They carve with their bodies unplanned statues, and I record them like models—right leg behind and head forward; head behind and arms forward; eyes above and hands below; open mouths and closed eyes; hand grasping the heel; elbows pressed backwards, hands close to the body and legs open; legs close together and hands reaching up; both hands forward and the left leg behind; head thrown backwards and arms dangling down; one arm above and the opposing leg forward.

While I record them, the alley stands still. When I turn my back to them, it comes alive. Black clouds of smoke are ascending from far-off tires. A few shots are heard in the west. Yehudah, Reuven, and Amsalem are playing cards in one of the hotel's inside rooms. Fathers and mothers are watching us from the windows; a few kites—maybe twenty—are flying toward the setting sun.

Most of the children cannot last more than four turnarounds. In the end, they move a hand or a foot, or they can't keep quiet and let some unclear sentence slip. I see everything through my telescope, and I motion to them to go back once more to the starting point. Two boys with cropped hair manage to cross sixty meters before they lose their balance and bump into each other. They whisper, *"Al Yahud"* and go to the back. One girl with taped eyeglasses has survived eight turn-arounds without being caught. On the ninth turnaround, she can't keep quiet and bursts out laughing. When I motion to her to return to the starting point, she makes a "V" with her little fingers and breaks into tears.

But there are two children—a boy and a girl—who are getting very close to the doorway of the Hotel Semiramis and are seriously threatening my observation position. All my attempts to catch them in mid-motion are for naught. They have already crossed more than one-hundred-and-fifty meters and have left all the other children behind. Their quickness and balance awaken in me admiration mixed with concern. One of them is the boy with the slingshot. Yehudah continues playing cards in an interior room of the hotel, so the boy with the slingshot permits himself to wander freely and devote himself to the game. The girl who is advancing next to him is Raḥel, the Moroccan from Shaarei Ḥesed. She is still in first grade; she has a wide colorful dress and no underpants. She has a lot of brothers and sisters, and her family is isolated in Shaarei Ḥesed. Her mother cleans houses in Reḥavia, and I was one of the few children of Reḥavia who agreed to let her join in our games. In hide and seek, we would find a joint hiding place—there she would pull up her skirt and show me. After that I would show her. Now she is advancing at a slow pace, and I am not able to catch her in movement. Even though I make my sudden about-faces ever sharper, they always react more quickly than I do.

I start to worry and deliberate whether I should call for help from the card players. The moment the boy with the slingshot sees Yehudah, he will lose his balance; then I will be able to catch him in movement and make him go back. Rachel will not be able to bear up without him and will lose her balance. She still has no underpants under her colorful dress. I follow her with the telescope. In a few more months, she will finish first grade, and she still doesn't know how to read and write.

In fact, her father is a construction worker, and her mother is a house-cleaner, and her big brothers are delinquents—meaning, they don't study and they don't work; they only sit veiled on the roadside fences of the main street of the neighborhood and tempt us—the girls and boys of first grade—to throw stones at cars and set tires on fire.

AT ONCE, HUNDREDS OF CHILDREN STOP THEIR MOTION AND STAND LIKE STATUES.

By evening, I and all the children of Pumbedita *quarter are playing the most perfect version of "red light, green light."* I *lean my head on the parapet and count like in "hide and seek"– one thousand and one, one thousand and two, one thousand and three.* Sometimes I

count up to one thousand and twenty. Sometimes, I *even approach one thousand one hundred.* Suddenly, I *turn my head around and call out,*"Red *light green light–one two three."* At *once, hundreds of children stop their motion and stand like statues.* I *study them very carefully through my telescope as they try very hard not to move and not to say a word.* Whoever *cannot stay immobile returns to the starting place at the edge of the alley.*

The fifth day of the curfew.

A lot of crying in the houses. The crying of shut-in children, the screams of shut-in babies, and the shouts of shut-in mothers. Confined fathers hang out the wash for fear we will observe their wives. They hang a sheet and smoke a cigarette; hang a white tablecloth and smoke another cigarette; hang diapers and diapers. Diapers and more diapers. From parapet to parapet, smoke another cigarette, and move the antenna as if it was a punching doll. As if it was the crescent of Islam on a mosque roof. As if it was the soles of a muezzin whose head reaches heaven and between whose shoulders lies a cotton-wool cloud soaked in benzine.

The curfew is becoming unbearable. Nobody can stand it any more. Especially me. The ceaseless crying drives me mad. My idyll has been completely destroyed. I want to come down, and I can't. I'm confined like everybody else.

I raise the level of my telescope's revolving seat and try to ignore the sounds of crying. The seat revolves just like Mama's piano seat: she turns in all directions and accompanies her song of *"Maoz Tzur"* or "Ḥanukkah." I rise higher, focus the telescope and see a youth of about nineteen getting off a blue bus in El Arish's Shekem Square. I magnify the telescope even more to make sure this is El Arish. No doubt about it. Here are the bold palm trees between the pristine sea and the asphalt; there are the little shepherd girls and the black goats. No doubt. Today must be a very clear day if you can see all the way to El Arish.

I mark the precise coordinates of Shekem Square in El Arish and continue to follow the youth. His cheeks are still smooth, and the rank of corporal is fixed carelessly on to one sleeve. He leaves one dune, sits on the top of another dune, and writes something down in a little notebook. In the square are parked dozens of Dan and Egged buses: this is the last rest stop for soldiers coming to Refidim and the Canal.

I continue to follow the young man. He is trying to get away from the crowds and only has fifteen minutes. He hides himself behind a dead sector of the dune and moves his pen from right to left. He forces himself to write. Refugee children are shining shoes for the encamped soldiers. They are actually forcing them to let them shine their shoes. They have black brushes and red brushes and shoe polish arrays from Izmir and Isfahan.

I see all this tumult, and I can't hear anything. The young man looks for an area even more dead and disappears behind a dune. I wait for him through my telescope at the exact spot where he last appeared. I know that he has to come out in fifteen minutes because the buses parked in the shoe shiners' square are continuing on, and new buses are coming in to park, and others are leaving, and thousands of soldiers are milling around Shekem dairy kiosks and Shekem meat kiosks, reading with great interest the extensive sports sections of Sunday's newspapers, and punching each other on the shoulders.

Suddenly, in an instant, everybody gets on the bus and drives away very fast. The shoe shiners' square is left empty, and the young man has still not appeared from behind the dune.

I sharpen the focus on my telescope and continue to wait for him at the coordinates at which he was last seen.

The Little Prince in Retirement

Once upon a time, we were little princes from battalion 2. We played in the giant sandbox they call the Sinai Desert. From first light to last light, we climbed up the dune hills and fell off them. We never asked why we fell. We just ran to climb again, and we fell, and ran and climbed and fell. We didn't ask why we fell. We fell. And the sands were as soft as down. At recess, between shells, we would spill the soft sand into burlap bags. We filled millions of bags with sand, and we fastened the filled bags and piled them on top of each other. And built barricades, pillars, pits, trenches, palaces. Walls of fixed sand on soft sand. When the shells fell, the filled bags caught some of the shrapnel and saved part of the lives of some of us.

At the end of the 60s, we bearers of holy restlessness went down to the sandbox we call Sinai. The elite corps of Bren, Sharon, and Yofeh were a lamp at our feet. Every junction in the Sinai was legendary for us, and every soldier was standing clear in the turret.[4] We were a generation of phantoms. Infra-red. A generation of little princes flying from a terminal in Refidim to the Land of Israel for a free weekend. Forty years in half an hour. The dust of the desert on the upholstery of a Boeing. An Uzi with a folding barrel and oxblood shoes. Beautiful and dirty. Fighters in bloom.

In November 1969, I discovered the little prince's magic telescope for the first time. It was set up behind a sandbagged post in the first fortification of my life. Between shellings, I would risk my life and survey the palm tree grove that is west of the Suez Canal. Egyptian soldiers in light uniforms spoke among themselves with far-off hand gestures. Large rusted-out ships were at anchor between me and them. With my state-of-the-art telescope, I tracked the moving lips of the Egyptian soldiers. During many bad days, I saw fascinating hostile voices, and I recorded them in my imagination.

Exactly four years later, at the beginning of November 1973, I found myself stationed in the palm tree grove I had observed in November 1969. The Egyptian soldiers had crossed over to stay at the place that I had been in then, and I continued to survey their fascinating movements through my telescope. The war had caused us to exchange positions, but the rusty ships continued to lie at anchor between us.

A year later, the border drifted forty kilometers east of the Canal. In the summer of 1975 I sat forty days and forty nights in that year's temporary observation post, a tower standing in the midst of the sands of nowhere and in it a 20×120 telescope—a far more perfect telescope than the one I had access to at the end of the '60s. With the aid of this perfect telescope, I saw the large ships sailing the Suez Canal, which had opened for traffic a few months earlier. I couldn't see the water—it was hidden behind the dunes. Using the coordinates in the telescope, I had to report to headquarters about the type of ship, its length, its height, its flag, and the direction it was traveling.

For forty days and forty nights, I recorded this marvel with great dedication, and I reported to headquarters. Forty days and forty nights, I surveyed large ships traveling on land, but I wasn't privileged to see the tens of thousands of slaves pulling the ships with transparent cords.

A few years later, the border drifted east. Once again I was stationed at a temporary border point that had been erected on the road that had once connected Refidim and Naḥal-Yam—seventy kilometers southeast of the ship-lookout-post of the summer of 1975. I set up an observation tower next to the ragged road; I put my ever-faithful telescope on it, and I moved into it. Some of the soldiers below me played backgammon with the Egyptian soldiers. The rest set folding mats out on the road and took sunbaths.

I had no border left to survey. No giant rusty ships had sunk in the waters. No shining giant ships were being dragged over dry land. Only the spots of sunset and sunrise continued to show me the approximate direction of North. Purple clouds gathered together over the setting sun, and other purple clouds gathered above the orange rising sun. Always orange, just as in November 1969 and the summer of 1975.

A month later, the border continued to move eastward. In one of the Shabbat supplements of the afternoon newspapers, the bold headline read: "And they left Refidim and encamped in Kadesh Barnea," and in giant photographic essays, the newspaper depicted the wandering of the Israeli Defense Forces to the new border. The temporary new border.

Divisions and battalions moved east. Millions of sandbags disintegrated in the abandoned West. They piled up like memorial tels in the shifting sands. The wandering sands erased tens of millions of traces of the heavy treads of armored equipment. And the traces of thousands of contractors of dust and contractors of water and contractors of fortifications and journalists . . . .

Since then I wander between many borders with my tower and my telescope. With this telescope, I document sunrises and sunsets. And collect inspirations for the gray days between reserve duty and reserve duty. Each dawn, I see how the sun breaks out through the darkness over Gaza and how, just as

THE SANDBOX THEY CALL THE SINAI DESERT.

Once upon a time, we were little princes from batallion two. We played in the giant sandbox they call the Sinai Desert. From first light to last light, we climbed up the dune hills and fell off them. We never asked why we fell. We just ran to climb again, and we fell, and ran and climbed and fell. We didn't ask why we fell. We fell. And the sands were as soft as down. At recess, between shells, we would spill the soft sand into burlap bags. We filled millions of bags with sand, and we fastened the filled bags and piled them on top of each other. And built barricades, pillars, pits, trenches, palaces. Walls of fixed sand on soft sand. When the shells fell, the filled bags caught some of the shrapnel and saved part of the lives of some of us.

in November 1969, it sends forth its early flashing rays into the morning skies. Behind purple clouds, shaped like camels and rabbits, the sun climbs like a giant bulb. And her rays penetrate strongly upward; barely fifteen minutes later, they hang down like roots sent forth by a tall giant sunflower. The flower most distant from earth.

To this very day, I continue to be a compulsive collector of sunrises. The dune hills have changed into tortured cities, but the dazzling sunrises remain the same.

To this very day, I am fascinated by the burning ground at my feet, as if you cannot see from here what you can see from there, like poinciana trees and kites and the crescents of mosques. And black columns ascend in a glorious ghost dance from flowing wells of bubbling tires.

I am such an embellisher of pains, documenter of calamities. A little prince in his golden years. A morality trader since the dawn of his pleasure-laden youth. One who rejoices over suffering without causing it. One who rejoices at the view without breaking contact. Who enjoys all possible worlds and takes pleasure from anarchy. Like a sad captain enraptured at the sight of his sunken ships, like Nero on the roof, getting high at the sight of his burning city.

Like Allah—lover of the scent of burnt tires. The dense black bubbling incense is a savory aroma to Him. If they didn't extinguish them right at the start, then the skies would be dark at noon, and tens of thousands of little gold stars would fly at noon among the kites, and tens of thousands of little princes on the rooftops would swing on swings from horizon to horizon, while they are weighed in scales between the conquered land and the black skies.

Black skies, intercede for me. Don't bring me to the conquered land; don't bring me in confusion to a minyan of men of my father's age who sweep the streets in the darkness before dawn by the dazzling light of projectors that little Givati-legion princes hold in their hands.

Black skies, intercede for me. Don't bring me into contact with the miserable and dangerous refugees. One of them might yet throw a Molotov cocktail at me and darken my face in public. After all, I identify with his struggle completely—don't let him throw burning bottles at me.

Please, black skies, I beg you, consider my tender emotions. Don't send me to Gaza. Why will you not let me continue to observe the green line between Kerem Shalom and Kadesh Barnea? Why will you not let me continue to love the desert sunrises, as I loosen for you the belts and the oppressed and the downtrodden? Haven't you noticed this is what I have been doing for the last twenty years?

Why don't you keep in Gaza two or three professional battalions which will cast their terror on the hostile population. They will continue to receive from us the full unseen backup, that is, an elegant objection, local words of protest, and solid demonstrations of opposition in Malkei Israel Square. Why must you dirty my hands and disfigure my soul? Why do you have to force me to speak ill of us? In the end, it doesn't pay for you. Types like me are obsessively tender spirits. They come out of everywhere with their spiritual beauty intact. Even from Gaza.

DEATH BY A KISS.

Alma Dee is waiting at his observation post between the green line and the violet line—from the dreamed of side of the Jordan. He looks out over all the places that he may see but may not touch and sees thousands of Shabbat candles through his perfect army telescope. On the plains of Moab before Jericho. He looks for spies through his telescope, who will come from the plains of Moab, cross the river, pass between the mines, cut through the chain link, hover over the sand-pit of no-man's land, climb the desert, scatter at the mountain, and gather him up on their way back to the man from the Tent of Meeting who is still on the way to the land of Israel.

Alma Dee is a member of the wilderness generation in reverse. He was born in the land of Israel and goes to wander in the wilderness for at least forty years. Among the longed-for generation is Alma Dee, planted in sand, at fortifications, tense all the time, always careful not to defame, always looking through telescopes. From reserve duty to reserve duty, he perfects his telescope. From reserve duty to reserve duty, he waits for them to take him to the Tent of Meeting. To the man who knows how to see this land from afar, without a telescope. (Telescopes break the most longed-for land into its components.) The man who knows this land from afar will teach Alma Dee to stand opposite, to touch with his eyes all the Shabbat candles, every day, every light, until sunset. And every day, before the sun dies, at the very start of their 121st year—Alma Dee and the man from the Tent of Meeting will clasp hands, close their eyes, and die with a kiss.

Notes

Sha'ar Atzmi: My Own Gate

1. This is indeed a mysterious stammering version of the Mourner's Kaddish. Literally it means:

   "Magnified and sanctified be God's great name in the world that . . .
   In the world that . . . magnified and sanctified be God's great name.
   God's great name in the world that . . . be magnified and sanctified."

2. Michael, Gabriel, Uriel, and Raphael are the four archangels. This sentence is from the traditional prayers before going to sleep.
3. BT Eruvin 54a.
4. BT Yoma 72b.
5. Ibid. Perhaps a similar emendation should be made to the sentence: "There he placed *(sam)* rules and judgments." If we read *sam* (poison) for *śam (placed),* we get: "All the rules and judgments are poison for him."
6. Normally *aliyah* is inward migration to Israel; *yeridah* is outward migration from Israel.

Sha'ar Tzion: Zion Gate

A Jew Is Anyone Who Looks at Him or Herself in the Mirror of History and Sees a Jew

1. This phrase is from Gershom Scholem, "Who is a Jew?" (Hebrew). In *Devarim Bego,* edited by Abraham Shapira. Am Oved (1975): 591-597.
2. Probably even later, in the Geonic period.
3. Gershom Scholem, "Who is a Jew."
4. Ibid.
5. As quoted by Martin Buber *Netivot BeUtopia.* Edited by Abraham Shapira. Am Oved 1983. This is the Hebrew translation of the work known in English as *Paths in Utopia.*

High and Low, Low and High—Nobody Here But You and I

6. BT Hagigah 11b.
7. Ibid.
8. Bereshit Rabbah 1.
9. Exodus 32:20.
10. From Bialik's *Sefer Ha'aggadah,* p. 48, legend 34, on the basis of Shmot Rabbah 3. See also other opinions in Shmot Rabbah, and compare the source with Bialik's version.
11. Yosef Ḥayyim Brenner, editorial for *Hame'orer,* London, 1905.
12. Now published in English: Ḥayim Naḥman Bialik and Yehoshua Hana Ravnitzky, *The Book of Legends: Sefer Ha'aggadah.* Translated by William G. Braude. Schocken, 1992
13. Ravnitzky, an author in his own right, was a member of Bialik's circle and his collaborator on *The Book of Legends.*
14. In English one can have an expanded reading:

    The two of us balanced here from birth/between the heaven and the earth/balance here before we die/above the earth, beneath the sky/ weighed in on a balance scale/under heaven, over hell. (Translator's note)

The Voice Is the Voice of Esau and the Hands are the Hands of Jacob

15. BT Ketubot 111b, interpreting Jeremiah 27:22.
16. See BT Ketubot 111b.
17. See BT Shabbat 30a.
18. According to BT Berakhot 26a, Abraham established morning prayers *(Shaḥarit),* Isaac established the afternoon prayers *(Minhah),* and Jacob established the evening prayers *(Ma'ariv).*
19. Moshe Shamir's book, *He Went in the Fields,* is a classic novel about the Palmach generation.
20. *Heritage of Battle* is an Israeli army manual.
21. In Hebrew the wordplay is between Esau and *asiyah* (to do); Esau and "essay" was as close as I could get in English. (Translator's note)
22. The Hebrew here has *megalgel einayim ḥelmoniot; ḥelmoni* literally means "yolky," like the yolk of an egg. In context it means "rolling saucer eyes" and contains a play on the word "dreamy" *(ḥolmani).* In English, the play "Ḥelmish" seemed irresistible. (Translator's note)
23. Shenkin street, named after a Zionist thinker, became the "in" place for Boheme, like 8th Street in Greenwich Village and South Street in Philadelphia. The "in" place changes every few years, so now Shenkin is Shenk-out.

24. *Mashiaḥ-lo-metalphen,* sung by Shalom Hanoch, was a hit rock song in the eighties. Hanoch sang about Mashiaḥ who doesn't telephone; he really meant the Messiah.

Sha'ar Hagai: Ravine Gate (Bab el Wad)

The Torah as Esther

1. For this interpretation of Proverbs 5:18-19, see BT Eruvin 54b and BT Ketubot 77b.
2. See Ginsberg, *Legends of the Jews.* Esther is similarly compared to the moon (Shemot Rabbah 15) and to the morning star (Shoḥer Tov 22).
3. BT Yoma 29a.
4. Esther 2:14.
5. Esther 2:17.
6. BT Hullin 139a.
7. BT Megillah 13a.
8. Midrash Shoḥer Tov 22.
9. BT Sukkah 39a.
10. BT Pesahim 49b.
11. BT Berakhot 57a.
12. Song of Songs Rabbah 4.
13. Shemot Rabbah 41. Twenty-four is the traditional numbering of the books of the Bible.
14. BT Berakhot 63b.

The Olympus that Moses Discovered on High

15. For this midrash, see Bereshit Rabbah 1 and parallel texts.
16. BT Eruvin 21b.
17. BT Brakhot 63b.

Pomegranate Nectar

18. *Knesset Yisrael* (the Congregation of Israel) is the people pictured as a woman beloved by God.
19. BT Brakhot 57a; BT Eruvin 19a; BT Sanhedrin 37a.

Learning Is Delight

20. Pirkei Avot 1:3.

Moshe Rabbenu's Cow

21. Steinsalz Talmud, Bava Metzia 85a.
22. BT Megilla 16b.

Reḥumi's Love Triangle

22a. This poem, *Magash Hareset* by Natan Alterman, is read at all *Yom hazikaron* (Memorial Day) commemorations.
23. The word "home" in Aramaic, *beita,* also refers to his wife (sometimes *deveithu.)* Aramaic makes a real distinction between "woman," *iteta,* and wife, *deveithu* (lit. "of his house"). Modern spoken Hebrew refuses to make a distinction between "wife" and "woman," rejecting other options for "wife," in favor of "my woman," or "your woman." In our context, both "home" and "wife" are implied and "he came to his house" every Erev Yom Kippur has double connotations.
24. *Shma'ata* can be translated by any number of terms such as halakhah or study. The closest translation is "the portion" (the *sugya*)—not just any *sugya,* but an intricate one containing many different possibilities for creative intellectual diversions and thereby addictive. So, too, in the next story about Yehuda son of Rabbi Ḥiyya, and so with Neḥemiah b. Ḥanilai, whom the *shma'ata* allured so that he transgressed the Shabbat boundaries (BT Eruvin 43) and Ada bar Ahava whom Rav Ḥuna allured with a *shma'ta* (BT Ta'anit 20b). In Masekhet Pesaḥim there is an explicit rule: A *talmid ḥakham* cannot learn Torah on the night the *ḥametz* (leaven) is to be burned, lest the portion allure him and cause him to refrain from observing the mitzvah of burning the ḥametz. (BT Pesaḥim 4a).
25. The expression, *ḥalshah da'ata* (lit. "her mind weakened") is a conspicuous motif in the stories of the Babylonian Talmud. The term refers to a weakening of the spirit, a state of deep depression connected with loss of control. Generally when the spirit of one of the heroes of these stories weakens, he becomes dangerous. We are all afraid of what he might do to us since he has lost control over himself. That is the strength of the very weak—we are afraid of them.
26. "Insult," *'ona'at devarim,* is an injury to another person's psyche. Unlike financial or physical injury, it does not leave any external signs, but penetrates inward and leaves a hidden, eternal wound.
27. The wives of *talmidei ḥakhamim* and other women in the Babylonian Talmud have no names. The few names known to us are the exceptions that prove the rule. The two best known are Ima Shalom and Beruriah, and relatively little is recorded even of them. In addition we meet Ḥuma, the wife of Abbaye, Yaltah the wife of Rav Naḥman, and a few others. Rabbi Akiva's wife is not called Rachel in the Talmud but acquires this name later. The talmudic wives are known from their relationship to a man: Rav Ḥisda's daughter, Rabbi Akiva's wife, Mar Uqba's wife, Abba Ḥilkiya's wife, Rab-

ban Gamliel's wife, etc. Needless to say, there is no woman *Tanna* or woman *Amora.* More women with names are remembered from the Bible, and the talmudic tradition remembers by name seven biblical prophetesses, among them: Deborah, Ḥuldah, Miriam and, of course, Esther.

Hallelujah at the Death of God-Accursed Children

28. The story appears immediately after the statement that the marital sexual obligation for *talmidei ḥakhamim* is from Shabbat to Shabbat. In other contexts, "at twilight" also refers to Erev Shabbat.
29. The marital obligation, the *onah,* is the sexual attention that the Talmud decrees a man owes to his wife.
30. Ecclesiastes 10:5. The sense is that a ruler's decree, even if made by mistake, remains the law.
31. According to BT Ketubot 77b, the column of fire appears only to one or two in a generation.
32. Ten things were created on Erev Shabbat at twilight according to Avot 5:6.
33. "A star once dared" is a well known Israeli poem by Nathan Zach.
34. There is a connection between this curtain and the fence that separated the beauteous daughter of Yossi from Yokrat from the masses. When Yossi from Yokrat saw a man who could not stop himself and made a hole in the fence to gaze on his daughter, he approached and said to her, "My daughter—you are bringing trouble to creatures—return to your dust so that men do not fail because of you." (BT Ta'anit 24a) And when it was revealed to him that his son publicly took fruits from a date palm in a miraculous manner, he approached and said to him, "My son, you forced your Creator to take fruits from a date palm before its time, so you too will be "gathered" before your time." (Ibid.) These cursed children—like Yehudah—were threatening because of the directness of their contact with the ethical-normative system, which is nondirect by nature. Their fathers—appointed to administer the normative system—are ethical fathers according to Kierkegaard's categories. Note: In Kierkegaard the pious fathers sacrifice their innocent children; here, the ethical fathers sacrifice their pious children. Rabbi Yannai and Yossi from Yokrat have to cast their children aside in order to guard the system. Such children have no right to exist in a world of observing commandments. They have no grounding in this world. Their ethical fathers decree their death and sacrifice them.
35. This sentence doesn't appear in the Hebrew. I don't remember adding it, but somehow it showed up in the English text. Perhaps . . . . (Translator's note)

The Father, The Son, and the Goad

36. Some manuscripts say, "He grabbed an axe," others "the pole" *(alah)*. I have chosen the word "goad" as the translation of *alah* to echo the Hebrew play on words between *alah* and *elah,* with "goad" and "goddess." (Translator's note)
37. At this point the Gemara brings "some say" (your dove) *yonatka*. It is clear that this is late. Bialik, of course, opts for the more polite reading and puts it into the body of the story. One should also note that the annotations to our Gemara bring also "Were you thinking of your partner" *(zugatka)*. Clearly, considerable effort has been expended to soften the blows carried by the phrase "Were you thinking of your whore?"
38. The Aramaic here has *lo mar ipsik velo mar ipsik,* playing on the word *psk,* which is the leitmotif of this story. The same word *psk* means "decide, decree" and is used in the sentence: **They decreed three years for him.** In this sentence, it means "end, conclude" and refers to the fact that the two never resolved their dispute. However, as Rashi points out, it can also refer to the concluding meal just before the fast on Yom Kippur, which is known as the *se'uda mafseket.* The two never prepared properly for the fast on Yom Kippur: They never concluded their fight, and they never ate the concluding meal. When Bialik relates the story in the *Sefer Ha'aggadah* (Hebrew, p. 327), he puts Rashi's explanation into the body of the story.
39. This is the literal meaning of *naḥah nafsho.*

The Father, the Son, and the Goddess

40. Note that Rabbi Shimon has taken this verse out of context. Deuteronomy 11 refers to the reward for fulfilling the commandments. (Translator's note)
41. The text says *ḥatan* (son-in-law) and Soncino translates accordingly. The context makes this doubtful: Why would his son-in-law have been his master before his years in the cave? Heiman, *Toldot Tannaim VeAmoraim,* notes that the Zohar suggests "father-in-law." See also, Steinsaltz, Ishim. (Translator's note)
42. Albeck, *Bereshit Rabbah* (p. 945) gives the sources.
43. Breshit Rabbah 79.
44. For commerce, see Ta'anit 21a.
45. On prayer: "Rava saw Rav Ḥimnuna taking a long time at prayer and said, 'You put aside eternal life and busy yourself with life of this world (the moment) . . . .'" (BT Shabbat 10a).

45a. Tiberias is not named in the Banli. However, the sources from the land of Israel name Tiberias.

The Infinite Despair of the Babylonian Ḥoni

46. Grotto-cave. The Aramaic says *meshunita.* Rashi translates "crag"; Bialik, "cliff." And see Jastrow.
47. See Yonah Frankel, *Inquiries into the Spiritual World of the Aggadic Story (Hebrew, p. 25).*
48. *Pirkei Avot 3:7.*

The Most Beautiful Man in Pumbedita

49. The historical Rabbi Yoḥanan lived in Tiberias. We cannot draw historical conclusions from this literary story about Babylon and certainly not about Israel; the story has no parallel in Israel sources. Every historical argument that depends solely on this story has nothing to depend on. Despite this, no less an authority than the *Encyclopedia Ivrit* in the article about the Babylonian Talmud tries to use this story as historical evidence for the way people learned in the academy of Rabbi Yoḥanan in Israel, acknowledging, nevertheless, that the Talmud does not preserve any *sugyot* in which there are twenty-four questions and responses, and even the portions of discussion between Rabbi Yoḥanan and Resh Lakish contain only seven or eight. In my opinion, this story points to the Babylonian reality.
50. See BT Bava Metzia 84a.
51. The concepts of *Torah nilmedet* and *Torah metzavah*—the Torah of learning and the commanding Torah—are developed in previous chapters.
52. See the discussion of this issue above pp. 64–65.
53. For this image, see BT Sanhedrin 24a.
54. **"Sorah and Eshta'ol were two large mountains; Samson used to uproot them and grind them against each other."** (BT Sotah 9b)
55. BT Sanhedrin 99b.
56. JT Berakhot 5:1.
57. See BT Ta'anit 8a.
58. See BT Bava Kama 117a.
59. A section of the Mishnah dealing with the Law of Purities.
60. A tractate of Seder Ṭaharot that focuses on the purity and impurity of vessels and tools.
61. BT Bava Metzia 58a.
62. See Frankel, *Inquiries,* op cit. n. 47, p. 75.

The Broken Threads of the Sabbath Boundary

63. For an unwitting adulterer, see BT Sanhedrin 99b, and the previous chapter p. 111.
64. See Pirkei Avot 3:7.
65. Inadvertent acts, *shegagot,* are misdeeds committed without awareness. Here they arise from the multifold ardor, *shigionot* that Resh Lakish

enjoys with his Torah.

66. For Nehemiah see BT Eruvin 43a.
67. For awareness, surrender, and despair, see BT Bava Metzia 22.
68. See the story in BT Hagigah 14a. The *pardes* is the special garden of paradise, of esoteric knowledge, and mystical speculation.

Sha'ar Ha'ashpot: The Dung Gate

1. See BT Brakhot 58b.
2. The real prison camps are called Ansar. Sura was the rival academy to Pumbedita in Babylonia.
3. This is how you spell *haftarah* (the weekly synagogue reading from the prophetic books of the Bible) over the radio to a secular Israeli soldier who doesn't recognize the word.
4. *Standing Clear in the Turret,* by Shabtai Tevet, was one of the most important books to come out of the Six Day War.

Glossary

aggadah the non-halakhic literature of Judaism, generally consisting of stories and exegetical explanations of Scripture that convey theological and philosophical ideas. Also more generically, legends, legendry.

aggadic part of the *aggadah* or similar to it.

ahalan "ahoy," a cry of greeting.

aliyah literally, "going up," frequently refers to going up to read the Torah and to immigration to Israel.

Allah hu akbar "God is Great," the central creed in Islam.

am ha'aretz the common people, or folk. The term has two plurals: *amei ha'aretz,* the normal plural, and *amharatzim,* a perjorative plural meaning "the ignorant ones."

Amidah The silent prayer said three times a day, also called the Eighteen Benedictions.

Amoraim the Rabbis who created the Talmud. They came after the *Tannaim.* Roughly third to sixth century CE.

apikores, apikorsim person or people with heretical, non-normative views. Ultimately derived from the word "Epicurean."

ba'al Mussaf the person who chants the Mussaf.

Bavli the Babylonian Talmud.

batei midrash study houses.

beigele an Arab bread something like a soft pretzel.

beit midrash a study house; also used for a talmudic academy.

bitul Torah wasting time by doing anything other than studying.

cubit a biblical measure from the elbow to the tip of the middle finger. Approximately eighteen inches. "Four cubits" is a talmudic phrase that occurs many times with the sense of "personal space."

darshan a preacher.

datti Israeli Orthodox, explained in the text.

Egged Israel's bus company.

Eli, Eli literally, "my God, my God." The line here is Psalms 22:1.

Eliyahu The prophet Elijah.

Elul the last month of the Jewish calendar year, a month for reflection and repentance in the anticipation of the New Year.

Erev Yom Kippur the day before Yom Kippur.

Gabriel one of the main angels.

galabiya Arab robe for men.

galut exile. The Diaspora of Jews that began with the destruction of the second Temple in the Roman period.

Gehinnom, Gehenna Hell; literally, "The Valley of Hinnom."

gemara the essential part of the Talmud, loosely organized as commentary on the Mishnah.

Gra Gaon of Vilna, Vilna Gaon;

Gushdan the Greater Tel Aviv metropolitan area.

haftarah a set reading from the prophets that accompanies each weekly Torah portion, and holiday Torah portions. The haftarah is chanted after the Torah reading.

halakhah the entire system of normative rules of behavior, sometimes called "the law."

ḥalutzim the pioneers; the Zionist settlers of Israel.

ḥametz leaven—that which may not be possessed on Passover.

HaShem literally, "the name"; a pious way to refer to God.

ḥasidic belonging to a Jewish movement that began at the beginning of the eighteenth century and stressed fervor in prayer.

Ḥazal acronym for "our Sages of Blessed Memory"; the classic Rabbis of the Mishnah, Tosefta, Talmud, and Midrash.

Ḥelmish belonging to Helm, the traditional "city of fools" in Jewish folklore; therefore, "foolish," "simple-minded."

ḥerem excommunication; an extreme form of banishment used rarely but powerfully. It had the effect of removing someone from the Jewish people.

ḥevruta study partnership.

ḥiloni literally, "secular"; the meaning is explained in the text.

Hineni The prayer chanted by the peron designated to lead the mussaf prayers on Rosh Hashannah and Yom Kippur. The prayer expresses the hope that the prayer-leader will be worthy of having his (now sometimes her) prayer listened to.

Ḥumash the Five Books of Moses, the Pentateuch.

Jihad Arabic for Holy War.

Kaddish an ancient Aramaic prayer said at various parts of prayer services and also specially recited by mourners.

Kadosh Barukh Hu literally, the Holy One Blessed Be He, an epithet of God used frequently in rabbinic literature. Here translated as the Holy Blessed One.

kibbutz Israeli collective village.

Kiddush Levanah prayers said outside at the new moon. The prayers are printed in very large letters so they can be read outdoors by the dim light of the not-yet-full moon.

kippah, pl. ***kippot*** the round head covering worn by observant Jews and even by *ḥiloni* students as they study "Jewish studies" and by Jewish males (and some females) during prayer services.

Knesset Israel the people of Israel portrayed collectively as a woman.

Kodesh-Barukh-Hu The words *kadosh barukh hu* mean "the Holy One Blessed be He," or (more inclusively) the Holy Blessed One. European Jews who speak Yiddish or Ashkenazi Hebrew say *Kodesh-Baruch-Hu* as a name of God and pronounce it as one word.

Kol Nidrei The opening prayer of Yom Kippur, chanted three times to a haunting melody as the sun is sinking.

Korban Minḥah a traditional siddur.

Ma'ariv evening prayer service.

Mamilla Street before 1967 there was a "no-man's-land" between Mamilla Street and the walls of the Old City (the border between Jordan and Israel).

mashiaḥ Messiah.

Megillat Esther the scroll of Ester, read aloud on Purim.

meḥitzah divider between women and men at prayer.

Michael one of the main angels.

midrash pl. **midrashim** the creative interpretation of texts that extends their meanings in many directions. Also used specifically to refer to the Rabbinic literature containing these interpretations and to individual examples of the genre.

mikvah a ritual bath for purification. Traditionally used monthly by women after their menstrual period and the seven "white days" that follow before the resumption of marital relations.

Minḥah afternoon prayer service.

minyan literally the quorum of ten Jews needed to have a public prayer service. It sometimes means the prayer service itself.

Mishnah a rabbinic listing of regulations arranged and promulgated in the second century CE.

mitokh shelo lishma yavo lishmah literally, "from doing it not for her sake, he will come to do it for her sake"; a proverbial statement that the right action will eventually cause the actor to have the right motive.

mitzvah literally, "a commandment"; also used in the sense of a religious good deed.

Moshe Rabbenu "Moses our Master, Moses our Rabbi"; a traditional way of referring to Moses.

muezzin the one who calls Moslems to prayer.

Mussaf the prayer service added on Sabbath, festivals, and Yom Kippur.

Ne'ilah the final prayer service of Yom Kippur.

niggun wordless melodies used as song.

oral law, Oral Torah the corpus of Rabbinic literature, particularly the Mishnah and the Talmud, believed to have been revealed along with the Written Torah but not written down until long after.

Oranim the college of the Kibbutz movement. See "Preface."

Palmaḥ Israel's crack troops of the Israeli War of Independence.

pardes literally "orchard, garden"; it is the source of the English word Paradise (for Garden of Eden) and often refers to the "garden of mystical learning and esoteric knowledge."

pilpul learning by debating.

poskim learned rabbis who make decisions about halakhic matters.

Pumbedita site of one of the two great talmudic academies in Babylonia.

rabbani, pl. ***rabbanim*** literally, "rabbinic"; the term is explained at length in the book.

Raphael one of the main angels.

ribboni, pl,. ***ribbonim*** literally, "like a master"; the term is explained at length in the book.

Rosh Yeshivah head of the academy.

Sabras native born Israelis.

samgad an assistant batallion commander in the Israeli army.

savta grandma.

Second Aliyah the foundational wave of Zionist immigration to Israel, informed by Zionist and communitarian principles.

Shabbat Sabbath.

Shabbat boundaries According to Jewish law, one should not walk more than 2000 cubits on the Sabbath. These are counted from the last house in the settlement, thus creating a ring around the town.

Shaḥarit morning prayer service.

Shekem the Israeli PX.

Shekhinah the presence of God in the world; sometimes envisioned as a winged female.

Shema the central credo of Judaism, recited daily evening and morning. The name refers to the line "Hear O Israel, the Lord is our God, the Lord is One." The bedtime Shema is the set group of prayers traditionally said at bedtime.

Shma'ata the study portion; the term is explained more fully on p. 172, n. 24.

shtetl Yiddish word for a small European market town with a Jewish population.

shuckling "swaying," the back-and-forth rocking of many traditional Jews during prayer.

Shulḥan Arukh the classic codification of Jewish Law, produced by Joseph Caro in the sixteenth century.

siddur the Jewish prayer book.

Stamaim the unnamed Rabbis who edited the Talmud in the sixth and seventh centuries.

sugya a unit of Talmud study.

sukkah ceremonial hut used for eating and sometimes sleeping on the festival of Sukkot in the fall.

Sura site of one of the two great talmudic academies in Babylonia

tallit prayer shawl.

talmid ḥakham literally, "the disciple of the wise"; it means the talmudic sage or Torah scholar. The plural is *talmidei ḥakhamim.*

Talmud the documents produced by the rabbinic study of the Mishnah. There are two: the Babylonian Talmud and Jerusalem Talmud.

talmud Torah traditional Torah study.

Tannaim the rabbis of the first few centuries CE.

Torah lishmah "Torah for her own sake"; normally refers to the act of study for the sheer joy of it.

Toshba the acronym for *torah shebe'al peh,* "the Oral Torah," i.e., rabbinic literature.

tefillin sometimes called "phylacteries"; these are ritual boxes containing biblical passages written on parchment that are strapped to the forehead and arm during morning worship.

tzaddik an absolutely righteous man.

tzitzis (modern Hebrew *tzitzit*), the ritual fringes on the end of a tallit. Also a garment with these fringes worn under the clothes.

Uriel one of the main angels.

Yedid Nefesh hymn often sung at the beginning of Friday night services and as a Sabbath table song.

yeridah literally, "going down"; it also means emigration from Israel.

yeshivah school of traditional Jewish learning.

yeshivah in the skies the academy in Heaven where the fortunate study for eternity.

yeshivah shel ma'alah the academy in the skies.

yetzer literally, "impulse." Usually short for *yetzer hara',* the evil impulse.

Yiddishkeit the flavor of being Jewish, composed of traditional expressions, customs, melodies, and foods.

Yishuv the settlement of Jews in Israel.

Yom Kippur the Day of Atonement.